# The Warmth of the Welcome

## Is Atlantic Canada a Home Away From Home for Immigrants?

Edited by

Evangelia Tastsoglou
Alexandra Dobrowolsky
Barbara Cottrell

CAPE BRETON UNIVERSITY PRESS
SYDNEY, NOVA SCOTIA

Cape Breton University Press recognizes the support of the Province of Nova Scotia, through the Department of Communities, Culture and Heritage and the support received for its publishing program from the Canada Council for the Arts Block Grants Program. We are pleased to work in partnership with these bodies to develop and promote our cultural resources.

FILM & CREATIVE INDUSTRIES
NOVA SCOTIA

Canada Council     Conseil des Arts
for the Arts        du Canada

Cover image: *Picnic on Snow*, 2014, by Najma Sharif, Halifax, NS.
Cover design: Cathy MacLean Design, Chéticamp, NS
Layout: Mike Hunter, Port Hawkesbury and Sydney, NS
Copyediting: Katie Yantzi, Toronto, ON
First printed in Canada.

Library and Archives Canada Cataloguing in Publication

Tastsoglou, Evangelia, author
     The warmth of the welcome : is Atlantic Canada a home away from home for immigrants? / Evangelia Tastsoglou, Alexandra Dobrowolsky, Barbara Cottrell.

Includes bibliographical references and index.
Issued in print and electronic formats.
ISBN 978-1-927492-99-4 (pbk.).--ISBN 978-1-927492-15-4 (pdf).--
ISBN 978-1-927492-16-1 (epub).--ISBN 978-1-927492-17-8 (kindle)


     1. Immigrants--Atlantic Provinces.  2. Immigrants--Cultural assimilation--Atlantic Provinces.  3. Naturalization--Atlantic Provinces. 4. Immigrants--Atlantic Provinces--Attitudes.  I. Dobrowolsky, Alexandra Z. (Alexandra Zorianna), 1964-, author  II. Cottrell, Barbara, 1945-, author  III. Title.

JV7220.T37 2015          305.9'0691209715          C2015-901163-9
                                                    C2015-901164-7

Cape Breton University Press, 1250 Grand Lake Road, Sydney, NS B1P 6L2 CA
www.cbupress.ca

# The Warmth of the Welcome

## Table of Contents

—

## Section 3: Immigration in Small Communities

—

## Section 4: Building Belonging

# Section 1

## Welcoming Communities?
## The Backdrop to Immigration in Atlantic Canada

# At Home, Down East?
# Immigration, Integration
# and Belonging in Atlantic Canada

*Evangelia Tastsoglou*
*Alexandra Dobrowolsky*
*Barbara Cottrell*

## I. Why Look at Immigration, Integration and Belonging in Atlantic Canada?

Atlantic Canada, comprised of the four eastern-most Canadian provinces (New Brunswick, Newfoundland and Labrador, Nova Scotia and Prince Edward Island) is a region of many fine features and inviting qualities. It is renowned for its lengthy coastlines and rural expanses, along with a smattering of lively, smallish cities, a reputedly slower pace and its people who are often portrayed as welcoming, warm and friendly. The allure of Atlantic Canada has been widely publicized to assorted, targeted groups. For example, alongside colourful pictures of stunning seascapes, "we have it all!" is the emphatic catchphrase used to draw tourists to the region (http://www.atlanticcanadatourism.com/).

To attract immigrants, mayors in Atlantic Canada have promoted the region's purportedly high quality of life, contrasting it with the challenges of "big city" existence. In the mayors' pitch to newcomers, healthy and safe communities and a lower cost of living, including lower housing prices, are featured in the hope that these considerations will entice immigrants to move to, and settle in, Atlantic Canada (see http://www.canadavisa.com/quality-of-life-will-attract-immigrants.html). But for immigrants especially, how much of this is rhetoric, and how much of this is reality? Is Atlantic Canada truly welcoming, and what really makes it a home away from home for newcomers in the region? These queries lie at the heart of this edited collection. Such questions, and the answers to them, are timely and relevant because, in recent years, alongside the mayors' appeals noted above, an array of constituencies (e.g., multiple levels of government, businesses, academics, community representatives) across Atlantic Canada have become much more concerned with the attraction and retention of immigrants to the region. For instance, several chapters in this volume examine the launch and evolution, over the last decade or so, of provincial immigration agreements with the federal government in the form of provincial nominee programs (or PNPs). At the same time, not only the public sector (federal, provincial and municipal), but the private and voluntary sectors have been enlisted to attract and retain newcomers to Atlantic Canada. Other chapters illustrate how community groups and individuals, even in remote areas, have also engaged in concerted campaigns to create a more "welcoming" environment for newcomers.

This growing awareness of the need for immigrants to come and to stay in the region corresponds to several worrisome socio-economic, political and demographic developments. Today, Atlantic Canada faces a series of grim demographic challenges that include: low birth rates; an aging population; and issues around rural de-population (Akbari and Mandale 2005; Murphy and de Finney 2008; Yax-Fraser and Tastsoglou 2008). Historically and presently, the region has also experienced recurring problems with out-migration and fluctuating immigrant retention rates (Dobrowolsky and Ramos 2014). Concomitantly, its economic health and growth potential varies from province to province, and especially from urban to rural locales. Politicians, business people and economists have identified Atlantic Canada's close to zero population growth (ZPG) condition as representing an economic problem, because it contributes to lower rates of growth in the economy (Freedman 2011: 173). Immigration has, in turn, been identified not only as the answer to these demographic shortfalls, but also as the key to boosting the region's economic competitiveness. These connections were stressed most recently in Nova Scotia's Commission on Building a New Economy recommendations, commonly referred to as the Ivany Report (Ivany et al. 2014).

The roots of the present situation run very deep. For example, as will be discussed in more detail below, Atlantic Canada's history of out-migration can be traced as far back as the early years of Canada's very existence. This country's first Prime Minister, Sir John A. Macdonald, not only encouraged western colonization, but concentrated manufacturing in the centre of Canada with his first National Policy. With this shift of the population and economic and industrial weight westward, de-industrialization, resource and population depletion occurred in eastern parts of the country and have continued ever since (Brodie 1990). For the same reasons that those born in Atlantic Canada left (and still leave) the area, most new waves of immigrants bypassed the region on their way west. As Canada's growing population concentrated in its major and mid-sized metropolitan centres, the Atlantic region remained relatively rural in comparison to other parts of the country (Desjardins 2011: 292).

Relatedly, we will also see how and why only a limited number of racially and ethnically diverse communities (i.e., beyond First Nation, Acadian and African-origin) were established. Those communities that did take hold were too small to attract significant numbers of compatriots. More specifically, for all Atlantic provinces, the non-European groups are very small, usually less than one per cent of the population (see table 1.1 at the end of this chapter). The ethnic makeup of Atlantic Canada continues to be similar to what it was when Canada was founded—mostly people from the British Isles and France (Tastsoglou 2011). Unlike many other parts of Canada, then, Atlantic Canada remained (and continues to be) less ethnically heterogeneous. Due to low numbers and visibility of diverse groups, assimilationist pressures held sway in Atlantic Canada, despite Canada-wide official policies of and constitutional commitments to multiculturalism (Jabbra 1992, 1997). This lack of diversity is significant for many reasons including the fact that research has shown ethnic networks to be paramount in the initial settlement location choice of newcomers (McDonald 2003). Consequently, Atlantic Canada's small ethnic communities and scattered immigrant populations have not been able to provide the critical mass to precipitate new waves of immigration or form ethnic hubs attracting new immigrants from other regions. The region's share of annual immigrant inflows compared to its population remains small: For example, in 2006, Atlantic Canada, with a population of 7.2 per cent of the total Canadian population, attracted only 2 per cent of immigrants who arrived in Canada (Akbari et al. 2007).

Yet immigrants have come to the region and continue to arrive, as the chapters in this volume illustrate. In fact, in recent years, the Atlantic region is slowly but surely diversifying its population (Akbari 2012). The problem that persists, however, is that many of these newcomers still do not stay. Although these numbers have recently improved, retention rates are patchy across the Atlantic provinces. Moreover, the "econocentric" approach that is now utilized to attract investors and skilled immigrants, in agreement with a similar federal approach, has come under serious criticism for undermining social and cultural factors necessary for immigrant integration to enhance Atlantic Canada's diversity and address its demographic needs (Dobrowolsky and Ramos 2014). Finally, negative net-migration is still, by and large, the pattern for the region's rural areas (Desjardins 2011: 296).

All of these developments, old and new, require close and careful scrutiny, as they raise a host of critical policy questions (and ethical concerns) for provincial and local governments and for communities in Atlantic Canada: Does the region truly

provide a welcoming environment, a "home away from home" for immigrants? If not, why not? What are the obstacles? How can they be removed so that greater numbers of immigrants come, and stay, in Atlantic Canada? What opportunities arise for immigrants here that are unique to Atlantic Canada? What are the key features and elements of living in Atlantic Canada that those immigrants who choose to stay especially appreciate? How can the four provinces further build upon and enhance such opportunities, features, and elements? These questions, and the answers to them, are explored in the chapters contained in this collection.

In so doing, the chapters in this volume underscore that a welcoming environment consists not simply of local people's reception of and encounters with newcomers and immigrants in everyday life. Beyond this human "warmth of the welcome," which is usually emphasized by government, in official literature and by the general public, there are also several institutional and structural layers that constitute and frame a welcoming environment. These layers can include the following: favourable political-economic conditions; receptive community relations including inter-ethnic group relations; the existence of local, national and transnational family networks; and the presence of policies and practices that not only concern immigration, settlement and integration, but also address such issues as adequate, accessible and affordable housing or childcare. This more well-rounded welcome, encompassing a range of layers from the individual and interpersonal to institutional and structural, ultimately leads and corresponds to a broadly defined notion of citizenship that Tastsoglou and Dobrowolsky have identified in an earlier work (2006) as encompassing intertwined and interrelated economic, social, political/civic and psychological/emotional aspects and processes.

This volume ultimately focuses on what immigrants find attractive about Atlantic Canada, its people and communities, and on the components that really make or would make them feel "at home" here, despite leaving their countries of origin. The concept of "home away from home," coined first by Vertovec (1999), refers to a kind of diaspora consciousness characterized by dual or multiple identifications, an awareness of being "here and there." Due to the nature of edited collections, our treatment in the various case studies of the reasons why immigrants do or do not feel that their Atlantic Canadian community is a "home away from home," and why they do or do not stay, cannot be exhaustive. Nevertheless we do attempt to situate these studies in an analytical framework, and in relation to several core themes.

In relation to the analytical framework, we identify several layers of "welcome." These extend from the micro to the macro–level continuum (i.e., individual, familial, community, policy/practice and political economy). Stemming from the present case studies (and drawing on a select number of other relevant studies), we make two core claims. First, that all of these levels of "welcome" need to be taken into account in order to begin to understand the complexities of the present picture for newcomers in Atlantic Canada, and to be able to improve it through policy. Second, although the layers can theoretically exist independently, they are, in reality, highly interdependent. For example, immigration and integration policies affect immigrants' familial relations and their reception by local communities, as well as their efforts at economic and professional integration. Many of these considerations (e.g., family networks, social or professional integration) subsequently affect immigrants' sense of belonging to the receiving communities. This sense of belonging can then, in turn, have an impact on immigrants' civic and political engagement and so forth.

With regard to the thematic considerations of this volume, chapters are arranged according to four interwoven themes. The introductory theme, *Welcoming Communities? The Backdrop to Immigration in Atlantic Canada,* provides the context for and a snapshot of current migration trends across the region. The subsequent themes explore several core concerns that can reflect both the similarities and differences across Atlantic Canada. Divergences are to be expected as the volume showcases research from all four Atlantic provinces, includes work in predominantly

English-speaking regions as well as the officially bilingual province of New Brunswick, and encompasses the rural-urban spectrum. Thus, in theme two, *Immigration and Settlement Policies and Immigrant Experiences,* multiple vantage points and the often devastating realities (including downward class mobility, homelessness and violence) faced by immigrant men and women are highlighted. Unique circumstances of other kinds—such as the fact that the region has relatively few large or even medium-sized cities—are taken into consideration in theme three, when examining *Immigration in Small Communities.* And finally, in theme four, three chapters explore the opportunities and constraints of different dimensions of *Building Belonging.*

The remainder of this introductory chapter will contextualize the case studies of the volume with a brief overview of the history of immigration practices in Atlantic Canada. As was alluded to above, a number of historical and political-economic reasons help to explain why the Atlantic region, despite the commonly remarked upon "friendliness" of its people, has traditionally not been very inviting to or receptive of immigrants. This chapter then addresses whether this trend continues in the late 20th, and into the 21st century, and if so, why.

In doing so, we unpack the notion of "welcoming communities" much utilized in policy circles and then raise the thorny question of the possibility of conceptualizing "Atlantic Canada" as a region with a common identity. In turn, this helps to frame our discussion of the concept of "home," which is as contested as the notion of the Atlantic region. As the chapters in this volume confirm, in a contemporary globalized world, "home" is not unitary, it can have different meanings for people of different origins and cultures, and it is often multi-sited. This is reflected in the last part of our introductory comments, which provides highlights from the chapters that follow.

Overall, the reasons for and the unique strengths of this volume showcase the rich empirical research being conducted on immigration across the four Atlantic provinces. It also traces connections between flourishing provincial and local studies, and the establishment of the Atlantic Metropolis Centre of Excellence (AMC). The AMC, in many cases, helped to inspire, spearhead and support such research since the Centre's inception in 2003 and until it closed its doors in 2013. The volume is also organized around key theoretical questions although it contains various methodologies, multiple dimensions and levels of analysis. For instance, it not only considers structural and institutional opportunities and constraints, but fleshes out and analyzes the experiences of immigration at the individual level, and demonstrates the links between public policies and individual experiences. Finally, this collection aims to feature, explore further and better comprehend the gendered impact of immigration and settlement processes in Atlantic Canada.

## II. Encounters with "Others": Immigration History and Research in Atlantic Canada

Atlantic Canada's longstanding and varied First Nations' settlements (e.g., Mi'kmaq, Maliseet, Innu or Montagnais-Naskapi Indians, and Inuit) were first colonized by the French and then the British. Thus, Atlantic Canada historically drew its immigrant population from Europe. Initial colonization took place by the French Acadians in the early 17th century. Caught in the conflicts between New England and New France, the Acadians were given the option to leave within a year or become British subjects under the Treaty of Utrecht in 1713. They were subsequently expelled during the Grand Dérangement (1755 to 1764), while later the British authorities allowed the Acadians to resettle in the Atlantic colonies of Canada (Basque 2011). Immigration continued from the British Isles but also, in the 18th and 19th centuries in Nova Scotia specifically, by "foreign protestants," New England "planters," and Loyalists, including "Blacks," in the aftermath of the American Revolutionary War and the War of 1812 (Withrow 2002; Walker 1980). The English and Acadians comprised the majority of the population and new migration flows (Carrigan 1988; Jabbra and Jabbra 1987; Jabbra 1992, 1997; Tastsoglou 2011), with some notable exceptions as when in the 20th century Caribbean immigrants were sought to work in Cape Breton coal mines (http://blackhistorycanada.ca/theme.php).

Canada's early immigration policies from Confederation (1867) to 1893 were oriented westward in an effort to populate the West and create an expanded yet self-sufficient national economy with internal rather than external economic linkages and trading ties. They were also geared toward preserving the British character of Canada by according preferential treatment to British settlers or those with British sympathies and by excluding others with variable degrees of intensity (Dobrowolsky and Tastsoglou 2011).

These policy choices had a huge impact on Eastern Canada. The Maritime provinces were among the earliest non-Aboriginal settlements in Canada and on the road to industrialization in the 1870s and 1880s. Yet, with Confederation and the first National Policy, Eastern Canada lost out as nation-building priorities centered on colonization of the West and the creation of transportation and communication links by railway construction. The latter in turn helped to concentrate manufacturing in central Canada, via favourable freight-rate and tariff politics (Brooks 2012). And so, federal government policies culminated in the Maritimes' de-industrialization by the 1920s, as the region experienced a massive loss of jobs, industry and corporate power, as well as a huge out-migration movement.[1] The region's economic decline turned into a long-term process, continuing to our days (Brodie 1990).

After Newfoundland joined Confederation in 1949, the term Atlantic Canada came into common usage and the region as a whole was often portrayed as economically "peripheral" and "disadvantaged." In Harold Innis's earlier "staples thesis" (Innis 1999 [1930]) and in other longstanding Canadian political economists' critiques of the privileged metropole, including Levitt's study influenced by dependency theory's core/periphery models (Levitt 2002 [1970]), it was clear that the federal government was not an innocent bystander in this process as, time and again, its major economic policies operated in ways that were "slanted towards the interests of central Canada" (Brooks 2012: 110). Here it is also important to acknowledge that some provinces in Atlantic Canada were harder hit than others, as reflected in divergent employment and income levels across the region. For instance, Newfoundland and Labrador, New Brunswick and PEI have traditionally been the poorest provinces in the country with personal income levels running at around 80 to 85 per cent of the Canadian average (Brooks 2012).

In spite of such notable differences, Atlantic Canadian provinces have shared some broad commonalities. Since 1945, population growth rates in the region have declined continuously and even became negative in the early years of the 21st century. Declining fertility rates and net out-migration have been the major causes of low (and in some cases zero) population growth rates (Desjardins 2011). What is more, the region was not immune to policy shifts taking place at the federal level. Despite a history of increasingly liberalized federal immigration policy from the 1960s onward (abandonment of the "white settler" policy; the adoption of the points system in 1967; the official *Multiculturalism Act* of 1971; and the 1976 *Immigration Act* favouring family reunification and removing other explicit barriers from Canadian immigration policies), Canada's reputation and practices around a more "open" approach to immigration began to change in the 1980s and 1990s (Abu-Laban and Gabriel 2002). Various neoliberal market reorientations designed to boost the ranks of "independent" and "worthy" immigrants reflected shifts in immigration priorities at the federal level, providing opportunities for some (e.g., business class immigrants), and constraints on others (family class immigrants and refugees) that, nevertheless, had an impact on the Atlantic region (Dobrowolsky and Tastsoglou 2011).

A more detailed examination of these issues is found in subsequent chapters, but for now, suffice it to say that a growing neoliberal marketization trend in federal immigration policy, along with devolutionary tendencies, such as the downloading of immigration matters from the federal to provincial levels from the late 1990s onward, have resulted in immigration agreements with each of the Atlantic provinces and substantial new provincial immigration programs (Dobrowolsky 2011; Dobrowolsky and Tastsoglou 2011). These aggressive provincial efforts have produced better numerical results in Atlantic Canada since 2001 (Murphy and de Finney 2008), in the sense that they have contributed to greater numbers of, and more diverse newcomers to, the region (consider here Baldacchino's chapter in this volume on recent migration patterns in PEI). However, the socio-economic and political costs of such programs across Atlantic Canada continue to be weighed, as indicated in this volume not only by Baldacchino, but also by Ramos and Yoshida as well as Dobrowolsky, Bryan and Gardiner Barber.

Nonetheless, all the provinces in the region have gone on to sign these agreements with the federal government that work to expedite immigration processes for desired nominees, and these agreements in turn have sparked other developments. For instance, new stand-alone provincial bodies responsible for immigration have been created and immigration strategies with set immigration targets each year have been adopted, becoming part of more defined and concerted immigration strategies for all the Atlantic provinces (Murphy and de Finney 2008). Alongside these efforts, there have also been a number of community initiatives—see chapters by Yax-Fraser and Cottrell; Tastsoglou, Cottrell and Jaya; as well as Tirone, Gallant, Sullivan, Shannon and Robertson in this volume. These initiatives have been developed not only in municipalities, but also in some rural areas—see Flint's, Hanson's and Wilson-Forsberg's respective chapters in this volume. Overall, through settlement and voluntary sector organizations, various mechanisms have been put in place to increase attraction and retention of immigrants in Atlantic Canada (Akbari and Mandale 2005; Yax-Fraser and Tastsoglou 2008; Clark 2009).

The immigration scene in Atlantic Canada has evolved over time, but aside from the dramatic shifts that occurred early on in the region, some of the most significant changes have occurred relatively recently. In the context of its political-economic, social and immigration history, it is no wonder Atlantic Canada has not been the focus of migration or ethnic studies research in

Canada. While there has been significant work on the Scottish pioneers (Campey 2004), Acadian (Arsenault 1965; Doucet 2004) and "Black" Nova Scotian and Maritime communities (Henry 1973; Walker 1976, 1980; Pachai 1987a, 1987b, 1990; Grant 1990; Saunders 1992), academic studies on a wider array of more recent immigrants and ethnic communities had been limited until recently (e.g., Gekas 1981; Medjuck 1986; Dogra 1987; Jabbra and Jabbra 1987; Abucar 1991; Hartzman 1991; Jabbra 1992, 1997; Gerrits 2000; Hartzman 2000; Thomas 2000; Waseem 2000). Moreover, research with a gender perspective or a focus on women had been lacking, with some exceptions (Thomas 1988; Ralston 1988, 1991, 2000; Miedema and Tastsoglou 2000; Tastsoglou and Miedema 2003). Major studies of Canada's ethnic groups still only barely touch on the different experience of living outside the major Canadian metropolitan centres with large concentrations of ethnic and diasporic communities.

However, in 2003, a new federal Metropolis Centre of Excellence for research on immigration and diversity was established in Atlantic Canada, the Atlantic Metropolis Centre of Excellence (AMC). Its creation, along with a renewed federal and provincial interest in immigration in Atlantic Canada, stimulated a wave of new research projects on immigration and immigrant and ethnic communities (cf. Crocker et al. 2007; Abdul-Razzaq 2008; Byers and Tastsoglou 2008; Murphy and de Finney 2008; Cottrell, Tastsoglou and Moncayo 2009; Dobrowolsky and Tastsoglou 2011; Tastsoglou and Jaya 2011; Dobrowolsky 2011, 2012; Bryan 2012). It also brought immigration studies in Atlantic Canada to the forefront and on par with similar research in other parts of Canada. The more significant rationale for the establishment of the AMC, however, was to study the reasons why immigrant attraction and retention in Atlantic Canada have lagged behind and how attraction and retention can be improved.

Consequently, research on integration and belonging in Atlantic Canada has flourished alongside and since the establishment of the AMC. Consider here a few illustrative studies selected for their range, scope and relevance to this collection. Baker et al.

(2012) discuss refugee youth's experiences of feeling at home in St. John's and argue that their perception of "home" is where they feel comfortable mixing elements of their "old" and "new" culture, selectively, resulting in the formation of a hybrid "congruent" Canadian identity. Structural elements, from security and the ability to engage in valued roles in the community (such as employment and education) are important elements of a welcoming community for these youths.

Benimmas's (2010) research among immigrant parents and Education students who are pre-service teachers in Francophone schools in Moncton, New Brunswick, reveals the impact (on teachers, parents and pupils) of the dynamics of schooling in an environment where French is a minority language and, more broadly, the processes of immigrant integration in a minority cultural context. Francophone schools are perceived by the parents of immigrant pupils as both sources of "opening" but also stigmatization. These findings point to gaps in the education of pre-service teachers who need to be able to teach in an environment of cultural diversity and communicate with immigrant parents.

Abdul-Razzaq (2008) examines Arab immigrant women's narratives of "home" and belonging in Halifax. Her findings reveal major divisions and differentiations among people identified as being of Arab or Middle-Eastern origin, falling along lines of class, gender, religion, history and country of origin. Her research challenges essentialist media portrayals and stereotypes of Arabs and Muslims, especially since 9/11. She argues, instead, that we must conceive of "identification" rather than "identity" as a constant process of adjustment rather than as something engraved in stone.

In a series of articles and book chapters elsewhere, Tastsoglou and Miedema (2003; 2005) and Tastsoglou (2006) draw on qualitative research into immigrant women's diverse experiences and focus on integration and belonging in two Maritime provinces (Nova Scotia and New Brunswick). The immigrant women in these studies, despite their qualifications, past work experience and willingness to work, find themselves marginalized in a labour market that raises systemic barriers. Yet, in order to overcome them, these women engage in community work, and thereby contribute to the social development of their communities and to social change. Thus, community involvement is identified as an important pathway in the integration process. Such experiences with work and community involvement have a direct impact on identity and on identity re-negotiation at the "borderlands" (Tastsoglou 2006).

In their work on security and immigration (2007), Crocker, Dobrowolsky, Keeble, Moncayo and Tastsoglou explore the changes and challenges arising from the security and immigration laws that took effect in Canada in the aftermath of 9/11. The researchers were particularly concerned with the impact of these changes on ethnic and immigrant groups, utilizing a multi-method research design, data derived from six cities, and a gender-based analysis. They were able to document a number of tendencies such as securitization and marketization of migration, reinforcement of state boundaries, new forms of racialization, and increased invisibilization of women.

Ku, Doyle and Mooney (2011) examine the (un)settlement experience of newcomer women in New Brunswick through a framework that integrates race, class and gender in transnationality, as well as in local and national processes. Jaya and Porter (2011) focus on the integration experiences of immigrant and refugee women in Newfoundland and Labrador. The researchers illustrate the negotiation and creative adaptation strategies that the immigrant and refugee women deployed in their new environment in order to cope with the challenges they experienced.

Topen's work (2011) outlines the labour market integration experiences and challenges of immigrant women from Sub-Saharan Africa in Halifax as well as their coping and resistance strategies. Amaya's research (2011) maps out the socio-cultural, gender and educational obstacles faced by male and female immigrant and refugee youth in Nova Scotia high schools. Brigham and Walsh (2011) explore the experiences and challenges of immigrant female teachers in Halifax. Weerasinghe's research (2011) deals with questions of accessibility to health for ethno-racial immigrant women in Atlantic Canada. Cottrell and VanderPlaat (2011) study the parenting of teens in immigrant families in Halifax and the special challenges for both groups. Yax-Fraser (2011) focuses on the "cross-cultural mothering" experiences of immigrant women in Halifax. Tirone and Sweatman (2011) examine how leisure is experienced by immigrant women and men in Halifax.

In sum, Atlantic Canada has experienced rapid, recent transformations both in the practices and study of immigration. Yet difficulties persist with respect to immigrant attraction and retention in the region. And while substantially more research in and on the region is being conducted than in the past, much more is required, especially in light of the unique Atlantic Canadian context and the gaps in information that remain. Here various issues come into play such as: a greater proportion of rural communities and small towns that are less attractive to immigrants; lack of knowledge about Atlantic Canada in other parts of the world; an economy that struggles to provide sufficient jobs even to the native-born; the misperception that immigrants "steal" jobs from the "locals" and a lack of appreciation for the former's contributions to the local economy and society; and insufficient resources devoted to immigration by all levels of government (Akbari and Mandale 2005).

It is with these challenges and changes in mind that we problematize key core concepts, in relation to the discourses and policy formulations around welcoming communities, the idea of Atlantic Canada, and notions of "home."

### III. "Welcoming Communities": Conceptual Clarifications and Recent Policy Directions

Although the concept of "welcoming communities" has been much utilized in policy circles since the 1990s, it has generally been understudied in scholarly literature. The concept encapsulates efforts to explore the host community's ability to integrate immigrants over the long term. A variety of reception strategies and services for newcomers have been increasingly adopted by small and mid-sized cities as illustrated in the journal *Our Diverse Cities* (issues from 2004 to 2012). The concept of a welcoming community was also utilized by the National Working Group on Small Centre Strategies' *Attracting and Retaining Immigrants: Tool Box of Ideas for Smaller Centres* (2007, 2nd edition, originally published in 2005).

The "Welcoming Communities Initiative" (WCI) has been Citizenship and Immigration Canada's (CIC) contribution to the Government of Canada's larger effort to reduce discriminatory barriers, referred to as "Canada's Action Plan Against Racism" (CAPAR). The latter was launched in 2005 and included a series of initiatives and strategies within a number of federal departments and agencies. The long-term goals of CAPAR are to strengthen social cohesion and economic inclusion and enhance Canada's legal frameworks by having the federal government take leadership in the areas of diversity, human rights and the elimination of racism (Citizenship and Immigration Canada 2011). Finally, the National Metropolis Project identified "Welcoming Communities" as a research policy domain in 2009.

Analytically, the concept includes: (a) a spatial element, a connection to a location (i.e., city, small community, region) and (b) a new discourse of responsibility for integration, placed upon all stakeholders, governments, cities, municipalities and individuals—both newcomers and native-born (Belkhodja 2009). These components imply that the locality has the agency to undertake initiatives that facilitate integration, that the integration effort and strategy is a collective one, assumed in partnership by the various stakeholders, and that the "location has the capacity to meet the needs and promote inclusion of newcomers as well as the machinery in place to produce and support these capacities" (Esses et al. 2010: 9).

This conceptualization of welcoming communities also reflects CIC's "two-way street" model of integration, focusing on creating connections between Canadians and newcomers through a number of measures including eliminating barriers to integration and educating against racism. Based on this model, a welcoming community goes beyond measuring inputs for achieving integration, but also measures outcomes, such as integration itself. This reflects in turn Canada's increasing awareness that basic settlement services are not sufficient for integration but that we should be concerned with social engagement, a sense of belonging, social cohesion and citizenship, with sensitivity to regional and local needs (Esses et al. 2010: 8).

To elaborate further, some scholars view welcoming communities as a means to achieve integration—defined as the social, cultural, political and economic incorporation of a newcomer's life into the receiving society, demonstrated by indicators at structural, community and individual levels (Frideres 2008). More recently, scholars increasingly agreed that welcoming communities go beyond input and include outcomes, such as the accomplishment of integration itself (i.e., they converge on a more substantive definition of "integration"). Esses et al. (2010), for example, emphasize the "capacity" of welcoming communities to achieve integration. Vatz Laaroussi (2010) also includes in her model of *"collectivités accueillantes"* systemic and structural outcomes and processes (e.g., social, human, political and cultural capital, and community development, resilience and vitality), which also go beyond inputs into the integration process. Clark's (2009) conceptualization of welcoming communities attempts to recognize and integrate the previous two perspectives. She defines a welcoming community as a social inclusion approach to the reception of immigrants at federal, provincial and municipal levels. She acknowledges the normative dimension of social inclusion and that, depending on whether it is conceptualized and operationalized as a set of structural or liberal strategies (Richmond and Saloojee 2005), a welcoming community can be more or less effective as an instrument for integration.

Our perspective dovetails better with these broader and deeper formulations of welcoming community. It goes beyond mere inputs and includes integration outcomes. It does so by acknowledging and grappling with the complex, multi-layered processes at play that are encapsulated in more all-encompassing notions of citizenship. This means that while socio-cultural, economic and political integration into the realm of broadly defined citizenship are critical, so too is social engagement on several levels including the psychological sense of belonging (Tastsoglou and Dobrowolsky 2006). To be sure, belonging is also very much a part of economic considerations, as researchers have pointed out the centrality of economic experiences of immigrants in shaping their feelings of attachment as well as social and cultural integration in Canada (e.g., Kazemipur 2012; Tastsoglou 2006). And so, we show how feeling "at home" includes this psychological/emotional dimension of citizenship—the sense of belonging—which in theory may exist independently of the other dimensions of citizenship such as rights and governance issues, but in practice is intertwined and interdependent with them. In short, the way we conceptualize the "warmth of the welcome" includes structural, political and institutional, as well as interpersonal and even psychological/emotional components.

Last but not least, our understanding of feeling "at home" encompasses the fact that, in Canada's multicultural society, "home" may entail belonging to multiple collectivities on various levels (Tastsoglou 2006). Claiming "home" involves a political act of claiming a place as one's own (Brah 1996), but one that can be informed by intersecting identities built on multiple localities. Therefore, in the chapters that follow, it becomes apparent not only that "home" can be pluri-local and based on intersecting identities, but also that these "homes" do not necessarily undermine each other but can, on the contrary, build upon, strengthen one another, and contribute to feelings of belonging.

## IV. What is Atlantic Canada? Questions of Integration and Belonging

Before proceeding any further with our discussion of integration and belonging experiences in Atlantic Canada, it is important to address the issue of whether we can consider Atlantic Canada as a distinct region with a unitary identity that can, in fact, interface with immigration, shaping the integration experiences, identities and senses of belonging of immigrants in similar ways.

Sociologists, political scientists, geographers, historians and economists all define regions in different ways, using different criteria (Brym 1986; Bickerton and Gagnon 2009; Stewart 2011). Moreover, there are various theories of and approaches to regionalism, from modernization paradigms to institutionalism and Marxist analyses (Bickerton and Gagnon 2009). Our intent here is not to review this vast literature, but rather emphasize a few key issues around understandings of the "Atlantic region" while acknowledging that this in itself is a highly contested term. Therefore, rather than treating the region as a "discrete, sharply bounded, static" unit that fits together in an "unambiguous way," our perspective accords more with the view that "the world is not structured in such a neat manner; to the contrary, regions disappear and reappear as they are transformed by various economic, political, and cultural factors" (Väyrynen 2003: 25).

Janine Brodie argues in *Political Economy of Canadian Regionalism* (1990), that Canadian regions are neither defined by internal parameters of climate, land, geography and natural resources, nor reducible to provinces. Rather, they are formed by their relationship to external units, either other regions or their relationship with a political centre, and shaped by political economic processes of development and capitalist accumulation. At the same time, their similar responses to external factors over time may have resulted in cultural, political and economic similarities among provinces to the extent that one can speak of a "region."

For example, the effects of the first National Policy in Canada at the time of Confederation triggered very similar responses of, first, economic development and, second, economic bust and long-term crisis across the region. Although there were variations in the degree of economic diversification, industrial production, and natural resources among the three Maritime provinces, nonetheless, the larger process of economic restructuring that resulted from their congruent relationships to the national economic and political "centre" or "core" launched comparable economic marginalization processes in the East Coast "periphery." The second and third National Policies that followed in the post-war era seem to have consolidated such processes, despite compensatory policies, decentralization of "national development" and regional development efforts (Brodie 1990: 135-228). As a result, these National Policies ultimately worked to re-cast the fates, achieving a degree of shared socio-economic and political disadvantage among the four Atlantic provinces (including Newfoundland and Labrador after 1949).

In addition, a number of interprovincial bodies and policies, emerging at various local, provincial and federal levels, exemplify as well as serve as a glue for this regional bond, such as the Council of Atlantic Premiers (CAP), the Atlantic Provinces Economic Council (APEC), the Atlantic Innovation Fund (AIF), the Atlantic Investment Tax Credit, various professional associations, think-tanks (e.g., Atlantic Institute for Market Studies (AIMS)) and Atlantic Canada Studies programs (Locke 2011), as well as collaborations across municipalities in the region of the kind referenced at the start of this chapter. In 2006, there was even a political party established with the objective of achieving "a political union of the four easternmost provinces of Canada" (Stewart 2011: 260), the "Atlantica Party."

Such initiatives notwithstanding, there is by no means agreement among scholars as to whether Atlantic Canada can be considered a "reality," even "a region in the making," or a myth. The "myth" claim argues that while there are common interests—including a strong sense of grievance of the provinces' treatment within the Confederation, shared historical experiences including similar out-migration histories, a significant sense of "place" and interprovincial collaboration on a number of issues—the provinces are also distinguished by sharp differences, historical and present, including intense competition on resource issues, in particular, and protracted legal disputes as a result. Geography by itself cannot settle the question of a common region and regional identity.

The question of conceptualizing Atlantic Canada as a region is significant because of policies that may or may not be associated with such a view. If being seen as a region leads to "one size fits all" approaches, then this might be detrimental in that it overlooks or sidesteps provincial specificities. At the same time, however, regional recognition may mean strength in numbers in the form of collaboration for benefits that accrue to every province. As Locke concludes, "Is Atlantic Canada a myth or a reality? Yes, it just depends on the context" (2011: 253).

In this volume, mindful of the above discussion in the literature, we do not start from an *a priori* definition of "Atlantic Canada" as a distinct region. We use the term mostly in a geographical sense; we view it through a political economy lens; and we consider Atlantic Canada as being one of many nested identities. But we also attempt to understand any further meaning empirically, by drawing out broad similarities and differences among the studies at hand. Even so, we are aware that any conclusions as to the "region" being a "home away from home" for immigrants (i) only provide a partial and contingent picture of a far more complex reality of settlement, integration and belonging and (ii) constitute by no means generalizations about a common "character" of the region.

With these caveats and conceptual clarifications in mind, and in light of the key questions, analytical framework and themes discussed above, this collection contains broad-ranging, informative studies that address diverse immigrant experiences, barriers and enabling factors of making a home and belonging in a particular province, city, locality or other community of Atlantic Canada.

## V. The Structure of This Volume

This introductory chapter, along with the first chapter by Ramos and Yoshida, contribute the contextual background for theme one, *Welcoming Communities: The Backdrop to Immigration in Atlantic Canada*. In their chapter entitled "From Away, But Here to Stay? Trends in Outmigration among a Cohort of Recent Immigrants to Atlantic Canada," Ramos and Yoshida offer a descriptive sketch of economic and non-economic factors associated with out-migration from Atlantic Canada to other provinces. Using data from the first two waves of the Longitudinal Survey of Immigrants to Canada, the authors find that immigrants who leave the region are underemployed; more educated; tend to have family in Canada; perceive discrimination; and are more likely to be male than female. By extension, then, this chapter offers a grounded account of why Atlantic Canada will not become a "home away from home" for the many immigrants who leave the region.

Theme two of the volume, *Immigration and Settlement Policies and Immigrant Experiences*, consists of three chapters which deal with selected immigrant experiences in Atlantic Canada that reflect existing immigration, settlement and integration policies or the lack thereof, as well as their gendered nature and repercussions. In "Choices, Calculations and Commitments that Help to Create a Home Away from Home," Dobrowolsky, Bryan and Gardiner Barber provide a vivid snapshot of a failed Nova Scotian immigration initiative that was well-intentioned but ultimately fell well short of expectations. This study of the "economic" category of the Nova Scotia Nominee Program (NSNP) serves to illustrate how and why an attempt to create a "home away from home," even for a group of immigrants strategically selected for class (and arguably, for gender and for race and ethnicity as well), can become fraught with difficulties and result in disappointing outcomes for all concerned. It suggests that part of the problem lies in the imbalance between social and economic wants and needs, along with an appreciable "disconnect" between the priorities of provincial immigration officials and the newcomers in question. From this the authors argue that new immigration strategies must work harder at achieving a greater equilibrium between economic and social priorities, and at balancing the choices, calculations and commitments of state officials with those of newcomers.

Chapter 4 is about immigrant women's search for a "home away from home" when they do not have access to safe and secure housing. The chapter starts from the premise that the need for security constitutes a key migration rationale for many immigrant women fleeing from political instability, war, economic crises, natural disasters, systemic gender violence, organized crime and narco-trafficking in their countries of origin. Having a roof over one's head and a physical space of comfort that one can call one's own is vital to the development of this sense of security, of feeling "at home" and belonging. It is therefore an important part of the successful integration of immigrants and refugees into a new society. And yet, when they come to Canada, immigrant women do not always find that sense of security. In "Home, Housing and Homelessness: Can Migrant Women Call Halifax 'Home' If They Don't Have a Dwelling Place?" Yax-Fraser and Cottrell argue that a number of newcomer women to Halifax suffer "invisible homelessness" and make the distinction between absolute and relative homelessness to provide a broader and more inclusive understanding of migrant women's homelessness. This chapter thus raises awareness about the fact that immigrant women's homelessness has to be understood as a continuum of tenuous housing arrangements intricately tied to the sexual division of labour and to women's social vulnerabilities.

In "Women, Immigration and Violence: Focusing on Atlantic Canada," Tastsoglou, Cottrell and Jaya argue that culturally appropriate intervention services in support of immigrant women and families in crisis are not only much needed measures to deal with violence, but are also indispensable tools of an integration strategy for immigrant women. This chapter, deriving from a 2007 mixed-method, multi-site study incorporating community feedback, examines the various forms of violence that immigrant women of diverse ethno-cultural backgrounds experience in their daily lives in five urban centres of Atlantic Canada. It assesses the impact of violence in women's lives and those of other family members, as well as the consequences of such experiences for adaptation. Starting with a broad framework on violence, the researchers explore violence in the family, in the workplace and in the public arena, from the immigrant women's own perspectives. The study also examines the ways in which immigrant women interfaced with and were constructed by social institutions such as settlement, social, criminal justice, employment and education services when it came to issues of violence. Finally, the authors discuss women's strategies for coping with/resolving the violence and their identification of service needs. The narratives of immigrant women illustrate their resilience and agency and the complex intertwining of violence with integration, in particular how the former (violence) may act as a powerful barrier to the latter (integration).

Theme three of the collection homes in on *Immigration in Small Communities,* and consists of three chapters that provide accounts of small-town and rural experiences of immigration in the different provinces of Atlantic Canada. In "Why do Immigrants Want to Come Here? A Case-Study of Immigration in Colchester County," Flint provides a case study from rural Nova Scotia. Based on data obtained from thirty semi-structured interviews, Flint develops a typology of immigrants who arrived with different expectations and who faced different problems. For example, his study suggests that immigrants who are visible minorities, have difficulties with English or are female find it hardest to integrate into this rural community, and that even the desperately needed immigrant professionals have difficulties with credential recognition. Flint's study also shows that immigrants are usually first attracted to this rural area of Nova Scotia through personal relationships or family ties with area residents, and that the strength of these ties correlates with the likelihood that immigrants will remain.

In "Community Support for the Leisure and the Well-being of Immigrant Families in Small Atlantic Canadian Communities," the second chapter in the theme on Immigration in Small Communities, Tirone, Gallant, Sullivan, Shannon and Robertson address immigrants' experiences of well-being and the role of leisure in facilitating their well-being. The authors provide an overview of the efforts being made by twenty-four Atlantic Canadian communities to support the social well-being of new immigrants. Their focus is on communities with populations between 5,000 and 12,000, as these medium-sized communities in this region are interested in recruiting immigrants to address population declines due to aging and out-migration. The authors recognize that immigrants settle in places primarily based on the availability of jobs, but job satisfaction is only one aspect of well-being. This study enhances our understanding of immigrants' lives beyond the workplace, and how small communities may facilitate initiatives that support social inclusion that may in turn contribute to immigrants remaining in the long term.

Chapter 8 is a small-town New Brunswick study that focuses on youth and belonging. In "Immigrant Adolescents' Journey to Belonging in New Brunswick: Making Friends with Local-Born Peers," Wilson-Forsberg argues that making Atlantic Canada a "home away from home" for immigrant adolescents is a particularly crucial consideration given that these are the citizens of the future. Her chapter documents the everyday worlds of immigrant adolescents as they adjust to their new lives and gradually acquire a sense of belonging in a small city and rural town in the province of New Brunswick. The research findings suggest that, for immigrant adolescents, the development of friendships in a small urban community is quite different from that of a rural community. In Fredericton, there is little purposeful contact between immigrant adolescents and their New Brunswick-born peers, while informal and spontaneous efforts of friendly engaged citizens in Florenceville-Bristol appear to ease the development of friendships and intra-group relations. Despite this difference, the immigrant adolescents in both communities appeared to have undergone similar journeys to belonging resulting in, for the most part, relatively positive outcomes.

Finally, theme four, *Building Belonging*, consists of three chapters. The first chapter in this thematic unit is about the importance of small communities' real willingness to "welcome" immigrants in their midst and for immigrants to settle in order for successful integration to take place. In "A 'Stopover Place' at Best? Recent Trends in Immigrant Attraction and Retention on Prince Edward Island," Baldacchino critiques immigration studies as often including an assumption that immigrants have a desire to settle, and that host communities have a desire to, or interest in, supporting such settlement. Recent migration to Prince Edward Island, the smallest of the Atlantic provinces, suggests that these assumptions are not currently tenable. Just under 80 per cent of the 5,839 immigrants to PEI between 2008-2010 have entered under the Provincial Nominee Program (PNP) under the investor class, and most of these have opted to migrate to PEI mainly for strategic reasons relating both to the ease and speed of case processing and to the level of required financial investment. They see less benefit in taking any initiatives to integrate with the host PEI society when their long-term plan is to leave for larger cities (particularly Toronto and Vancouver), where they can connect with their relatives and friends in their own ethnic or national diaspora, partake in ethnic food, speak their native language, share in common events, and place their children in what they consider to be better schools. Within these plans, PEI comes across as a convenient stepping stone, a "stop-over place." Meanwhile, this disposition connects with a host society that rhetorically proclaims the importance of immigrants from demographic and labour market perspectives, but which, in practice, has very little appetite, interest, skill or disposition to act as a "welcoming community."

The second chapter of this theme (Chapter 10) is a comparative study of highly skilled Turkish immigrants' experiences in Toronto and Halifax. In "Is 'Home' Where We Fill Our Stomachs? Turkish Professionals in Halifax and Toronto," Sevgur provides an account of the perceptions of "home" based on a qualitative study conducted with immigrant professionals of Turkish origin, which explored their identities, belongings and network participation. Although there were differences based on the starkly different cities in question, the perceptions of "home" and social processes via which "home" was formed were surprisingly similar for participants from these two different cities. Sevgur highlights the presence of loved ones and portability as two defining features of "home." Local, national and transnational networking practices facilitated the building and maintenance of "home" by the respondents, who either saw Canada as their only home or as one of their two homes.

Finally, in chapter 11, the last chapter of this theme, "Why here? Immigrants' Decisions to Stay or Leave Maritime Communities: Research from Miramichi, New Brunswick," Hanson uses qualitative research to explore the decision-making process surrounding staying or leaving this rural New Brunswick community. The data addresses what interviewees considered positive and negative aspects of living in Miramichi, whether they felt welcome, and if they were going to remain there. The findings indicate the important influence of social and cultural factors on decisions to stay in a community. This case study clearly supports the idea that a welcoming community, from a socio-cultural perspective, can help to retain those immigrants initially attracted to an area, and that this may be even more important in smaller cities such as Miramichi. However, the author also underlines certain immigration issues that need to be addressed across all levels of government in order to facilitate the immigration process in general.

Given the foregoing, it is our intention to provide an array of engaging, accessible analyses from across the region that helps us to outline and assess how to extend a more substantively "warm" welcome to newcomers, and how to truly make Atlantic Canada a lasting "home away from home" for immigrants. We sincerely thank all the authors for their efforts in contributing to and helping us to realize this ambitious project. Let us now turn to their invaluable insights.

**Note**

1. 300,000 Maritimers left the region between 1900 and 1930 with nearly half of them emigrating during the 1920s (Brodie 1990: 124).

| TABLE 1.1 POP. BY SELECTED ETHNIC / REGIONAL ORIGINS | | | | |
|---|---|---|---|---|
| | NS | NB | PEI | NL |
| Total population 2011 | 921,727 | 751,171 | 140,204 | 514,536 |
| Other North American Origins (American, Canadian, Acadian, etc.) | 376,285 | 394,995 | 53,800 | 253,255 |
| French | 154,130 | 199,970 | 28,950 | 28,845 |
| Acadian | 20,505 | 32,005 | 3,760 | 395 |
| German | 97,605 | 34,870 | 7,160 | 8,190 |
| Dutch | 32,520 | 16,370 | 4,240 | 1,860 |
| North American Aboriginal Origins | 52,930 | 37,900 | 4,460 | 43,395 |
| Northern European (except British Isles) | 14,640 | 10,405 | 2,115 | 3,095 |
| Western European (except French) | 125,775 | 50,725 | 11,625 | 10,180 |
| Italian | 14,305 | 7,195 | 955 | 1,825 |
| Southern European | 26,440 | 12,245 | 2,370 | 3,985 |
| Eastern European | 26,515 | 10,840 | 2,650 | 3,575 |
| Other European (Jewish, Roma, Basque, Slavic n.o.s.) | 5,125 | 1,875 | 300 | 515 |
| West Central Asian and Middle Eastern Origins | 14,710 | 4,610 | 1,300 | 1,295 |
| Lebanese | 7,245 | 2,645 | 700 | 630 |
| East and Southeast Asian | 11,360 | 6,940 | 2,560 | 2,800 |
| Chinese | 7,065 | 2,945 | 1,920 | 1,970 |
| Filipino | 2,110 | 1,155 | 95 | 375 |
| Korean | 1,165 | 1,865 | 140 | 120 |
| South Asian | 5,935 | 3,090 | 500 | 2,000 |
| African origins | 15,115 | 4,435 | 500 | 1,445 |
| Caribbean | 4,215 | 1,620 | 305 | 750 |
| Latin, Central and South American | 2,380 | 1,650 | 445 | 500 |

*Table 1.1 - Statistics Canada, 2011 National Household Survey: Data Tables (by province, total single and multiple ethnic origin responses)*

## References

Abdul-Razzaq, Dalal. 2008. Discourses of Citizenship and Community: Arab Immigrant Women and their Narratives of Home and Belonging in Halifax, N.S. *Working Paper No 13.* Halifax: Atlantic Metropolis Centre.

Abucar, Mohamed H. 1991. *Peoples of the Maritimes: Italians.* Tantallon, NS: Four East Publications.

Abu-Laban, Yasmeen and Christina Gabriel. 2002. *Selling Diversity: Immigration, Multiculturalism, Employment Equity and Globalization.* Peterborough: Broadview Press.

Akbari, Ather H. 2012. *Socioeconomic and Demographic Profiles of Immigrants in Nova Scotia.* Halifax: Atlantic Metropolis Centre of Excellence. A Report.

Akbari, Ather H., Scott Lynch, James Ted McDonald and Wimal Rankaduwa. 2007. *Socioeconomic and Demographic Profiles of Immigrants in Atlantic Canada*, 65. Halifax: Atlantic Metropolis Centre. Report.

Akbari, Ather H. and Maurice Mandale. 2005. A Survey of Selected Presentations of the Conference on Immigration and Outmigration: Atlantic Canada at a Crossroads. *Canadian Ethnic Studies* 37 (3), 150-60.

Amaya, Benjamin. 2011. The Experience of Gender, Culture, and Ethnicity in Nova Scotia High Schools. In *Immigrant Women in Atlantic Canada. Challenges, Negotiations, Re-constructions*, ed. Evangelia Tastsoglou and Peruvemba S. Jaya, 175-207. Toronto: Canadian Scholars' Press/Women's Press.

Arsenault, Bona. 1965. *Histoire et généalogie des Acadiens. Tome 1 et 2.* Québec: Le Conseil de la Vie française en Amérique.

Baker, James, Chris W. Martin and Jonathan Price. 2012. "Home Is Where the Self Is: The Intersection among Security, Role, and Identity." Presentation at the Research Symposium *Atlantic Canada: A Home Away from Home? Gender and Intersectional Perspectives on Immigration* (St. John's, NL, Atlantic Metropolis, September 28-29, 2012).

Basque, Maurice. 2011. Atlantic Realities, Acadian Identities, Arcadian Dreams. In *Shaping an Agenda for Atlantic Canada*, ed. John G. Reid and Donald J. Savoie, 162-77. Black Point, NS: Fernwood.

Belkhodja, Chedly. 2009. Toward a More Welcoming Community? Observations on the Greater Moncton Area. In *Plan Canada. Welcoming Communities: Planning for Diverse Populations*, 96-98. Ottawa: Citizenship and Immigration Canada, Canadian Institute of Planners and Metropolis.

Benimmas, Aïcha. 2010. L'intégration des élèves immigrants, la relation école-familles immigrées et l' adhésion à la mission de l' école francophone acadienne selon les perceptions des parents immigrants et des futures enseignantes. Working Paper No 26. Halifax: Atlantic Metropolis Centre.

Bickerton, James and Alain G. Gagnon. 2009. Regions and Regionalism. In *Canadian Politics*, ed. James Bickerton and Alain G. Gagnon, 71-93. Toronto: University of Toronto Press.

Brah, Avtar. 1996. *Cartographies of Diaspora: Contesting Identities*. London: Routledge.

Brigham, Susan and Susan Walsh. 2011. Having Voice, Being Heard, and Being Silent: Internationally Educated Teachers' Representations of Immigrant Women in an Arts-Informed Research Study. In *Immigrant Women in Atlantic Canada. Challenges, Negotiations, Re-constructions*, ed. Evangelia Tastsoglou and Peruvemba S. Jaya, 209-34. Toronto: Canadian Scholars' Press/Women's Press.

Brodie, Janine. 1990. *The Political Economy of Canadian Regionalism*. Toronto: Harcourt Brace Jovanovitch.

Brooks, Stephen. 2012. *Canadian Democracy*. Don Mills: Oxford University Press.

Bryan, Catherine. 2012. Gendered Returns, Ambivalent Transnationals: Situating Transnationalism in Local Asymmetry. *Anthropologica*, 54 (1): 133-42.

Brym, Robert. 1986. *Regionalism in Canada*. Richmond Hill: Irwin.

Byers, Michèle and Evangelia Tastsoglou. 2008. Negotiating Ethnocultural identity: The Experience of Greek and Jewish Youth in Halifax. *Canadian Ethnic Studies* 40 (2).

Campey, Lucille H. 2004. *After the Hector: The Scottish Pioneers of Nova Scotia and Cape Breton, 1773-1852*. Toronto: Natural Heritage Books.

Carrigan, D. Owen. 1988. The Immigrant Experience in Halifax, 1881-1931. *Canadian Ethnic Studies* 20 (3): 28-41.

Citizenship and Immigration Canada. 2011. *Evaluation of the Welcoming Communities Initiative*, Appendix A. http://www.cic.gc.ca/english/resources/evaluation/wci/appendixA.asp (accessed February 6, 2013).

Clark, Natasha. 2009. *Welcoming Communities and Immigrant Integration in Newfoundland and Labrador*, 77. Unpublished MA Thesis, Ryerson University.

Cottrell, Barbara, Evangelia Tastsoglou and Carmen Celina Moncayo. 2009. Violence in Immigrant Families in Halifax. In *Racialized Migrant Women in Canada: Essays on Health, Violence and Equity*, ed. Vijay Agnew, 70-94. Toronto: University of Toronto Press.

Cottrell, Barbara and Madine VanderPlaat. 2011. My Kids Want To Eat Pork: Parent-Teen Conflicts in Immigrant Families. In *Immigrant Women in Atlantic Canada. Challenges, Negotiations, Re-constructions*, ed. Evangelia Tastsoglou and Peruvemba S. Jaya, 267-96. Toronto: Canadian Scholars' Press/Women's Press.

Crocker, Diane, Alexandra Dobrowolsky, Carmen Celina Moncayo and Evangelia Tastsoglou. 2007. *Security and Immigration, Changes and Challenges: Immigrant and Ethnic Communities in Atlantic Canada, Presumed Guilty?* Ottawa: Status of Women Canada, Policy Research Fund and Canadian Heritage.

Desjardins, Pierre-Marcel. 2011. Demographic Challenges for Atlantic Canada's Provinces: An Urban-Rural Analysis. In *Shaping An Agenda for Atlantic Canada*, ed. John G. Reid and Donald J. Savoie, 292-301. Black Point, NS: Fernwood.

Dobrowolsky, Alexandra. 2011. The Intended and Unintended Effects of a New Immigration Strategy: Insights from Nova Scotia's Provincial Nominee Program. *Studies in Political Economy* 87 (Spring): 109-41.

———. 2012. Nuancing Neoliberalism: Lessons Learned from a Failed Immigration Experiment. *Journal of International Migration and Integration*. Published online 15 February, 2012. DOI: 10.1007/s12134-012-0234-8.

Dobrowolsky, Alexandra and Howard Ramos. 2014. *Expanding the Vision: Why Nova Scotia Should Look Beyond Econocentric Immigration Policy*, 1-37. Nova Scotia: Canadian Centre for Policy Alternatives.

Dobrowolsky, Alexandra and Evangelia Tastsoglou. 2011. Continuity and Change in Immigration Policy: Canada, Atlantic Canada and the Future of Citizenship. In *Shaping an Agenda for Atlantic Canada*, ed. John G. Reid and Donald S. Savoie, 263-292. Black Point, NS: Fernwood.

Dogra, Ravi. 1987. *Peoples of the Maritimes: Indo-Canadians.* Tantallon, NS: Four East Publications.

Doucet, Clive. 2004. *Lost and Found in Acadie.* Halifax: Nimbus Publishing.

Esses, Victoria M., Leah K. Hamilton, Caroline Bennett-AbuAyyash and Meyer Burstein. 2010. *Characteristics of a Welcoming Community.* A Report to Citizenship and Immigration Canada.

Freedman, Bill. 2011. Environmental Change and Legacy in Atlantic Canada. In *Shaping An Agenda for Atlantic Canada*, ed. John G. Reid and Donald J. Savoie, 169-231. Black Point, NS: Fernwood.

Frideres, James. 2008. Creating an Inclusive Society: Promoting Social Integration in Canada. In *Immigration and Integration in Canada in the Twenty-first Century*, ed. John Biles, Meyer Burstein and James Frideres. Kingston, ON: McGill-Queens University Press.

Gekas, George Andrew. 1981 [1979]. *The Greeks in Cape Breton.* The Department of the Secretary of State. Province of Nova Scotia.

Gerrits, G. H. 2000. *Peoples of the Maritimes: Dutch.* Tantallon, NS: Four East Publications.

Grant, John N. 1990. *The Immigration and Settlement of the Black Refugees of the War of 1812 in Nova Scotia and New Brunswick.* Dartmouth, NS: The Black Cultural Centre for Nova Scotia.

Hartzman, Carole A. 1991. *"Not yet Canadians..." The Latin American Immigrant Experience in Nova Scotia.* Halifax: International Education Centre, Saint Mary's University.

———. 2000. *Peoples of the Maritimes: The Latin Americans.* Tantallon, NS: Four East Publications.

Henry, Francis. 1973. *Forgotten Canadians: The Blacks of Nova Scotia.* Don Mills, ON: Longman Canada.

Innis, Harold A. 1999. *The Fur Trade in Canada: An Introduction to Canadian Economic History.* Toronto: University of Toronto Press.

Ivany, Ray, Irene d'Entremont, Dan Christmas, Susanna Fuller and John Bragg. 2014. *Now or Never: An Urgent Call to Action for Nova Scotians.* Final Report of the Nova Scotia Commission on Building Our New Economy. http://onens.ca/wp-content/uploads/Now-or-Never-Nova-Scotia-Final-Report-with-Research-Engagement-Documentation.pdf

Jabbra, Nancy W. 1992. Immigrant Culture Change in Atlantic Canada. In *Migration and the Transformation of Cultures*, ed. Jean Burnet,

Daniell Juteau, Enoch Padolsky, Anthony Rasporich and Antoine Sirois, 145-62. Toronto: Multicultural History Society of Ontario.

Jabbra, Nancy W. 1997. Politics and Acceptance: The Lebanese in Canada's Maritime Provinces. *Canadian Ethnic Studies* 29 (1): 99-118.

Jabbra, Nancy W. and Joséph G. Jabbra. 1987. *Peoples of the Maritimes: Lebanese*. Tantallon, NS: Four East Publications.

Jaya, S. Peruvemba and Marilyn Porter. 2011. Asking for Apples from a Lemon Tree: Experiences of Immigrant Women in Newfoundland and Labrador. In *Immigrant Women in Atlantic Canada. Challenges, Negotiations, Re-constructions*, ed. Evangelia Tastsoglou and Peruvemba S. Jaya, 111-41. Toronto: Canadian Scholars' Press/Women's Press

Kazemipur, Abdie. 2012. Employment and Social Integration of Immigrants: The Intersection with Gender and Religion. Presentation at the Research Symposium *Atlantic Canada: A Home Away from Home? Gender and Intersectional Perspectives on Immigration* (St. John's, NL, Atlantic Metropolis, September 28-29).

Ku, Jane S., Judith Doyle and Nicola Mooney. 2011. Consolidating the Self: Immigrant Women's Settlement in New Brunswick. In *Immigrant Women in Atlantic Canada. Challenges, Negotiations, Re-constructions*, ed. Evangelia Tastsoglou and Peruvemba S. Jaya, 79-11. Toronto: Canadian Scholars' Press/Women's Press.

Levitt, Kari. 2002 (1970). *Silent Surrender: The Multinational Corporation in Canada*. Montreal and Kingston: McGill Queen's University Press.

Locke, Wade. 2011. Atlantic Canada: Myth or Reality? In *Shaping an Agenda for Atlantic Canada*, ed. John G. Reid and Donald J. Savoie, 235-57. Black Point, NS: Fernwood.

McDonald, James Ted. 2003. Location Choice of New Immigrants to Canada: The Role of Ethnic Networks. In *Canadian Immigration Policy for the 21st Century*, ed. Charles M. Beach, Alan G. Green and Jeffrey G. Reitz, 163-95. Montreal and Kingston: John Deutsch Institute for the Study of Economic Policy, Queen's University and McGill-Queen's University Press

Medjuck, Sheva. 1986. *Jews of Atlantic Canada*. St. John's, NL: Breakwater.

Miedema, Baukje and Evangelia Tastsoglou. 2000. But Where are you from, Originally? Immigrant Women and Integration in the Maritimes. *Atlantis* 24 (2): 82-91.

Murphy, Terry and James de Finney, ed. 2008. *Our Diverse Cities*. Special Issue on the Atlantic Region. Atlantic Metropolis, Citizenship and Immigration Canada and Canadian Heritage, Spring (5).

National Working Group on Small Centre Strategies. 2007. *Attracting and Retaining Immigrants: A Tool Box of Ideas for Smaller Centres*. Inter-Cultural Association of Greater Victoria. 2nd ed. http://eae.alberta.ca/documents/WIA/WIA-EN_Toolbox.pdf (accessed February 3, 2013).

Pachai, Bridgal. 1987a. *Beneath the Clouds of the Promised Land: The Survival of Nova Scotia's Blacks. Vol. 1: 1600-1800*. Halifax: Black Educators' Association of Nova Scotia.

———. 1987b. *Peoples of the Maritimes:Blacks*. Tantallon, NS: Four East Publications.

———. 1990. *Beneath the Clouds of the Promised Land: The Survival of Nova Scotia's Blacks. Vol. 2: 1800-1989*. Halifax, NS: Black Educators' Association of Nova Scotia.

Ralston, Helen. 1988. Ethnicity, Class and Gender among South Asian Women in Metro Halifax: An Exploratory Study. *Canadian Ethnic Studies* 20 (3), 63-83.

———. 1991. Race, Class, Gender and Work Experience of South Asian Immigrant Women in Atlantic Canada. *Canadian Ethnic Studies* 23 (2), 129-39.

———. 1996. *The Lived Experiences of South Asian Immigrant Women in Atlantic Canada: The Interconnections of Race, Class, and Gender*. Lewiston, NY: Edwin Mellen Press.

———. 2000. Mothers and Daughters in the Diaspora: A Comparative Study of Identity Construction among Women of South Asian Origin in Canada and Australia. Paper presented at the Fifth International Metropolis Conference, Vancouver, BC.

Richmond, Ted and Anver Saloojee, ed. 2005. *Social Inclusion: Canadian Perspectives*. Halifax: Fernwood Publishing.

Saunders, Charles R. 1992. *Spirit of Africville*. Halifax: Formac.

Statistics Canada, 2014. *2011 National Household Survey: Data Tables* http://www12.statcan.gc.ca/nhs-enm/2011/dp-pd/dt-td/Rp-eng.cfm?LANG=E&APATH=3&DETAIL=0&DIM=0&FL=A&FREE=0&GC=0&GID=0&GK=0&GRP=1&PID=105396&PRID=0&PTYPE=105277&S=0&SHOWALL=0&SUB=0&Temporal=2013&THEME=95&VID=0&VNAMEE&VNAMEF (accessed October 10, 2014).

Stewart, Ian. 2011. Region and Atlantic Canada. In *Shaping an Agenda for Atlantic Canada,* ed. John G. Reid and Donald J. Savoie, 258-62. Black Point, NS: Fernwood.

Tastsoglou, Evangelia. 2006. Gender, Migration and Citizenship: Immigrant women and the Politics of Belonging in the Canadian Maritimes. In *Women, Migration and Citizenship: Making Local, National and Transnational Connections*, ed. Evangelia Tastsoglou and Alexandra Dobrowolsky, 201-30. Aldershot, U.K.: Ashgate.

———. 2011. Women, Gender and Immigration: Focusing on Atlantic Canada. In *Immigrant Women in Atlantic Canada. Challenges, Negotiations, Re-constructions*, ed. Evangelia Tastsoglou and Peruvemba S. Jaya, 1-51. Toronto: Canadian Scholars' Press/Women's Press.

Tastsoglou, Evangelia and Alexandra Dobrowolsky, ed. 2006. *Women, Migration and Citizenship: Making Local, National and Transnational Connections.* Aldershot, U.K.: Ashgate.

Tastsoglou, Evangelia and Baukje Miedema. 2003. Immigrant Women and Community Development in the Canadian Maritimes: Outsiders within? *Canadian Journal of Sociology* 28 (2): 202-34.

Tastsoglou, Evangelia and Baukje Miedema. 2005. Working Much Harder and Always Having to Prove Yourself: Immigrant Women's Labour Force Experiences in the Canadian Maritimes. In *Gender Realities: Local and Global*, 201-33. Advances in Gender Research vol. 9. Ed. Marcia Texler Segal and Vasilikie Demos. Oxford: Elsevier/JAI Press.

Tastsoglou, Evangelia and Peruvemba S. Jaya, ed. 2011. *Immigrant Women in Atlantic Canada. Challenges, Negotiations, Re-constructions.* Toronto: Canadian Scholars' Press/Women's Press.

Tastsoglou, Evangelia and Valerie Preston. 2005. Gender, Immigration and Employment Integration: Where We Are and What We Still Need to Know. *Atlantis: A Women's Studies Journal* 3 (1): 46-59.

Thomas, Geraldine, T. 1988. Women in the Greek Community of Nova Scotia. *Canadian Ethnic Studies* 20 (3): 84-93.

———. 2000. *Peoples of the Maritimes: Greeks.* Tantallon, NS: Four East.

Tirone, Susan and Mary Sweatman. 2011. You Suddenly Have a Different Life: Leisure, Gender, and the Experiences of Immigrants Living in Halifax, Nova Scotia. In *Immigrant Women in Atlantic Canada. Challenges, Negotiations, Re-constructions*, ed. Evangelia Tastsoglou and Peruvemba S. Jaya, 325-53. Toronto: Canadian Scholars' Press/Women's Press.

Topen, Amanda. 2011. Selective Welcome: Labour Market Experiences of Immigrant Women from Sub-Saharan Africa. In *Immigrant Women in Atlantic Canada. Challenges, Negotiations, Re-constructions*, ed. Evangelia Tastsoglou and Peruvemba S. Jaya, 143-73. Toronto: Canadian Scholars' Press/Women's Press.

Vatz-Laaroussi, Michèle. 2010. Vers un modèle d'analyse des collectivités accueillante. Key-Note Talk at Symposium on Small Welcoming Communities and New Arrivals in Atlantic Canada, Moncton, Université de Moncton, April 28-29.

Väyrynen, Raimo. 2003. Regionalism Old and New. *International Studies Review* 5:25-51.

Vertovec, Steven. 1999. Conceiving and Researching Transnationalism. *Ethnic and Racial Studies* 2 (2): 447-62.

Walker, James W. St. G. 1976. *The Black Loyalists: The Search for a Promised Land in Nova Scotia and Sierra Leone, 1783-1870*. London: Longman and Dalhousie University Press.

———.1980. *A History of Blacks in Canada: A Study Guide for Teachers and Students*. Hull, QC: Minister of State, Multiculturalism.

Waseem, Gertrud. 2000. *Peoples of the Maritimes: Germans*. Halifax: Nimbus Publishing.

Wayland, Sarah V. 2006. The Politics of Transnationalism: Comparative Perspectives. In *Transnational Identities and Practices in Canada*, ed. Vic Satzewich and Lloyd Wong, 18-34. Vancouver: UBC Pres.

Weerasinghe, Swarna. 2011. Healthcare Accessibility in Atlantic Canada: Immigrant Women's Perspective. In *Immigrant Women in Atlantic Canada. Challenges, Negotiations, Re-constructions*, ed. Evangelia Tastsoglou and Peruvemba S. Jaya, 235-266. Toronto: Canadian Scholars' Press/Women's Press.

Withrow, Alfreda. 2002. *Nova Scotia's Ethnic Roots*. Tantallon, NS: Glen Margaret Publishing.

Yax-Fraser, Maria Joséfa and Evangelia Tastsoglou. 2008. *Attraction, Promotion and Retention of Immigrants in Atlantic Canada: A Synthesis of Existing Research*. Citizenship and Immigration Canada.

Yax-Fraser, Maria Joséfa. 2011. Mothering Across Cultures: Immigrant Women's Experiences in Halifax. In *Immigrant Women in Atlantic Canada. Challenges, Negotiations, Re-constructions*, ed. Evangelia Tastsoglou and Peruvemba S. Jaya, 297-323. Toronto: Canadian Scholars' Press/Women's Press.

# 2

# From Away, But Here to Stay?
# Trends in Out-migration Among a Cohort of Recent
# Immigrants to Atlantic Canada

*Howard Ramos and Yoko Yoshida*

In Canada, immigration is often seen as a remedy for declining fertility, aging populations, out-migration and economic stagnation. This is evidenced by high rates of immigration to the country over the last twenty years sparked by federal policy. However, interest in immigration is not limited to the national agenda and in the last decade-and-a-half provinces have developed their own immigration strategies to attract newcomers. Yet, many recent immigrants cluster in major urban centres, and of those who do migrate to less populous regions, many leave. This is particularly pronounced in Atlantic Canada, which has seen a large share of its recent immigrants move to other provinces or leave the country altogether. As a result, the primary aim of this chapter is to examine out-migration trends of a cohort of recent immigrants to Atlantic Canada. In exploring these trends, the chapter offers a preliminary descriptive sketch of economic and non-economic factors associated with out-migration.

During the 1990s, Canadian immigration policies changed in an attempt to attract a "large and steady flow" (Green and Green 2004: 131) of immigrants to offset the country's declining population and to generate economic growth (cf. Aydemir and Robinson 2006: 5). One of the regions most struck by population loss and slow economic development is Atlantic Canada. For decades, migration researchers and policy-makers have tracked out-migration from the region to Ontario and more recently to Alberta (Ostrovsky, Hou and Picot 2008; Minister of Industry Canada 2002; Newfoundland 2006; Prince Edward Island 2008; Nova Scotia 2006; New Brunswick Population Growth Secretariat 2007). As a response to out-migration, not to mention increasingly aging populations and slow economies, all of the Atlantic Canadian provinces have turned to immigration.

Evidence of the region's interest in immigration can be seen in the generation of Provincial Nominee Programs (PNPs), starting with New Brunswick and Newfoundland and Labrador in 1999, then Prince Edward Island (PEI) in 2001, and last Nova Scotia in 2002 (Everden 2008: 13). Each of these provinces signed agreements with the federal government to gain the ability to screen and nominate immigrants who match their needs (Citizenship and Immigration Canada 2008). In a review of Atlantic Canadian immigrations Everden argues that provincial government interest in immigration is also found in the development and publication of immigration strategies (2008: 15). Front and centre in these strategies is the importance of immigration to alleviate demographic and economic obstacles. Two Atlantic provinces, Newfoundland and Labrador and Nova Scotia, have gone as far as launching provincial commissions into these issues.

The appeal of attracting immigrants is apparent not only at the level of government, but is also more broadly evident among individual Atlantic Canadians. A poll by the Centre for Research and Information on Canada (CRIC) found that 38 per cent of Atlantic residents felt "that support for immigrants should be increased" (Quell 2005: 3), which was the highest level of endorsement across Canada. The same spirit can be found in policies geared to generating "welcoming communities," as seen in Newfoundland and Labrador and Nova Scotia (Newfoundland and Labrador 2012; Nova Scotia 2009). According to the same CRIC poll, Atlantic

Canadians also believe that newcomers quickly identify with the region, perhaps also signalling their openness to migration "from away."[1] Ironically, as Quell (2005: 2) shows, newcomers find the region second-most difficult in Canada to adopt as a new home and as Godfrey Baldacchino's chapter in this book among others illustrates, polling and interviews show mixed and highly nuanced support for immigrants in Atlantic Canada. As a result, there is a disjuncture between the desire to attract migrants and their actual experiences.

This disjuncture, in turn, contributes to at least two trends: (a) a concentration of immigrants in large urban centers and (b) secondary migration of immigrants who originally settle outside them. Numerous researchers and policy-makers have shown that new immigrants overwhelmingly settle in the country's three major cities—Montreal, Toronto and Vancouver, what some refer to as MTV—at the cost of rural communities and less developed regions like the Prairies and Atlantic Canada (Derwing and Krahn 2008; Boyd 2005; Metropolis 2003; Green and Green 2004; Houle 2007; McDonald 2004; Yoshida and Ramos 2013). For example, using 2001 Census data, Radford (2007: 47) shows that 74 per cent of immigrants arriving during the 1990s settled in MTV, and Houle (2007: 16) found that only 23 per cent of immigrants settled outside of the seven largest urban centres. With the advent of PNPs, this concentration has lessened somewhat in the 2000s, but is still overwhelmingly concentrated in those three cities. According to the 2012 Facts and Figures, about 60 per cent of new immigrants landed in MTV. Of the small number of immigrants who do migrate outside of MTV, especially those moving to less populated and less economically developed regions, many do not stay, which leads to high rates of onward or secondary migration. This is commonly seen in Atlantic Canada, leading some to argue that the region suffers from "chronic" out-migration.

Despite the need for research on immigration outside of MTV (Radford 2007: 47), much of the existing literature, especially large-scale quantitative analysis, overlooks Atlantic Canada. In part this is because of the small number of recent immigrants settling there. According to Citizenship and Immigration Canada the Atlantic Provinces received just 2.5 per cent of immigrants landing in 2012 (Citizenship and Immigration Canada 2012). The figure is in line with immigration trends over the previous decade and makes the population difficult to enumerate in national surveys. This in turn leads to problems associated with small sample size, resulting in limited power in multivariate analysis and violation of confidentiality compliance policies of Statistics Canada.

Consequently, much of the existing literature on Atlantic Canadian immigration has tended to be qualitative, focusing on the narratives and experiences of immigrants (cf. Tastsoglou 2008; Tastsoglou and Miedema 2003; Dobrowolsky 2011, 2012; Flint 2009, 2008; Gallant 2008; Corbette 2005, 2007; Jabbra 1988; Ralston 1988, 1991). There are notable exceptions; for example, Akbari (2005, 2008, 2011) or Akbari and Dar (2005) who estimate rates of out-migration; however, they do not explicitly examine the factors associated with it. There are also others who look at interprovincial migration of immigrants and/or foreign born Canadians in general (Edmonston 2002; Day and Winer 2006; Finnie 2001, 1999, 2004; Newbold 1996, 1999, 2006) but they tend to focus on region as just one of many covariates in larger models rather than engaging the question of what factors specifically relate to the experiences of out-migration from Atlantic Canada.

In addition to the small number of immigrants to the region, data access has also been an issue limiting quantitative research on Atlantic Canada. Much research on secondary migration has used Census data (cf. Akbari and Dar 2005; Edmonston 2002; Everden 2008; Liaw and Qi 2004; McDonald 2004; Newbold 1999, 1996; Newbold and Bell 2001; Ram and Shin 2007). It is easily attainable through its Public Use Micro File (PUMF), or through the Research Data Centre (RDC) program. However, these data have at least two obstacles to studying the interprovincial out-migration of Atlantic Canadian immigrants. First, as noted above, the small number of immigrants to the region makes analysis difficult, especially for multivariate analysis. Second, the Census contains questions on place of residence one and five years previously, but

is structured cross-sectionally, making analysis of repeat migration difficult and limiting the ability to research migration over
time because at best only quasi-cohorts can be created. A number
of researchers have already commented on problems associated
with this (e.g., Aydemir and Robinson 2006). The new National
Household Survey, moreover, does not serve the region well either.
Statistics Canada cautions that the results of the survey are less
reliable in small cities and regions (Statistics Canada 2013). Given
that Atlantic Canada is disproportionately rural, this presents
significant barriers for analysis.

For these reasons, others have looked to alternate data
sources to overcome such limitations, including the Longitudinal
Immigration Database (also known as: IMDB) and other taxation
and/or landing record-based data. However, such data are not
easily available for non-governmental researchers because they
are not distributed in PUMF format or the RDC program. This
has meant that much of the analysis is limited to government
documents and is conducted by Citizenship and Immigration or
Statistics Canada employees or researchers who gain access to that
data through contracts with various federal government agencies
(see Everden 2008; Ayedmir and Robinson 2006; Finnie 2004,
1999; Ostrovsky et al. 2008; Day and Wiener 2006). Much of this
data, unfortunately, do not contain measures of broader social and
cultural factors that might be associated with migration, leading
most analysis to focus on economic or human capital causes of
migration.

Thus, the release of the Longitudinal Survey of Immigrants to
Canada (LSIC) was met with much excitement, seen as potentially
offering data that could be accessed through the RDC program,
that is longitudinal, and that contain a wide range of economic,
social and cultural measures that allow for a broader engagement
of Canadian immigration, and possibly out-migration of immigrants from Atlantic Canada. Using the first wave of the LSIC,
Newbold (2006) examined secondary migration of immigrants.
However, his analysis focused on differences between intended
settlement destinations and short distance migration, instead of

interprovincial, occurring within the first six months of arriving to Canada. Houle (2007) extended the analysis, using all three waves of the LSIC to examine interprovincial migration; however, his focus was on all immigrants and did not pay special attention to those in Atlantic Canada.

In response, the primary goal of this paper is to explore the data and provide a broad outline of economic, social/cultural, health and demographic factors associated with out-migration of the LSIC cohort of immigrants to Atlantic Canada. A secondary goal is to assess the dataset's potential for researchers interested in immigration trends of the region.

## Trends in Out-migration

Let us introduce the LSIC and how we define out-migration. The survey was first administered by Statistics Canada in 2001 and has results for three waves of data—following a cohort of immigrants six months, two years and four years after their arrival in Canada (Statistics Canada 2009: 5). It offers unique insight into the transitions immigrants experience after migrating. Unlike the census, it is longitudinal, and unlike the IMDB or other tax/landing record databases, it contains a wider range of information and is reasonably easy to access. Unfortunately, however, the LSIC still faces obstacles related to small sample size when it comes to studying recent immigrants in the Atlantic region. Our analysis focuses on Waves One and Two alone due to the substantial attrition rate over the four-year survey period and reports basic descriptive statistics and tables. Research by Houle (2007: 21) suggests that the majority of recent immigrants who move do so during this period. The sample analyzed in this paper includes only immigrants who resided in one of the four Atlantic Provinces in Wave One of the LSIC.

Previous researchers studying immigrant moves (secondary, onward or out-migration) operationalized them in various ways. Some engage the simple question of whether or not immigrants settle permanently or make subsequent moves within a city or province. Such analysis defines secondary migration in a very broad sense, looking at any move, whether it is local, interprovincial or international. Newbold's (2006: 12) research, based on the first wave of the LSIC, shows that many of the secondary moves of recent immigrants occur in the early months after arrival in Canada and they are local, often from temporary arrangements to more permanent housing. Such a broad operationalization of secondary migration mixes divergent trends, but does look at migration as a process. Others examine larger moves. Much of this research defines secondary migration in terms of moves among Census Metropolitan Areas (CMAs), provinces, or even outside of the country. Of those that examine secondary migration at this level, moving is largely defined as movement within a time frame that is proximate to the cross-section of the survey (seen among researchers using Censuses), or based on a change in either postal code, CMA, province or country for those using longitudinal data (like the IMDB or LSIC). Our research follows the design of longitudinal studies and looks at recent immigrants who settled in an Atlantic province in Wave One of the LSIC, but then moved out of the region to other provinces in Wave Two; this was used to generate the variable *Atlantic movers*. Interestingly, of those who made interprovincial moves during this period, all moved to a province outside of Atlantic Canada.

Research on interprovincial migration has tended to focus on economic and human capital factors that contribute to moving. It largely looks at employment, income, education and economic performance of different regions or other structural factors. To account for the potential impact of these factors we examine four variables. Previous scholarship has shown that high rates of unemployment act as a push factor contributing to out-migration. This is analyzed by looking at whether or not recent immigrants are *currently employed* in Wave One of the LSIC. Many researchers have shown that employment is one issue but underemployment is an equally important consideration. The lack of recognition of immigrant credentials has led many to work in underpaid job sectors (Alboim et al. 2005; Li 2001; Reitz 2005). This too may act as a push factor. We examine this by looking at family *employment income* in Wave One. Related to this is the role of education. Previous research on interprovincial immigration has shown that highly skilled and educated workers are more mobile and likely to pursue opportunities in other regions if the labour market is unable to reward their experience (see Ram and Shin 2007). To engage this we look at highest level of education obtained outside Canada in Wave One of the LSIC. Because of the small sample of recent immigrants in the Atlantic region and because of RDC release requirements that ask to report tables with cell counts that are ten or greater, we were forced to aggregate these data into a measure of *university and professional education*; those who we considered to have the most potential mobility. We examine economic and human capital factors further by also considering whether or not recent immigrants or a member of their family received *social assistance* income in the previous year at Wave Two of the LSIC. Existing scholarship is split on how this might affect secondary migration. Some argue it has no impact on migration (Lin 1995), while others consider it a push factor related to employment and income (Finnie 2000; also see Day and Winer 2006 for a good review of this literature). Given the overall high level of human capital of recent immigrants we expect the latter to be the case.

Although many have focused on the economic influences of migration, these alone do not account for why people move. Literature over the last decade has begun considering non-economic determinants. Much scholarship, for instance, has begun to assess the role of social capital and networks that support immigrants (Couton 2011; Aizelwood and Pendakur 2005; Reitz and Banerjee 2007). Others have also looked at the role of family ties and familial support (Deshaw 2006; Telegdi 2006); and yet, others have considered the role of "welcoming communities." We account for this by looking at three factors: the number of *groups or organizations* that recent immigrants are involved with; whether or not they have *extended family* living in Canada, and whether or not recent immigrants *experienced discrimination* since arriving. With the exception of the number of different types of groups or organizations, these are measured at Wave Two. We anticipate that recent immigrants' involvement in fewer organizations, along with more discrimination faced, will lead to increased out-migration from Atlantic Canada. We are agnostic to the role played by family ties because they might influence both staying in the region or moving to another, depending on where extended family lives.

We also consider health as a possible determinant of out-migration from the region. As a number of other chapters in this book note, health and access to leisure activities are often overlooked in the analysis of immigrant settlement. Here we agree and extend the claim to secondary or interprovincial migration. We believe that poor health is a proxy of poor living conditions and potentially a manifestation of stress or an unwelcoming community. Poor health, however, may conversely be an obstacle to migration. We consider this by looking at how recent immigrants self-assessed their *health* in Wave One of the LSIC. Respondents ranked their health on a five-point scale, where one indicated excellent health. We have no specific expectations of how health is associated with out-migration from the region, and are instead interested in seeing if there are any discernable patterns associated with it.

We lastly consider two demographic factors that may be linked to migration: *age* and *sex*. Existing scholarship has shown that age is inversely related to migration (see Finnie 2006). As people age they are less likely to move. We thus expect to find the same with recent immigrants to Atlantic Canada. Research on the region has found that sex is strongly related to out-migration. Corbett (2007) for instance has shown that women are more likely to move than men. We anticipate that this may also be the case with recent immigrants' interprovincial out-migration. We tried to also consider marital status, visible minority status and official language abilities; however, there were too few cases to allow release of the data from the RDC and are thus not reported.

As a result, our analysis examines economic, social/cultural, health and demographic factors that are associated with interprovincial out-migration of recent immigrants from the Atlantic regions.

### What do the Data show?

We first begin by examining overall trends of interprovincial migration in Canada of the LSIC cohort of immigrants. As the literature suggests, the Atlantic region faces a high rate of out-migration compared to other provinces. In fact, as seen in Table 2.1, 29 per cent of recent immigrants moved out of Atlantic Canada between six months and two years after arrival.[2]

| TABLE 2.1: INTERPROVINCIAL MOVERS AND STAYERS BY ATLANTIC REGION AND OTHER PROVINCES (%) | | |
|---|---|---|
| Province | Movers | Stayers |
| Atlantic provinces | 29.23 | 70.77 |
| Quebec | 2.21 | 97.79 |
| Ontario | 2.43 | 97.57 |
| Manitoba | 4.95 | 95.05 |
| Saskatchewan | 26.08 | 73.92 |
| Alberta | 2.62 | 97.38 |
| British Columbia | 3.24 | 96.76 |
| Total | 2.91 | 97.09 |
| Source: Statistics Canada LSIC | | |

This figure is in line with Houle (2007: 21), but diverges widely from Akbari (2008) who uses different data and methods to calculate out-migration from the region. In contrast, the provinces hosting MTV have much higher retention rates, as well as Alberta which was experiencing an economic boom during the period of analysis. These findings suggest that Atlantic Canada may indeed suffer from chronic out-migration.

We try to understand this further by examining the association of various factors with out-migration from Atlantic Canada. We first examined a series of economic and human capital vari-

| TABLE 2.2: ATLANTIC CANADIAN IMMIGRANT MOVERS AND STAYERS BY EMPLOYMENT STATUS AT WAVE 1 (%) | | |
|---|---|---|
| Atlantic Canadian Immigrants | Movers | Stayers |
| Employed | 30.41 | 69.59 |
| Unemployed | 28.30 | 71.70 |
| Total | 29.23 | 70.77 |
| Source: Statistics Canada LSIC | | |

ables. Table 2.2 shows the rate of moving by current employment. The result indicates that slightly more people who were employed moved compared to those who were unemployed.

Although there is only about a two percentage-point difference, this result is somewhat surprising, given that employment is usually a factor that retains migrants rather than contributing to out-migration. This is explored further by considering average income between movers and stayers. When this is done, we find that the average household income of recent immigrants in the LSIC cohort was over ten thousand dollars higher for stayers ($29,102) than movers ($18,958). These findings suggest that employment is not necessarily the issue contributing to out-migration, but rather underemployment associated with lower wages. This is even more apparent when human capital is considered. Table 2.3 shows that immigrants with university or professional education moved out of the region. Thirty-three per cent of these immigrants left, while only 23 per cent of those without it moved.

| TABLE 2.3: ATLANTIC CANADIAN IMMIGRANT MOVERS & STAYERS BY HIGHEST LEVEL OF FOREIGN EDUCATION AT WAVE 1 (%) | | |
|---|---|---|
| Atlantic Canadian Immigrants | Movers | Stayers |
| All other Education | 22.78 | 77.22 |
| University or Professional | 33.21 | 66.79 |
| Total | 29.83 | 70.17 |
| Source: Statistics Canada LSIC | | |

This finding is in line with existing research that shows a correlation between higher education and out-migration. Clearly the region is losing some of its most talented immigrants. This should be of concern to academics and policy-makers alike. One last economic measure analysed was whether or not recent immigrants or their family received social assistance benefits during the previous year.

It is worth noting that the majority of recent immigrants in the region do not receive social assistance. In fact, only about 14 per cent did. However, Table 2.4 shows that 60 per cent of those recipients, as compared to 26 per cent of non-recipients, moved. As mentioned above, we were uncertain about what relationship we would find; however, it appears that it is consistent with the other measures of economic determinants of out-migration and it is likely that poor economic integration is associated with moving.

| TABLE 2.4: ATLANTIC CANADIAN IMMIGRANT MOVERS AND STAYERS BY SOCIAL ASSISTANCE AT WAVE 2 (%) | | |
| --- | --- | --- |
| Atlantic Canadian Immigrants | Movers | Stayers |
| Recipient | 59.97 | 40.03 |
| Non-Recipient | 26.41 | 73.59 |
| Total | 31.04 | 68.96 |
| Source: Statistics Canada LSIC | | |

Economic factors, however, are not the sole impetus for out-migration. It is also important to consider social and cultural influences. We first examine recent immigrants' social capital. Overall, the LSIC cohort of recent immigrants to the region was not very involved in different groups or organizations six months after their arrival to Canada. When we calculated the average number of organizations they were involved in, we found that movers participated in roughly half as many different types of groups or organizations (0.45) compared to stayers (0.81). This finding hints at the potentially important role of social incorporation and networks. As one would expect, those who moved were less involved in organizations. We explore social ties further in Table 2.5 by looking at whether or not the LSIC cohort of recent immigrants to Atlantic Canada had extended family living in the country.

| TABLE 2.5: ATLANTIC CANADIAN IMMIGRANT MOVERS AND STAYERS BY EXTENDED FAMILY AT WAVE 2 (%) | | |
|---|---|---|
| Atlantic Canadian Immigrants | Movers | Stayers |
| Family | 41.59 | 58.41 |
| No Family | 23.64 | 76.36 |
| Total | 29.23 | 70.77 |
| Source: Statistics Canada LSIC | | |

Interestingly, almost double the proportion (42 per cent) of people with extended family living in Canada moved compared to those without (24 per cent). Some caution is worth mentioning: unlike other measures we were not able to look at this association in Wave One and the finding may reflect a pull factor contributing to their out-migration. Movers may have decided to leave to join family already living in other provinces. Further analysis is surely warranted. The last social/cultural measure we analyze is whether or not the LSIC cohort of recent immigrants to Atlantic Canada experienced discrimination since arrival.

A large share of recent immigrants to the region (29 per cent) experienced discrimination. This is a rather high rate and contradicts emphasis on generating "welcoming communities" and the reported openness to people "from away." This figure should be of interest to researchers and policy-makers and demands further investigation. The role discrimination plays in out-migration can be seen in Table 2.6. As one might expect, those who experienced it were five percentage points more likely to leave than those who had not.

| TABLE 2.6: ATLANTIC CANADIAN IMMIGRANT MOVERS AND STAYERS BY EXPERIENCE OF DISCRIMINATION AT WAVE 2 (%) | | |
|---|---|---|
| Atlantic Canadian Immigrants | Movers | Stayers |
| Discrimination | 33.03 | 66.97 |
| No Discrimination | 27.66 | 72.34 |
| Total | 29.23 | 70.77 |
| Source: Statistics Canada LSIC | | |

Perceptions of health are also considered in our analysis. The average self-assessment of recent immigrants' health was measured on a five-point scale, where one is considered excellent health. We found little difference in the perceived health of movers and stayers, with averages of 1.95 and 1.80 reported, respectively. Both movers and stayers thus report fairly "good" health. It appears that despite economic and social obstacles recent immigrants face, they do not report signs of poor physical or mental health.

The last two factors analyzed are demographic: age and sex. As one might expect, recent immigrants to Atlantic Canada are relatively young. When we calculated the average age of movers and stayers, we found that they were around thirty-six and thirty-seven years old respectively when they arrived. This is hardly a large difference and may signal that age plays only a subtle role in out-migration. In terms of sex, the differences are more apparent. Table 2.7 shows that proportionally more men moved out of the Atlantic region compared to women.

Roughly 37 per cent of men left the region as compared to 24 per cent of women. This trend may reflect a staggered approach to

| TABLE 2.7: ATLANTIC CANADIAN IMMIGRANT MOVERS AND STAYERS BY SEX (%) | | |
|---|---|---|
| Atlantic Canadian Immigrants | Movers | Stayers |
| Male | 36.68 | 63.32 |
| Female | 24.35 | 75.65 |
| Total | 29.23 | 70.77 |
| Source: Statistics Canada LSIC | | |

out-migration that is gendered, with men leaving to be followed by women and their families.

To summarize we found that poor economic performance and underemployment are associated with out-migration, as are low levels of non-familial social capital. Ties to extended family in Canada and the experience of discrimination also led to out-migration. Age showed no discernible pattern, and it appears that men are proportionally more likely to leave the region than women.

## Discussion and Conclusion

Overall, our preliminary analysis offers general insight into out-migration trends of a cohort of recent immigrants in the Atlantic region and allows us to identify some potential avenues for further examination. When economic factors were assessed we found that *under*employment in addition to unemployment needs to be engaged by Atlantic Canadian provincial policy-makers. Although immigrants as a whole face harsh employment prospects in the region, an analysis of income and education suggests that of those who did find work, many are not earning high levels of income, and on average the lowest earners and most educated leave the province. This should be of major concern to policy-makers who look to immigration as a way to boost the economy and see it as a potential long-term solution to population decline. Given that the Canadian immigration system has attracted highly educated and skilled workers and Provincial Nominee Programs aim to do the same, it is important to creatively engage how these patterns of employed and educated immigrants leaving the region can be reversed. For this reason we suggest that further investigation among economic outcomes and human capital is needed so that the Atlantic Provinces not only attract immigrants but also successfully integrate them for the *longue durée*.

Although economic concerns are important we also found evidence for the need to engage social and cultural disjunctures. As much scholarship would predict, immigrants who were least involved in groups and/or organization were those who were most likely to move out of the region. This was not a surprise. However, we were struck by the relationship between extended family and out-migration. It appears that immigrants who had relatives in Canada, perhaps in other regions, were more likely to leave than those who did not. Immigrant out-migration from Atlantic Canada may also have a gendered component as seen by the disproportionate number of men who left the province compared to women. It signals the potential for breaking apart families as men may be leaving the region to pursue better economic opportunities elsewhere, much in the same way other native-born Atlantic Canadian men leave families behind in pursuit of work in other regions of the country. These two findings suggest that it is important for policy-makers to consider broader conceptions of family ties that extend beyond the nuclear family and to also consider linking immigrants to broader family networks when they arrive in specific communities. It may prove fruitful to consider policies aimed at attracting families and reunifying families rather than individual migrants. This would be a radically different policy than the current economic-driven policies of both federal and provincial governments. Surprisingly we found evidence of a disjuncture between Atlantic Canadians' stated openness to those "from away" versus the high level of perceived discrimination by immigrants. This is a difficult issue to address because if it is not perceived as a problem by the dominant society little change may occur and many may silently leave the region. Atlantic Canadian provinces have recognized the need to develop "welcoming communities," and this is a good first step; however, we believe it will be important for provincial policy-makers to maintain their vigilance on this front and to monitor whether or not such an atmosphere is indeed created and maintained.

To properly engage these Atlantic Canadian findings, multivariate analysis is much needed. However, to conduct it, access to and collection of adequate data are imperative. The LSIC is an exciting dataset that has great potential for engaging interprovincial migration but its data still suffer from under sampling of smaller and poorer regions. It is also now dated. As noted above, moreover, census analysis can provide some insight but lacks the methodological sophistication of truly longitudinal data and its future is unclear. Its new replacement, likewise, appears to fall short when coming to analyze smaller communities. Taxation or landing record-based data still remains difficult for non-governmental researchers to access. It is thus important for the Atlantic Provinces to pursue data collection on their region which pays special attention to *their* concerns. This will be necessary for monitoring migration patterns and breaking the MTV concentration of immigration to Canada.

## Note

The researchers would like to thank Natasha Hanson and Patrick W. J. Pearce who contributed to the initial literature review. The research is supported by a pilot project grant from the Atlantic Metropolis Centre and data access through Statistic Canada's Research Data Centre program.

1. "Come from away" and "from away" are commonly used terms in the region referring to migrants and travelers to the region—both native-born and immigrant. For an extended discussion on this matter in Prince Edward Island, see Baldacchino (2012).

2. It should be noted that in recent years trends for Saskatchewan have largely changed for immigrants arriving after the LSIC cohort. There is also slightly more migration outside of MTV; however, trends in Atlantic Canada have largely remained the same.

## References

Aizlewood, Amanda and Ravi Pendakur. 2005. Ethnicity and Social Capital in Canada. *Canadian Ethnic Studies* 37 (2): 77-102.

Akbari, Ather H. 2005. Coming and Goings of Immigrants in Atlantic Canada. *The Workplace Review* (April): 30-37.

———. 2008. Introduction. *International Migration and Integration* 9: 341-44.

———. 2011. Labour Market Performance of Immigrants in Smaller Regions of Western Countries: Some Evidence from Atlantic Canada. *Journal of International Migration and Integration* 12 (2): 133-54.

Akbari, Ather H. and Atul Dar. 2005. Socioeconomic and Demographic Profiles of Immigrants in Nova Scotia. *A Report Prepared for the Atlantic Opportunities Agency.*

Alboim, Naomi, Ross Finnie and Ronald Meng. 2005. The Discounting of Immigrants' Skills in Canada: Evidence and Policy Recommendations. *Choices* 11 (2) (February). Montreal: Institute for Research on Public Policy.

Aydemir, Abdurrahman and Chris Robinson. 2006. *Return and Onward Migration among Working Men.* Analytical Studies Branch Research Paper Series. Statistics Canada: Catalogue no. 11F0019M1E (273).

Baldacchino, Godfrey. 2012. Come Visit, but don't Overstay: Critiquing a Welcoming Society. *International Journal of Culture, Tourism and Hospitality Research* 6 (2): 145-53.

Boyd, Monica. 2005. Immigration, Internal Migration and the Distribution of Canada's Population. Presented to the Population Change and Public Policy SSHRC cluster workshop. London, Ontario. February 3-4, 2005. http://sociology.uwo.ca/popchange/Boyd,%20Planning%20Workshop2.pdf (accessed September 9, 2009).

Citizenship and Immigration Canada. 2012. *Facts and Figures: Immigration Overview – Permanent and Temporary Residents.* Citizenship and Immigration Canada: Ci1-8/2012E-PDF

Corbett, Michael. 2005. Rural Education and Out-migration: The Case of a Coastal Community. *Canadian Journal of Education* 28 (1&2): 52-72.

———. 2007. All Kinds of Potential: Women and Out-migration in an Atlantic Canadian Coastal Community. *Journal of Rural Studies* 23: 430-42.

Couton, Philippe. 2011. The Impact of Communal Organizational Density on the Labour Market Integration of Immigrants in Canada. *International Migration.* DOI: 10.1111/j.1468-2435.2010.00673.x.

Day, Kathleen M. and Stanley L. Winer. 2006. Policy-Induced Internal Migration: An Empirical Investigation of the Canadian Case. *International Tax and Public Finance* 13 (5): 535–64.

Derwing, Tracey M. and Harvey Krahn. 2008. Attracting and Retaining Immigrants Outside the Metropolis: Is the Pie Too Small For Everyone to Have a Piece? The Case of Edmonton, Alberta. *International Migration and Integration* 9:185-202.

Deshaw, Rell. 2006. The History of Family Reunification in Canada and Current Policy. *Canadian Issues/Thèmes canadiens* (spring): 9-14.

Dobrowolsky, Alexandra. 2011. The Intended and Unintended Effects of a New Immigration Strategy: Insight from Nova Scotia's Provincial Nominee Program. *Studies in Political Economy* (87): 109-41.

———. 2012. Nuancing Neoliberalism: Lessons Learned from a Failed Immigration Experiment. *Journal of International Migration and Integration* (Spring): 1-22.

Edmonston, Barry. 2002. *Interprovincial Migration of Canadian Immigrants*. Research on Immigration and Integration in the Metropolis Working Paper Series No. 02-10.

Everden, Brian. 2008. Taking Up the Challenge: The Atlantic Provinces and Immigration. *Our Diverse Cities* 5 (Spring): 11-17.

Finnie, Ross. 1999. Inter-provincial Migration in Canada: A Longitudinal Analysis of Movers and Stayers and the Associated Income Dynamics. *Canadian Journal of Regional Science* XXII (3): 227-62.

———. 2000. Who Moves? *A Panel Logit Model Analysis of Inter-Provincial Migration in Canada*. Analytic Studies Branch Research Paper Series 11F0019MPE (142).

———. 2001. The Effects of Inter-provincial Mobility on Individuals' Earnings: Panel Model Estimates for Canada. *Research Paper No. 163*. Analytical Studies Branch. Ottawa: Statistics Canada.

———. 2004. Who Moves? A Logit Model Analysis of Inter-provincial Migration in Canada. *Applied Economics* 36:1759-79.

———. 2006. *International Mobility: Patterns of Exit and Return Canadians, 1982-2003*. Analytical Studies Branch Research Paper Series Catalogue no. 11F0019MIIE (288).

Flint, J. David. 2008. Recent Immigrants in a Rural Nova Scotia County: A Tentative Typology. *Our Diverse Cities* 5 (Spring): 40-44.

———. 2009. Developing a Typology of Recent Immigrants in a Rural Nova Scotia County: The Case of Colchester. Presented at Metropolis Brown Bag Series, Saint Mary's University, Halifax, Nova Scotia, April 24, 2009.

Gallant, Nicole. 2008. How Social Networks Help Attract, Integrate and Retain Immigrants: A Multidimensional Research Initiative. *Our Diverse Cities* Spring (5): 73-77.

Green, Alan G. and David Green. 2004. The Goals of Canada's Immigration Policy: A Historical Perspective. *Canadian Journal of Urban Research* 13 (1): 102-39.

Houle, René. 2007. Secondary Migration of New Immigrants to Canada. *Our Diverse Cities* Summer (3): 16-24.

Jabbra, Nancy. 1988. Household and Family and Lebanese Immigrants in Nova Scotia: Continuity, Change and Adaptation. *Journal of Comparative Family Studies* 22 (1): 39-56.

Li, Peter. 2001. The Market Worth of Immigrants' Educational Credentials. *Canadian Public Policy* 27 (1): 23-38.

Liaw, Kao-Lee and Mingzhu Qi. 2004. Lifetime Interprovincial Migration in Canada: Looking Beyond Short-Run Fluctuations. *The Canadian Geographer* 48 (2): 168-90.

Lin, Zhengxi. 1995. *Interprovincial Labour Mobility in Canada: The Role of Unemployment Insurance and Social Assistance.* Human Resources and Skills Development Canada IN-AH-220E-08-95. http://www.hrsdc. gc.ca/eng/cs/sp/hrsdc/edd/reports/1995-000311/page02.shtml (accessed August 24, 2009).

McDonald, Ted. 2004. Toronto and Vancouver Bound: The Location Choice of New Canadian Immigrants. *Canadian Journal of Urban Research* 13 (1): 85-101.

Metropolis. 2003. Regionalization of Immigration. *Metropolis Conversation Series* 9, February 21.

Minister of Industry Canada. 2002. 2001 Census: Analysis Series: Profile of the Canadian Population by Mobility Status: Canada, a Nation on the Move. Ottawa: Ministry of Industry. Catalogue no. 96F0030XIE2001006. http://www12.statcan.ca/english/census01/products/analytic/companion/mob/pdf/96F0030XIE2001006.pdf (accessed September 3, 2009).

Newbold, K. Bruce. 1996. Internal Migration of the Foreign-Born in Canada. *International Migration Review* 30 (3): 728-47.

———. 1999. Internal Migration of the Foreign-Born: Population Concentration or Dispersion? *Population and Environment: A Journal of Interdisciplinary Studies* 20 (3): 259-76.

———. 2006. Secondary Migration of Immigrants to Canada: An Analysis of LSIC Wave 1 Data. socserv.mcmaster.ca/rdc/RDCwp10.pdf (accessed August 24, 2009).

Newbold, K. Bruce and Martin Bell. 2001. Return and Onwards Migration in Canada and Australia: Evidence from Fixed Interval Data. *International Migration Review* 35 (4): 1157-84.

New Brunswick. 2007. *It is time to Act! Towards New Brunswick's Population Growth Strategy.* http://www.gnb.ca/3100/Promos/Reports/Disspaper-e.pdf (accessed September 3, 2009).

Newfoundland and Labrador. 2006. *Demographic Change: Issues and Implications.* St. John's: Department of Finance, Economics and Statistics Branch. http://www.economics.gov.nl.ca/pdf2006/demographyupdate.pdf (accessed September 3, 2009).

———. 2012. Together We Rock! Celebrate Cultural Diversity! http://www.nlimmigration.ca/news/together-we-rock!---nl-multiculturalism-week-2012.aspx (accessed December 9, 2012).

Nova Scotia. 2006. *2006 Census of Canada Nova Scotia Perspective: Release #1 Population and Dwellings.* Halifax: Department of Finance, Economics & Statistics Division. http://www.gov.ns.ca/finance/publish/census/2006/Release5.pdf (accessed September 3, 2009).

———. 2009. Nova Scotia Office of Immigration. http://www.novascotiaimmigration.com/nova-scotia-office-of-immigration (accessed August 24, 2009).

Ostrovsky, Yuri, Feng Hou and Gernett Picot. 2008. *Internal Migration of Immigrants: Do Immigrants Respond to Regional Labour Demand Shocks?* Analytical Studies Branch Research Paper Series Catalogue no. 11F0019M (318).

Prince Edward Island. 2008. *Prince Edward Island Population Report:* Second Quarter, 2008. Charlottetown: Provincial Treasury. http://www.gov.pe.ca/photos/original/pt_pop_rep.pdf (accessed September 3, 2009).

Quell, Carsten. 2005. An Overview of Regional and Multicultural Diversity in Canada. *The CRIC Papers: Diversity in Canada.* Centre for Research and Information on Canada.

Radford, Paul. 2007. A Call for Greater Research on Immigration Outside of Canada's Three Largest Cities. *Our Diverse Cities* 3 (Summer): 47-51.

Ralston, Helen. 1988. Ethnicity, Class and Gender Among South Asian Women in Metro Halifax: An Exploratory Study. *Canadian Ethnic Studies* 20 (3): 63-83.

———. 1991. Race, Class, Gender and Work Experience of South Asian Immigrant Women in Atlantic Canada. *Canadian Ethnic Studies* 33 (2): 129-39.

Ram, Bali and Y. E. Shin. 2007. Educational Selectivity of Out-Migration in Canada: 1976-1981 to 1996-2001. *Canadian Studies in Population* 34 (2): 129-48.

Reitz, Jeffrey G. 2005. Tapping Immigrant Skills: New Directions for Canadian Immigration Policy in a Knowledge Economy. *Choices* 11 (2) (February). Montreal: Institute for Research on Public Policy.

Reitz, Jeffrey G. and Rupa Banerjee. 2007. Racial Inequality, Social Cohesion, and Policy Issues in Canada. In *Belonging? Diversity, Recognition and Shared Citizenship in Canada*, ed. Keith Banting, Thomas J. Courchene and F. Leslie Seidle, 489-545. Montreal: Institute for Research on Public Policy.

Statistics Canada. 2009. Longitudinal Survey of Immigrants to Canada: Micordata User Guide –Wave 3. http://www.statcan.gc.ca/cgibin/imdb/p2SV.pl?Function=getSurvey&SDDS=4422&lang=en&db=imdb&adm=8&dis=2#4 (accessed August 24, 2009).

———. 2013. *NHS User Guide*. Statistics Canada: 99-001-X2011001.

Tastsoglou, Evangelia. 2008. Gender, Security and Immigration in Atlantic Canada. *Our Diverse Cities* 5 (Spring): 149-55.

Tastsoglou, Evangelia and Baukje Miedema. 2003. Immigrant Women and Community Development in the Canadian Maritimes: Outsiders Within? *Canadian Journal of Sociology* 28 (2): 203-41.

Telegdi, Andrew. 2006. Family Reunification: The key to successful integration. *Canadian Issues/Thèmes canadiens* (spring): 94-96.

Yoshida, Yoko and Howard Ramos. 2013. Destination Rural Canada: An Overview of Recent Immigrants to Rural Small Towns. In *The Social Transformation of Rural Canada: New Insights into Culture, Identity and Collective Action,* ed. John R. Parkins and Maureen G. Reed, 67-87. Vancouver: UBC press.

# Section 2

# Immigration and Settlement Policies and Immigrant Experiences

# 3

## Choices, Calculations and Commitments that Help to Create a Home Away from Home

*Alexandra Dobrowolsky*
*Catherine Bryan*
*Pauline Gardiner Barber*

This chapter provides a snapshot of a Nova Scotian immigration initiative that was well-intentioned but ultimately fell short of expectations for most concerned: the business and investor or "economic" category of the Nova Scotia Nominee Program (NSNP). It serves as a study of how and why an attempt to create a "home away from home" for even a select, strategic group of immigrants can become fraught with difficulties and result in disappointing outcomes. Our data suggest that part of the problem lies in what we (as researchers and students of immigration) perceive to be an imbalance between social and economic wants and needs, along with an appreciable "disconnect" between the priorities of provincial immigration officials and the newcomers in question.

The pages that follow not only tell the story of the failed "economic" stream of the NSNP, but also offer an analysis of the repercussions, both for theory and in practice. The main reason for engaging in this study of what is now an obsolete provincial immigration category is neither to revel in the scandals it spurred, nor to sensationalize the multiple challenges it inadvertently created for officials and migrants alike.

Rather, by exploring and evaluating the different sets of theoretical and practical implications and consequences of this economic stream saga, the hope is to contribute to a greater understanding of the promises and pitfalls of present-day immigration efforts, and to help inform more grounded, well-rounded immigration policies in the future.

These aims are especially timely and relevant, given the fact that at the time of writing, on October 8, 2013, a newly-elected Liberal government came to power in Nova Scotia on a general campaign promise of attending to immigration matters, as well as a specific commitment to reinstating an entrepreneurial stream in the NSNP. Concomitantly, in early 2014, Canadians received mixed messages with respect to the federal government's approach to immigrant investors. As part of its federal budget for 2014-15, and its primary objective to return to a balanced budget, the Harper government announced that it would shut down its Immigrant Investor Program (IIP). However, it then suggested that the IIP would be replaced by a new Investor Venture Capital Fund pilot project requiring immigrants to make substantial investments in the Canadian economy.

As a result, many lessons can be learned from this previous Nova Scotian immigration experiment gone wrong. The most crucial ones, in our view, are quite straightforward but still seem to have been overlooked in this unfortunate situation. They are that any new provincial immigration strategies must work harder at achieving greater equilibrium between economic and social priorities, and at balancing the choices, calculations and commitments of state officials with those of newcomers.

Our analysis stems from research completed for a pilot study funded by the Atlantic Metropolis Centre (AMC) in 2008. The project was comprised of a review of relevant government documents, an analysis of local media reports on the NSNP (gathered from the Newscan database) and eighteen qualitative interviews with immigrants who entered Nova Scotia between 2008 and 2009, mostly as economic nominees (sixteen), but also as federal skilled workers (two).

The chapter proceeds as follows: In part I, we begin by briefly explaining the nature and objectives of provincial nominee programs in general, and then move to the NSNP, and the specifics of the business and investor stream on which our research was based. In part II, after noting some key presumptions that underpin nominee programs, we illustrate how the experiences of Nova Scotia economic nominees run counter to these ideas and ideals. In particular, we highlight the extent to which social dimensions are often underdeveloped in immigration schemes, especially in those categories that are expressly aimed at increasing economic benefits. More specifically, we focus on how, for a significant number of Nova Scotia nominees, in spite of PNPs' explicit economic rationale, and despite the specific NSNP economic stream in question, migration represented a broader personal project of parenting and care related primarily to the reconfiguration of gendered roles within the household, as a means of enhancing quality of life for all family members. Part III explores how, with these gendered and social objectives of their migratory project largely unmet, nominees sought to redress the limitations of the NSNP and the consequences of these limitations for their short- and long-term plans. All of this informs our policy recommendations that are noted in Part IV as part of our conclusions.

## I: PNPs and the NSNP:
## Divergent Expectations and Outcomes

Provincial nominee programs are relatively new in Canada. Historically, even though immigration is a jurisdiction that is shared by both federal and provincial levels of government, the federal government tended to be the primary player when it came to dealing with immigration matters (Quebec providing the main exception). However, since the mid 1990s, federal officials began signing successive immigration agreements with a growing number of provinces. The focus here is on these "provincial nominee programs" or "PNPs" which allow provincial authorities to "nominate" immigrants to the federal government's Citizenship and Immigration Canada (CIC) department. While CIC approval seals the final deal, each province's program is fashioned to respond to its particular immigration needs. Today, all provinces and territories, save for Quebec and Nunavut, have launched these provincial and territorial programs (PTNPs).

The expectation is that provinces (and territories) will open new avenues of immigration, tailored to their particular contexts and demands (which typically correspond to their respective labour market needs), and that CIC will ultimately endorse their immigrant selections. This means that provinces have more control when it comes to immigration program design, implementation and, optimally, in terms of successful outcomes. Yet, the overarching objective of the PNPs is "to make an immediate economic contribution to the province ... that nominates them" (CIC 2013) and thus a premium is placed on immigrants who have the desired skill sets, education and work experience.

The hope is also that nominee programs can prove to be advantageous for certain kinds of migrants, particularly those with the requisite capital and skills (Dobrowolsky 2012). The expectation here is that they now have greater "choice" in the types of immigration programs on offer at both federal and provincial levels, and in terms of the variations in nominee programs across the country (although, the federal government has recently worked to standardize provincial streams). At the same time, with PNPs especially, given their speedier processing times, select migrants are able to "fast-track" the immigration system, and, in the end, citizenship processes (Seidle 2013: 5).

With these considerations in mind, the first Canada-Nova Scotia nominee agreement was signed in August of 2002 as a five-year pilot with the goal of introducing one thousand immigrants (Dobrowolsky 2011, 2012). It included three designated streams (skilled workers, community identified and economic nominees). As the first decade of the 2000s progressed, these were expanded to include a few additional categories (e.g., family business workers, international students, non-dependent children of Nova Scotia nominees and an agricultural stream), but, as of early 2014, the NSNP has reverted back to having three main streams (skilled workers, family business workers and community identified). However, in this chapter the focus is on the short-lived "economic" category. This designation not only underscored the federal government's economic priorities as determined by CIC, but also reflected the Nova Scotia government's attempt at innovation. As we shall see, by July 2006, as a result of numerous difficulties that will be detailed below, Nova Scotia stopped accepting these economic stream applicants. Nonetheless, it is important to emphasize that the NSNP, as a whole, continues to operate, and that both economic and demographic "returns" remain at the forefront of new nominee program developments. And again, here, the new Liberal government's consideration of an entrepreneurial stream provides a case in point.

In light of the particular challenges faced by the province, the business and investor stream initially held promise. As discussed in this volume, Nova Scotia grapples with interrelated demographic and economic concerns that include: historic and present out-migration; recurring difficulties with attraction and retention; an aging population; chronic de-population in rural areas; slow economic growth; and labour shortages in various sectors. In this context, we can understand why the economic stream of the NSNP would be viewed as an opportune strategy aimed at remedying serious provincial demographic and economic shortfalls.

Indeed, in time, the following objectives for the economic category became evident: (a) to increase the economic benefits for Nova Scotia, (b) to process and admit candidates as expeditiously as possible, (c) to attract and retain more immigrants and (d) to provide mentorship to give immigrants exposure and experience with Nova Scotia businesses.

To be sure, potential economic stream migrants also had to meet certain expectations. Eligibility was based on the following: candidates had to be between the ages of twenty to sixty years old; possess grade twelve education, or its equivalent; and have basic skills in English or French. They also had to have experience owning and operating a business and have documented proof of holding a minimum net worth of $300,000.

In addition, applicants were required to pay a fee of $130,500. This fee was broken down as follows: $100,000 went to a Nova Scotia company offering a paid work placement and "mentorship" (it would be paid in two installments of $50,000, and at least $20,000 of this amount was to be paid in salary to the nominee); $20,000 went to an international recruiter or immigration consultant in the nominee's home country (early in the program only $18,000 was paid to the consultant) (OAG 2008a); $10,000 would go to Cornwallis Financial Corporation, a Halifax-based financial consulting company, to oversee the process and prepare immigrant files; and $500 went to the province of Nova Scotia for an assessment fee (although the province dropped this portion of the fee on May 9, 2006). After provincial staff approved a nominee's application, it went to the CIC for final approval.

Clearly, these were select migrants who were strategically recruited. Principal applicants were wealthy individuals with business skills and because of the financial and business requirements, they were also more likely to be male than female. In fact, statistics provided by the Office of Immigration indicate that this was the case for provincial nominees overall. For example, by 2007, while 16 per cent of the total immigrants to Nova Scotia were male principal applicants to the NSNP, women constituted less than half of this number at 7 per cent (data on file with the authors compiled by the Office of Immigration (NSOI) in April 2009). Office of Immigration data also indicates that, between 2004 and 2006, the top source countries for provincial nominees were Korea (219), Iran (185), Taiwan (178) and the Philippines (103), followed by Britain (101) and the United States (71) (Office of Immigration 2007).

The economic stream entailed successful candidates landing in Nova Scotia and being matched with a business. Through their work with these business "mentors," nominees would gain the local experience and contacts that would serve them well when the nominees moved on to build and grow their own business ventures.

And so, economic stream nominees were required to participate in a six-month middle management employment contract chosen from a list of companies provided by the province. Again, program participants would receive $20,000 for the period and if they did not sign a contract with a business mentor within one year of landing, they would forfeit $100,000 of their application fees (Office of the Auditor General 2008a).

Unfortunately, many of these expectations were not met. Various aspects of the economic stream proved problematic, starting with the fact that the application fees were high, and in the end, there was little to show for the expenses incurred. For instance, many nominees were poorly matched with companies. Highly skilled professionals were assigned to inappropriate postings that included, in some cases, menial labour, and in others involved non-existent work assignments. As a result, not everyone who started a mentorship completed their six-month assignment.

A two-volume report released by Nova Scotia's Office of the Auditor General (OAG 2008a; 2008b) uncovered the depth of the economic stream's problems. For example, the Auditor General found that many of the companies offering mentorships did not comply with the stated criteria: some were smaller than required, while others provided placements that were clearly not at a middle management level.

Early evaluations of the program were not positive. The government released data that showed provincial targets were not being reached, while other indicators, such as those that would track the program's retention of migrants, were not forthcoming.

Controversies also arose with respect to the private consulting company, Cornwallis Financial Corporation, entrusted with running most of the logistics of the program. While this was meant to be a "public private partnership," the bulk of the administration fell to the private company. Early in the process newspaper reports flagged the fact that the contract was untendered, and that Cornwallis was among the top donors to the provincial Progressive

Conservatives, the party in government at the time (Flinn 2005). Increasingly, the high fees received by Cornwallis were also called into question, and Halifax Global Inc. was hired (this time, in a tendered competition) to review the money involved ("Immigrant fees reviewed" 2006). This, in turn, raised more questions in the press over the high fees going to Cornwallis (Flinn 2005; Jackson 2005).

On the government's side, initial oversight of the program came from the Office of Economic Development, but when Nova Scotia's Office of Immigration (NSOI) was created it took over responsibility for the "public" part of the nominee program "partnership." Still, the NSOI was markedly constrained in its capacities given its small staff and limited budget (in fact, the provincial government announced that the program would come at "no extra cost to the taxpayers of the province" (Flinn and Bauder 2013: 10)) and given Cornwallis's role; the program appeared to have operated on more of a privatized basis.

To make matters worse, when the Cornwallis contract expired and was not renewed, it launched four legal suits against the provincial government. These legal claims were consolidated into one by April 2008 (Nova Scotia 2009). A year later, an out-of-court settlement was reached between the corporation and the government of Nova Scotia (Jackson 2009) involving millions of dollars that drew on nominees' fees.[1]

Taken together, these challenges help to explain why Nova Scotia stopped accepting new NSNP economic category applications on July 1, 2006. However, it did continue processing applications received before that date and proceeded with mentor programs for economic nominees who had received permanent resident visas for Nova Scotia, some of whom arrived in the province as late as 2008.

Additionally, and in response to well-organized mobilization on the part of nominees, a year later, the provincial government found itself making a commitment to refund millions of dollars. By October 2007, local newspapers reported that the NSOI had posted a notice on its website indicating that those who had not started the program and could prove that they had lived in Nova Scotia for twelve consecutive months could be in line for the refund. Those who had started or had completed the program would not qualify (Jeffrey 2007). Six hundred people who had not yet signed a contract became eligible for a refund of $100,000. In the fall of 2008, the Nova Scotia government announced more refunds would be forthcoming with 206 people added to the list of those eligible for refunds.

In the end, we can safely conclude that many of the aims and expectations of the economic category of the NSNP failed to be realized. However, before exploring the actual assessments of some of the nominees involved, and why there was a "disconnect" between their expectations and priorities, and those of the Nova Scotia government, let us turn to and unpack the broader logic at work with such programs, and the ways in which this rationale fails to accommodate the expectations and objectives of individual nominees.

## II: Mismatched Expectations

Provincial Nominee Programs represent an effort at the subnational level to attract skilled and self-sufficient immigrants. They work from the assumption that migration is an inevitable process, based on the individual choices of migrants and the features of the receiving state that make migration desirable. These features or pull-factors are often framed in terms of economic opportunities: employment and investment. The PNPs seek to take advantage of this process by recruiting the most economically viable migrants—those with high levels of financial and human capital. In the case of the NSNP economic category, this was most obvious in the $130,500 fee, but also in the professional credential requirements.

Under the NSNP economic stream, "ideal migrants" (see Barber 2008a) were those who could afford the fee, and who sought to improve their economic standing through migration. The province, in turn, sought to capitalize on these individuals, their spending power, their investment in local business, and their overall contribution to the economy. In these ways, the NSNP economic stream mirrored global and national trends that increasingly cast immigration in economic terms. While it is true that provincial nominees arrive with a set of economic objectives (typically related to employment), by focusing solely on the economic incentives of migration, PNP logic masks the more multi-layered motivations and expectations of migrants and their families. It is to these unrealized outcomes that we now turn.

Despite the NSNP's emphasis on economic motivations and objectives, for the nominees interviewed, financial gain was not the primary reason for migration. Instead, nominees cited a number of social and familial motivations as having prompted their decision to come to Nova Scotia. Many of these reasons spoke to the nominees' perceptions of Nova Scotia and, more broadly, Canada, as well as to the attitudes and opportunities they expected to encounter there. For many of the nominees, these attitudes and opportunities diverged from those typically found in their respective countries of origin. Notably, in discussing the well-being of children, migration emerged very much as a means of redressing gendered constraints as they were perceived and experienced in the country of origin for both male and female children.

Although early research on international migration tended to overlook gender, over the last thirty years a vast body of work has emerged that documents and analyzes the relationship between gender and migration (Anderson 2000; Barber and Bryan 2012; Bryan 2012; Dobrowolsky 2013; Dobrowolsky and Tastsoglou 2006; Fouron and Glick Schiller 2001; Hondagneu-Sotelo 1992; Guendelman and Perez-Itriago 1987; Kofman 2012; Lamphere 1987; Parreñas 2000; Pessar 2003; Pessar and Mahler 2003; Piper 2007; Stasiulis and Bakan 2005). This scholarship recognizes that gender—understood as the socio-cultural meanings and values assigned to biological difference—informs migration opportunities and experiences. Moreover, it emphasizes the gendered outcomes of migration; in other words, how migration influences and alters gender relations and hierarchies.

Early accounts of gender and migration often view migration as an emancipatory experience that empowers women by providing enhanced employment opportunities (cf. Grasmuck and Pessar 1991; Lamphere 1987; Pessar 2003). Through their earnings, employed immigrant women are able to assert increased independence or authority in the country of resettlement. More recently, however, a number of studies have highlighted the extent to which the emancipatory potential of migration remains largely unachieved. These often focus on circular labour migration, and emphasize the extent to which women often migrate for employment that is itself constrained by traditional gender roles (Andersen 2000; Parreñas 2000; Stasiulis and Bakan 2005). A third subsection of this literature focuses on the ways gender—understood here as a process—is negotiated and renegotiated in different contexts. The emphasis on gender as process means that gender norms are simultaneously upheld, challenged, rejected and even harnessed in different settings to meet different objectives (Barber 2008b; Barber and Bryan 2012; Dobrowolsky 2013; Fouron and Glick Schiller 2001; Pessar and Mahler 2003; Tastsoglou and Dobrowolsky 2006).

Despite their entrance through an economically-driven program, the nominees saw migration as part of a broader project related to objectives of a decidedly social nature—a project in which considerations of gender and gendered roles figured prominently. The nominees typically self-identified as "liberal," and in many cases saw their values as discordant with the ideologies and practices of their states of origin. Many expressed anxiety concerning the authorities in their countries of origin, describing the political situation as unstable and dangerous. One family moved to Canada to avoid mandatory military service for their sons. Others left because they felt their children's mobility was curtailed by moral and legal codes. These feelings were particularly prevalent among nominees with daughters. For example, one Iranian nominee said, "I prefer to send my daughter to a different kind of country, a more free country, [where there is] more chance to have a better life." This "better life" was often understood in terms of increased opportunities, yet the focus was rarely economic in nature; rather, they tended to be social opportunities. These related to travelling unrestricted, meeting new people, interacting with different cultures, appreciating how different people live, accessing education and developing new language skills.

For many nominees, migration was also specifically intended to augment the opportunities available to female children, and in some instances to female partners/parents (see Bryan 2012). Concerning his spouse, one nominee said "my wife is a pediatrician. She is very interested in continuing to study. She is very sharp, and she can grow here." For these nominees, then, the decision to migrate to Nova Scotia was based on their understandings and expectations of gender equality in Canada. Much like conventional accounts of gender and migration, they anticipated that their female family members would achieve more in Canada—socially, economically and personally.

Gender also emerges as an important aspect of migration in relation to household responsibilities and the sexual division of labour. Several of the nominees hoped that migration would provide them with the opportunity to renegotiate household responsibilities and tasks, with men and women, and male and female children alike, engaging in a variety of household chores. It was believed by these particular nominees that a more flexible sexual division of labour would benefit both male and female children. In these ways, for most of the nominees the decision to migrate was part of a parenting strategy, a way of providing and caring for their children; rather than a purely economic one.

The decision to migrate, however, was made at the expense of other caring relationships, notably those with aging parents. The presence of aging parents in the country of origin was described as one of the more stressful and uncertain aspects of migration. Many of the nominees planned to redress the care deficit created in their absence by providing financial support and by returning to the country of origin regularly in order to provide respite for other family members (typically siblings).

In these ways, for many of the nominees, family migration was part of a larger strategy of redressing gender inequality and mitigating the perceived social constraints placed on both men and women, but particularly women, in the country of origin. Successful execution of this strategy was contingent upon gainful employment, but as expressed by the nominees, gainful employment was not the principle objective; it was a means to an end, rather than an end in itself. Further, it was also expected in several cases that the nominee—frequently being the most affluent member of his or her family—would continue to provide financial support for siblings and extended family. This was to be achieved through remittances. While some nominees were able to achieve these goals without employment, their savings enabling them to retire once in Nova Scotia, most were not. Unable to access the mentorship program and unable to find employment, most of the nominees were forced to modify their objectives and formulate new strategies. These resulted in a reversal of not only what the nominees expected but also of what the NSNP had anticipated.

Indeed, most nominees experienced a significant decline in their standard of living in Canada, something which was not unexpected, at least for the short term. Less predictable were the reported feelings of class humiliation, compounded by gendered cultural norms. For example, a businessman from a middle-eastern country, who described his previous circumstances as upper middle class, told us about the features of what we identify as significant downward social mobility. In his country of origin, he owned several properties, hired a driver for his car and a private English language teacher for his young son. While he anticipated a different lifestyle in Canada, he had not imagined just how different and challenging it would be. Because his placement with a suitable local firm did not materialize, he had to contemplate other options. One idea was to drive a taxi but he felt that he must maintain class appearances to provide stability for his young son; the idea of his father as a driver rather than the driver's employer was considered potentially traumatic for his transposed son.

Perhaps it would also be traumatic to a father wishing to provide a continuity of class status in his son's childhood.

While many of Canada's immigrants, historically and in the present, have experienced downward social mobility at least temporarily, most of them were not compelled here by a privately profitable immigration scheme, managed by a consulting firm, with the promise of business opportunities in Canada. Nonetheless, this immigrant told us, without bitterness:

> ...My son is a little child. He doesn't understand what happened to me and why the lifestyle is very different. I tried to do it in a way that he cannot recognize any difference between here and there. I arranged some programs, I bought a new car, and sometimes we go to good restaurants and ... when the weather is good, we go somewhere around the country and make some pleasure for him.

The concern with class in this example illustrates how the calculations made by nominees are carefully measured. However, the subjective and more demeaning aspects of the transnational class switch are incalculable. Our research suggests that while policy modification may lessen the extent to which these are experienced, they will persist unless we move beyond market driven immigration strategies.

## III: Nominee Strategies

The strategies developed by the nominees to mitigate the limitations of the NSNP and their subsequent unemployment span great distances, and they rely on familial, social and business networks in the country of origin. Unable to access the hoped-for benefits of the NSNP mentorship program, and unable to find appropriate employment, most of the nominees—at the time of the interviews—found themselves in difficult circumstances. Most were drawing heavily on savings, and some were beginning to seek out work and new investment opportunities in the country of origin. Continued employment in the country of origin was effective where one family income earner had been able to maintain employment in the country of origin. Although many female partners/parents were employed prior to resettlement, it was typically the male partner/parent who continued to work in the country of origin, commuting to and from Nova Scotia. Under this arrangement, women became fully responsible for the daily tasks of social reproduction and household management in Nova Scotia (Bryan 2012).

The strategy is itself gendered, drawing on divisions of reproductive and productive labour in the country of origin. More importantly, however, the outcome is also highly gendered; compromising the awaited social outcomes of migration, the increased mobility for female family members and, in a very real sense, diminishing the relative autonomy women had experienced through paid employment in the country of origin. Furthermore, efforts to establish a more equitable division of household labour were curtailed; separated from their children, nominee men were unable to engage in family and domestic life in Canada as they had hoped.

Through this we can observe an explicit reversal of the expected flow of remittances as both migrant and money move in the same direction: away from the country of origin and into Canada. This was exacerbated in situations where employment was unavailable in both Canada and the country of origin, and as a result, nominees came to require remittances sent from family—parents and siblings—in the country of origin.

The experiences of the nominees complicate conventional accounts of labour migration and the hoped-for outcomes of fast-track business-class and investor streams, with many of the nominees unable to secure employment, choosing to leave Nova Scotia for larger city centres such as Toronto and Vancouver. Their experiences also bring to light the limitations of immigration policies that are solely interested in the economic contributions of immigrants.

Migration is a relatively costly process for all categories of migrants, and even for those who must demonstrate wealth prior to departure. Because of this group's economic status, the NSNP failed to anticipate that they would face challenges similar to other newcomers. At the same time, what is clear through the narratives of the nominees is that while different groups of migrants may face similar difficulties, their socio-economic standing in their country of origin influences how those difficulties are experienced and resolved. For this group of nominees, the stress already associated with migration was compounded by a lack of financial security, loss of status and prolonged separation from or the unexpected need to rely on family, the consequences of which—as described by participants—included uncertainty, stress, anxiety, emotional distress and tension between spouses. Furthermore, for both men and women, normative gender roles were reassigned by the circumstances of resettlement. In other words, gender inequality as it was experienced in the country of origin was not rectified; rather, it was reinforced.

## IV: Conclusions

Our research indicates the need to deal with the "disconnect" occurring in immigrants' lives. This entails a more concerted effort to balance social and cultural aspects of migrants' lives—previously and post-immigration—with the government's economic priorities reflected in immigration policy. In particular, we suggest more attention be accorded to gender, class, cultural conditions and associated experiences in efforts to recruit immigrants across various social and economic backgrounds. Acknowledgment of immigrants' social standing and expertise should be reflected in policy development around the provision of support programs. Immigrant support groups already know these things; what they lack are adequate resources and support for the cross-cultural translation of the needs of their clients. Neoliberal policy takes for granted that class and money are commensurate with self-sufficiency; hence the underlying logic of the economically calculated immigration selection processes that suggest better-off economic migrants do not require settlement resources. Clearly they do, and ones better tailored to their needs.

Further, in recruitment practices for various skilled workers into particular occupational niches, such as in nominee programs, ethical best practices suggest working with professional associations, educational and other institutional partners in countries of origin. This is to ensure that (a) potentially negative outcomes caused by migration—disruption to family life, depletion of human capital in the community of origin, downward class mobility in Nova Scotia and unfulfilled expectations of livelihood (e.g., in the case of medical or other skilled professionals) and family relations—are minimized, and (b) Canada's reputation as a welcoming destination is deserved.

Otherwise, it would appear that our immigration policy represents a full commitment to a neoliberal market-driven model with little regard for immigrant dignity, and, in the case of PNPs, immigrant retention. Ultimately, in the intensified competition among western nations for "ideal" immigrants, Canada's reputation may slide. After all, immigrants who enter Canada are much better informed about immigration policy than in the past, and we can assume they are also making ever more calculated decisions of their own. The lesson learned here is that immigration policy that respectfully recognizes newcomers and their contributions to the social and economic fabric of communities, as well as how these are enhanced by emigration, will go a long way in making Nova Scotia a "home away from home."

**Note**

We are thankful for an Atlantic Metropolis Centre/SSHRC-funded pilot project grant that supported this research.

1. The Nova Scotia Immigration Minister Len Goucher announced that the lawsuit against the province, and the province's counterclaim, had been settled "'with the province getting at least $7.5 million and Cornwallis $1 million. All of the money will come from the fees paid by immigrants or from interest earned on those fees, not from taxpayers,' Mr. Goucher said.... Cornwallis president Stephen Lockyer didn't want to say much ... about the settlement.... The RCMP are still looking

at aspects of the immigrant nominee program" (Jackson 2009). See also
Nova Scotia (2009).

## References

Anderson, Bridget. 2000. *Doing the Dirty Work? The Global Politics of
Domestic Labour.* London: Zed Books.

Barber, Pauline Gardiner. 2008a. The Ideal Immigrant? Gendered Class
Subjects in Philippine Migration. *Third World Quarterly* 29 (7): 1265-85.

———. 2008b. Cell Phones, Complicity and Class Politics in the
Philippine Labour Diaspora. *Focaal: European Journal of Anthropology*
51:8-42.

Barber, Pauline G. and Catherine Bryan. 2012. "Value Plus Plus":
Housewifization and History in Philippine Care Migration. In *Twenty-
First Century Migration: Political Economy and Ethnography*, ed. Pauline
Gardiner Barber and Winner Lem, 215-35. New York: Routledge.

Bryan, Catherine. 2012. Gendered Returns, Ambivalent Transnationals:
Situating Transnationalism in Local Asymmetry. *Anthropologica* 54 (1):
133-42.

Citizenship and Immigration Canada (CIC). 2013. Provincial nominees.
http://www.cic.gc.ca/english/provincial/index.asp.

Dobrowolsky, Alexandra. 2011. The Intended and Unintended Effects
of a New Immigration Strategy: Insights from Nova Scotia's Provincial
Nominee Program. *Studies in Political Economy* 87:109-41.

———. 2012. Nuancing Neoliberalism: Lessons Learned from a
Failed Immigration Experiment. *Journal of International Migration and Integration.* Published online: February 15. DOI 10.1007/
s12134-012-0234-8.

———. 2013. Economic Migration and Women: Not the Usual Story,
Not the Usual Suspects. In *Migration, Globalization and the State*, ed.
Rachel K. Brickner, 79-100. Houndmills: Palgrave Macmillan.

Dobrowolsky, Alexandra and Evangelia Tastsoglou. 2006. Cross-
ing Boundaries and Making Connections. In *Women, Migration and
Citizenship: Making Local, National and Transnational Connections*, ed.
Evangelia Tastsoglou and Alexandra Dobrowolsky, 1-35. Aldershot:
Ashgate.

Flinn, Brian. 2005. One of Tories' Top Donors Got Untendered Immigration Contract. *Daily News.* 23 November.

Flynn, Emma and Harald Bauder. 2013. The Private Sector: Institutions of Higher Education and Immigrant Settlement in Canada. Ryerson *Centre for Immigration and Settlement Working Paper* 2013-9.

Fouron, Georges and Nina Glick Schiller. 2001. All in the Family: Gender, Transnational Migration, and the Nation-State. *Identities: Global Studies in Culture and Power* 7:539-82.

Glick Schiller, Nina. 2010. *Migration and Development without Methodological Nationalism: Towards Global Perspectives on Migration. Journal of Social Analysis* 53 (3): 14-37.

Grasmuck, Sherri and Patricia Pessar. 1991. *Between Two Islands: Dominican International Migration.* Berkeley: University of California Press.

Guendelman, Sylvia and Auristela Perez-Itriago. 1987. Double Lives: The Changing Role of Women in Seasonal Migration. *Women's Studies* 13:249-71.

Hondagneu-Sotelo, Pierrette. 1992. Overcoming Patriarchal Constraints: The Reconstruction of Gender Relations among Mexican Women and Men. *Gender and Society* 6 (3): 393-415.

Immigration Fees Reviewed. 2006. *The Daily News.* January 31.

Immigration Plan Province's Own 'Sponsorship Scandal'- NDP. 2009. *The Daily News.* February 9.

Jackson, David. 2005. Province to review fees immigrants must pay to enter NS. *The Chronicle Herald.* December 21.

———. 2009. Immigration Lawsuit Settled: Cornwallis Financial to get $1 Million, Province at Least 7.5 Million From Nominee Program Fees. *The Chronicle Herald.* May 12. http://thechronicleherald.ca/Front/1118541.html (accessed August 10, 2009).

Jeffrey, Davene. 2007. Rebate Quietly Offered to Immigrants: People Had Paid to Mentor Here. *The Chronicle Herald.* October 18.

Kofman, Eleonore. 2012. Rethinking Care Through Social Reproduction: Articulating Circuits of Migration. *Social Politics* 19 (1): 142-62.

Lamphere, Louise. 1987. *From Working Daughters to Working Mothers.* Ithaca, NY: Cornell University Press.

Ley, David. 2010. *Millionaire Migrants: Trans-Pacific Life Lines.* Malden, MA and Oxford: Wiley-Blackwell.

Nova Scotia. 2009. Nominee Program Legal Dispute Settled. http://www.gov.ns.ca/news/details.asp?id=20090424003 (accessed May 15, 2009).

Office of the Auditor General (OAG). 2008a. *Special Report to the House of Assembly on the Office of Immigration Economic Stream of the Nova Scotia Nominee Program*. Phase I.

———. 2008b. *Special Report to the House of Assembly on the Office of Immigration Economic Stream of the Nova Scotia Nominee Program*. Phase II.

Office of Immigration (OOI). 2007. Provincial Nominees to Nova Scotia: Nova Scotia Immigration Information and Fact Sheet. Released November 6. http://www.novascotiaimmigration.com (accessed May 20, 2009).

Parreñas, Rhacel Salazar. 2000. Migrant Filipina Domestic Workers and the International Division of Reproductive Labor. *Gender and Society* 14 (4): 560-80.

Pessar, Patricia. 2003. Anthropology and the Engendering of Migration Studies. In *American Arrivals: Anthropology Engages the New Immigrants*, ed. Nancy Foner, 75-98. Santa Fe, NM: School of American Research Press.

Pessar, Patricia and Sarah Mahler. 2003. Transnational Migration: Bringing Gender In. *International Migration Review* 37 (3): 812-43.

Piper, Nicola. 2007. International Migration and Gendered Axes of Stratification: Introduction. In *New Perspectives on Gender and Migration: Livelihood, Rights and Entitlements*, ed. Nicola Piper, 1-18. New York: Routledge.

Seidle, Leslie. 2013. Canada's Provincial Nominee Immigration Programs: Securing Greater Policy Alignment. *Institute for Research on Public Policy* 43 (Dec): 1-25.

Stasiulis, Daiva K. and Abigail B. Bakan. 2005. *Negotiating Citizenship: Migrant Women in Canada and the Global System*. Toronto: University of Toronto Press.

Tastsoglou, Evangelia and Alexandra Dobrowolsky, eds. 2006. *Women, Migration and Citizenship: Making Local, National and Transnational Connections*. Aldershot, U.K.: Ashgate.

UNDP 2009. Human Development Report 2009, *Overcoming barriers: Human mobility and development*. http://hdr.undp.org/en/reports/global/hdr2009 (accessed December 12, 2012).

4

# Home, Housing and Homelessness: Can Migrant Women Call Halifax "Home" if They Don't Have a Dwelling Place?

*Maria José Yax-Fraser and Barbara Cottrell*

*I think it is not easy to find good, safe and appropriate affordable housing, at least here in Halifax.—Asha*

## The Meaning of Home

Migrants, academics and those working with immigrants have brought forward a notion of home that refers not only to questions of territoriality, nationality and citizenship, but also to senses of belonging to particular communities and notions of identity. Home, in this context, is seen as a locus of emotional support, a physical and emotional connection to one's past, and as such is much more than merely a structure or a geographical place of everyday life (Simich 2010; Magat 1999; Mohanty 2003). Home is therefore seen not as something that is static, but as something that is created, recreated and "territorialized," as well as something that "we are" (Macgregor Wise 2000: 297, 300). In this chapter we acknowledge that the processes of making home are vital to the successful integration of a newcomer into her new place of settlement; and what is crucial to this process is having a dwelling place, a place one can "inhabit" and call one's own (Grant and

Danso 2000: 20; Novac 1999). We suggest that having a roof over one's head and a physical space of comfort that one can call one's own is vital to the development of a sense of feeling "at home" and that of belonging to a particular society.

In this context, we acknowledge the process of territorialization involved in making a home, including the intricate negotiations of identity, culture, belonging and attachment involved in migration processes (Macgregor Wise 2000). At the same time, however, we highlight the use of the word home to refer to the place of residence or the house where one lives and its relationship to the conceptualization of "home" as a place of safety and security. We argue that having a home—a place to live—is especially vital to a newly arrived immigrant woman in her process of making Canada her home, and concur with a small number of geographers, sociologists and anthropologists addressing homelessness and immigration, that the successful integration of immigrants and refugees into a new society involves the attainment of several basic needs, one of the most important of which is affordable, suitable and adequate housing (Teixeira and Halliday 2010).

Drawing on the research we conducted as part of the YWCA Integrated Housing Project, carried out in Halifax, Nova Scotia in 2009-2010 with ten migrant women, we shed light on both the "invisible homelessness" many migrant women experience, and their resilience to overcome barriers to access adequate housing in their process of settlement and integration into Halifax society. In addition, we examine the various dimensions of gendered homelessness and integration; the connection between access to affordable housing and the successful integration and inclusion of migrant and new immigrant women; and the link between newcomer settlement policy and housing policies and programs. We conclude with recommendations for improving the links between immigration, settlement and housing policies and programs to provide better opportunities for migrant women to secure housing and make Canada their home.

## The YWCA Integrated Housing Project

The YWCA Integrated Housing Project was developed to de-termine why new immigrant women were at risk of homeless-ness and the impact of their situation on their integration into Canada. The Federation of Canadian Municipalities defines "at risk of homelessness" as being in core-housing need. This includes singles and families spending 30 per cent or more of their income on housing, experiencing rooflessness (i.e., staying overnight in a vacant building, a public or commercial facility, a city park, a car or on the street) or living in an emergency shelter on a short-term or recurrent basis. It also includes "invisible homelessness," such as living with friends or relatives or exchanging favours in return for housing; and residing in long-term institutions because there is no suitable accommodation in the community. This term also refers to those who are temporarily and/or involuntarily living in unsafe, overcrowded homes or are sleeping on friends' couches, moving from place to place as one situation after another is no longer an option for them.

The project stemmed from an increasing awareness that new immigrant and migrant women who are homeless or at risk of homelessness do not panhandle on the streets of Halifax Regional Municipality (HRM) and thus constitute disturbing numbers of the "invisible homeless." The project was conducted by a team of two independent researchers (and authors of this chapter), a YWCA project manager and a project coordinator. It was de-signed to better understand what supports were needed to assist new immigrant women to remedy their housing situation, as well as to identify which interventions could help this demographic to secure housing and to address the challenges posed by the complex combination of systemic economic, gender and cultural barriers barriers that affect new immigrant women's capacity to find housing and suitable employment.

The women who participated in this project were born in Congo, Eritrea, Kenya, Rwanda, Sri Lanka, Sudan, Zimbabwe, Mexico and Iran. Among them were newcomer immigrant and migrant[1] women who were landed immigrants, Canadians born abroad, refugee claimants and international students who were experiencing core-housing need. Six came to Canada as refugees: four came under the Government Assisted Refugee (GAR) program, one came sponsored by a church, and one sponsored by her relatives. Three entered under different immigrant categories: one participant came under the family class category sponsored by her former husband, one came as an international student, and one came as a visitor and was a refugee claimant at the time of the study. The tenth participant immigrated as a Canadian citizen born abroad. The participants had been in Canada from six months to five years. In order to protect participants' identities, we use pseudonyms when referring to each participant individually; to acknowledge their journeying experiences and highlight their legal status to address their particular experiences of immigration and housing situation, we refer to all the participants as newcomers or as migrant women regardless of their legal status.

The YWCA project ran from September 1, 2008, to September 1, 2009, with two specific objectives. The first objective was to determine the extent to which an intervention with housing and multiple supports improved the long-term housing and settlement outcomes for newcomer women and their children. The second objective was to bridge federal agencies with coordinated local community supports and thereby create new mechanisms and partnerships across organizations and government departments. The project's multiple intervention approach encompassed the following: financial support, housing support, counselling, intercultural education, language skills and employment training. These interventions fell under the following two components of the project: (a) income supplement in the form of training allowance and housing supplement, and (b) support services including housing support, social engagement, employment support, language training and Canadian life skills support. Particular interventions were decided upon based on the development of an individualized work plan to assist each participant in solving her housing situation.

We draw from the data we collected throughout the project, including the entrance interviews conducted to better understand the participants' skills and needs; biweekly progress reports submitted by the program coordinator; and an exit focus group comprised of all participants to evaluate the success of the project. The information collected through the entrance interviews provided the project staff with background information on each participant and their precarious housing situations and it was used to develop a personalized plan and to determine monthly educational meetings. As researchers, we met with the project manager and coordinator on a monthly basis to review progress reports, lend support to the project staff and exchange information to facilitate the implementation of each participant's individualized plan. We also attended a number of the educational workshops. As will be elaborated upon in the following pages, the causes of women's housing insecurity were multiple, including, among others, economic instability, difficulties accessing support services, family structures, challenges in establishing social networks and lack of affordable and suitable housing availability. This chapter will point to the changes needed to better connect immigration and settlement and housing policies and programs in order to increase the opportunities for migrant women to secure suitable, adequate and affordable housing.

### Homelessness and Immigration: A Gender-based Analysis

Research in the area of homelessness has only recently begun to address the relationship with immigrant status, raising awareness of the changing portrait of homelessness in Canada (Balley and Bulthius 2004) and its gender dimensions. While immigration is crucial to Canada's population growth and economic well-being, growing evidence shows that immigrants arriving in Canada today increasingly face structures of inequality and barriers to full participation in the economy and society (Akbari et al. 2009; Tota 2004; Picot 2004; Wayland 2006). Despite being more highly educated and skilled than earlier immigrants, new immigrants have not fared as well in terms of employment and earnings and are more likely to live in poverty and be at risk of being homeless (Akbari 2009; National Homelessness Initiative 2003). Income insecurity, coupled with the rising cost of rent, results in not being able to pay for basic necessities, including housing, thereby raising the spectre of homelessness for newcomers to Canada (Wayland 2006). According to 2006 census data, published in 2008, about 28.5 per cent of immigrants were living in unacceptable housing conditions or in "core housing need" (core housing is defined by Canada Mortgage and Housing Corporation as suitable, adequate and affordable), compared to 18.6 per cent of the Canadian-born population. In Halifax, core housing need is greatest among Aboriginal peoples, visible minorities and immigrants (Ball 2002). Immigrants and refugees are over-represented in the at-risk population living in households that pay 50 per cent or more of gross household income on all shelter costs (Dempsey and Soojin 2004; Fleury 2007; Thurston et al. 2006; Tota 2004). And women, especially single mothers, are disproportionally affected by issues of affordability and discrimination (Ling 2008).

**Invisible Homelessness**

Our literature review demonstrated that defining "homelessness" in the Canadian context has been problematic and its extent not well documented due to narrow definitions of what constitutes being homeless (Thurston et al. 2006; Klodawsky 2006). Such narrow definitions of what constitutes homelessness and where that homelessness is located have contributed to the popular misconception that homelessness is a problem faced overwhelmingly by men. Consequently the portrait of the homeless in Canada fails to include migrant women's distinctive realities and fails to capture the specificities of migrant women's experiences of homelessness. For example, in Canada, homelessness for migrant women is less likely to constitute what feminists such as Fran Klodawsky (2006: 366) refer to as "absolute homelessness," or what we refer to as rooflessness or visible homelessness, such as sleeping on the street or in an emergency shelter. Rather, it is likely to constitute "relative homelessness," or what we refer to as being in core housing need, or invisible homelessness, such as living in a crowded house, sharing an apartment with other relatives, couch surfing, or paying more than 30 per cent of income on housing.

Making the distinction between absolute and relative homelessness is a significant feminist contribution to analysis of homelessness. This distinction not only provides a broader and more inclusive understanding of migrant women's homelessness, but raises our awareness that women's homelessness has to be understood as a continuum of tenuous housing arrangements intricately tied to the sexual division of labour and to women's social vulnerabilities as wives and mothers, and often as daughters as well (Klodawsky 2006; Watson 1988; Kappel Ramji Consulting Group 2002). It thus raises our awareness that the opposite of "homelessness" is not only having "housing" but also a "home" as suggested by UN researchers working on homelessness:

> Those who have no home and who live either outdoors or in emergency shelter or hostels, and people whose homes do not meet UN basic standards of adequate protection from the elements, access to safe water and sanitation, affordable prices, secure tenure and personal safety, and accessibility to employment, education and health care. (United Nations Year of Shelter for the Homeless 1987)

This broader definition of what being without housing means speaks to the increasing evidence that women's homelessness is more likely to be invisible. Women more often use informal strategies to avoid either the streets or emergency shelters. In her study of homeless men and women in New York, Joanne Passaro (1996) is sensitive to the spacial distribution of and different characteristics between homeless women and men, including access to public spaces such as "the street" or "the park" and access to facilities and services including shelters. She asserts that homeless women have little choice but to be active agents of their own subordination, and are complicit actors in a system that defines their place as home because women, more often than men, will tend to avoid living on the streets and will have better access to facilities and services (1996: 85). Passaro's conclusion makes an important point regarding the social construction by which women have been, both ideologically and materially, associated with the private and domestic spaces. However, our contention is that an analysis of homelessness should encompass an exploration of gender, bodies, culture and the urban in order to acknowledge the complex intersections of women's subjectivities in the context of urban homelessness. What is more, rather than perceiving homeless women as agents of their own subordination, we acknowledge that their strategies to avoid the streets, the parks and the shelters reflect immigrant women's resistance to their situation and their resilience.

Here, along with feminist theorists who have challenged liberalism's facile public-private dichotomization of social life, and its socialized gendered spaces (Ardener 1981), we consider the family, and by implication the home, as a political site and space. And yet, as we know from previous studies and well-documented evidence, the domestic environment does not always represent a sanctuary from the perils outside. Deprivations and physical, sexual and psychological violence are found within households. The link between home insecurity and domestic violence has also been well-documented (Assanand 2004; Brownridge and Halli 2002; Lenon 2002; Thurston et al. 2006). Women leaving abusive situations often find themselves in exceptionally vulnerable positions. Nevertheless, we also recognize that, even though women do not control physical or social space directly, this does not necessarily preclude them from being "determinants of, or mediators in, the allocation of space" (Ardener 1981: 17).

These navigations, negotiations and contestations of public and private become even more complicated for migrant women. As subjects whose bodies had been recipients of displacement and deterritorialization, most women in our study were well aware that even women in Canada feel increasingly at risk in the streets and roads of their own communities, particularly at night, and are often warned that they are at risk. At the same time, however, women in our study were not only wary of the public space of the street, but also of shelters. They attempted to avoid the physical spaces where the potential threat to their survival exists, including other humans as well as the natural environment. The multiplicity of often hidden places to which homeless migrant women must resort has contributed to the invisibility of immigrant women's homelessness. It has also prevented researchers' access to women who are experiencing relative homelessness, particularly in smaller cities like Halifax (Thurston et al. 2006).

Migrant women's avoidance of such "public" spaces does not suggest that they are active agents of their own subordination. It does, however, underscore how they act as mediators of public and private space and are conscious actors responding to the circumstances that force them to live at risk of experiencing absolute homelessness. Similarly, in the "private" realm, they also recreate and establish new family forms in their struggle to secure permanent, adequate and safe accommodations and environments, including what has been termed as single or lone parenting.

The participants in our study came to Canada in search of an opportunity to create and establish a home for themselves and their families—for those who were accompanied by their children—because they had lost both their place of safety and comfort as well as the roof over their heads. Political instability, war, economic crises, natural disasters, systemic gender violence, organized crime and narcotrafficking had made their countries of origin unwelcome and foreign places to live. The need for security constituted a key migration rationale for these women. Yet, after migrating to Halifax their experiences were such that they still found themselves in a space of insecurity in a continuum of tenuous housing arrangements. This constituted a significant obstacle to creating a home and feeling at home in Canada. Our research reveals that these women were conscious actors given their multiple efforts to construct and reconstruct a safe and secure home for themselves and their families. It provides some concrete suggestions as to how to break down some of the barriers and facilitate processes of integration. We now turn to explore these realities and to examine the scale and rationale of housing and immigration, settlement policy and services.

## Affordable, Suitable and Adequate Housing and Successful Integration of Immigrant and Newcomer Women

Peter S. Li claims that the integration discourse in policy statements, immigration debates and academic writing endorses the normative expectation of conformity as the desirable outcome of successful immigrant integration. This conformity model, Li suggests, is "based on a narrow understanding and a rigid expectation that treat[s] integration solely in terms of the degree to which immigrants converge to the average performance of native-born Canadians and their normative and behavioural standards" (2003: 1). Thus, immigrants are deemed economically well-integrated if they earn as much as "native-born Canadians," and socially integrated if they successfully adopt the English or French language, move away from ethnically concentrated immigrant enclaves, and participate in social and political activities of mainstream society. This perspective undermines and takes for granted what constitutes desirable integration for new immigrants.

According to the Canadian government, integration is a two-way process of accommodation and adjustment between new immigrants and Canadian society (Citizenship and Immigration Canada 2002). However, consistent with our understanding that the notion of home is complex for migrants, immigrants, nomads, transnationals and asylum seekers, we also acknowledge that integration is a multifaceted socio-cultural, economic and political process in which access to housing plays a crucial role in the settlement experiences of new immigrants and the entire living experiences of newcomers undergoing the process of integration in their new society. We recognize the interconnectedness between social, cultural, political and economic integration in the immigrant experience of making home; we recognize that there are multiple and diverse versions of integration including the concept of what successful integration means for the newcomer herself; and, thus, we recognize the importance of following a holistic approach to integration.

The women in our study had dreams and high hopes that they would be able to re-establish themselves and have a fulfilling and productive life, within a welcoming community and a politically stable environment in Canada. The majority of them had or were pursuing post-secondary education and a number of them had informal training and skills in areas such as subsistence farming, cooking and sewing. All of them had significant work experience in their country of origin or in their last country of residence be- fore they came to Canada. Most of them spoke, or were learning to speak, at least one official language. Nine spoke two or three other languages. Some of them were confident that they would be able to access secure and well-paid jobs, be financially secure and have opportunities for self-improvement. Those who hoped for career advancement believed they could easily transfer their skills and experiences to the Canadian job market and expected to be able to obtain jobs and practice in their professional fields of training. However, for many, these hopes were not realized because they had been unable to find suitable and secure employment. Not surprisingly, this had a negative impact on their housing options, which in turn negatively influenced their sense of "home."

We argue that the successful integration of newcomers into a new society, regardless of their reason for immigrating, involves the attainment of several basic needs, one of the most important of which is affordable, suitable and adequate housing. Ransford Danso (2001) suggests that the initial settlement experiences, as the first phase of the multistage, multidimensional process of integration, play almost a deterministic role in the successful es- tablishment of the immigrant community while the initial recep- tion of an immigrant and a feeling of acceptance by the receiving society plays an important role in whether integration will be suc- cessful or dysfunctional: "How a society receives and welcomes its new members goes a long way to affect the life chances of the newcomers" (8). Housing is a key component of the settlement experience that will determine the newcomer's first impressions of what a society can offer to them (Gajardo 2010) and is a key component of the process of making Canada one's home.

Most of the women in our study acknowledged that they had received a friendly welcome on arrival. In their view, Canada was a safe haven where some of the human rights they had lost in their countries of origin were restored to them. However, the majority of them also stated that the barriers they faced to becoming full members of their new community prevented them from living at the same standards as Canadian-born citizens. They felt that, regardless of their socio-economic status and education, they did not have the same access to goods and services as mainstream Canadians and rather than being accepted as equal members of Canadian society, they felt they became part of the underclass. In particular, they noted that their diverse experiences in their pathways to housing marked their settlement and integration experiences and the kind of welcome they felt they received from Canadian society. Some of the challenges they faced in finding per-manent housing included high rent, low income and inadequate sources of income. The factors they mentioned that conditioned their access to housing and affordable housing were their gender, race, immigration status, period of immigration, marital status, household composition and their need for a guarantor.

## Housing and Integration

As newcomers, the women participating in our study were confronted with the reality that a shortage of low-income rental housing has plagued Halifax for decades (Silver 2008). Accord-ing to the *Municipal Land Use Policy and Housing Affordability* report (HRM 2004), 44 per cent of renters in the Halifax Regional Municipality were spending 30 per cent or more of their income on shelter in 2001. Similar studies have shown that the proportion of Nova Scotian households paying more than 50 per cent of their income for housing is the highest in the country (Fairless 2004). For the women in our study, lack of access to affordable, suitable and adequate housing limited their access to a multiplicity of resources and their participation in all social, economic, cultural and political activities of urban life in Halifax, and it structured their opportunity for upward mobility.

Seven of the participants involved in our study found themselves in core housing need. Although most of them were living in adequate housing, it was not affordable. They were spending close to 50 per cent of their limited income on housing and jeopardizing other immediate needs, not to mention children's wants. Tiffany, who was waiting for her employment permit to arrive, was receiving social assistance. She found it very difficult to cover other costs after paying for rent and utilities:

> We receive only $620 for rent, but here we pay $675.... We have to pay the power, the phone. For me the phone is necessary because my lawyer call me, my doctor, if something is happening with my daughter ... and with what we have left, we try to make this last for the whole month. At times we have $50 a week for food and transportation. This is the highest amount that we count on some months. The social worker gives me a bus pass but not for my husband, my daughter, but we go to see the lawyer, or we go to ARIS, so that's where we spend some of that money.... Children like to have the things that other children have, such as treats like candy, and we cannot even afford to get her a candy. It makes you feel horrible. The weather here is different. It is very cold, and people are saying it will get colder. She does not have proper clothing for this weather. Another thing was the school supplies; we did receive $50 from social assistance but we spent $150 and we were not able to buy her shoes.... We buy milk only when we can afford it.

Michael Haan points out that "if you were an immigrant living in an urban area in Canada in 2006, the odds that you lived in a crowded house as defined by the National Occupancy Standard (NOS)[2] were about 1 in 14; if you were Canadian-born, they were roughly 1 in 60" (2010: 16). The NOS is calculated by looking at how individuals are distributed across bedrooms. It requires no more than two persons per bedroom; for parents to have their own bedroom; for members 18 or older to have their own bedroom unless they are married or living common-law; and for children age five or older to not share a bedroom if they are of the opposite sex (Canada Mortgage and Housing Commission 1991). Haan suggests that, residentially speaking, crowding is one of the biggest differences between immigrants, particularly recent immigrants, and those who are Canadian-born. Although research on housing for new immigrants is growing, little attention has been given to the topic of crowding, particularly in light of the fact that there are differences in how researchers define "crowding" and its subjective meaning for different groups of people. He suggests, for instance, that there are positive aspects of crowding as well as negative outcomes. One of the positive aspects is that it "allows households to pool resources, thereby enhancing their access to things such as more desirable schools, neighbourhoods, and business and investment opportunities" (2010: 16). Some of the "negative outcomes" of crowding, Haan asserts, include lower child academic performance and an increase in the risk of health problems. A number of our participants would add the loss of privacy and additional stress to this list.

For Hadil, a participant in our study, crowding was a strategy to pool her resources and those of her infirm mother-in-law. Although Hadil occasionally worked for the former Metropolitan Immigrant Settlement Association (MISA, now the Immigrant Services Association of Nova Scotia, ISANS) as an immigrant support worker, she had not managed to find permanent employment to improve her financial situation, and her housing options. As a result, she depended on social assistance but this support was insufficient to afford suitable rental housing for the size of her family which included three children ages 7, 9 and 16 years old. Hadil's and her mother-in-law's income came close to $1,250. They paid almost $800 for rent and utilities of a three-bedroom apartment. The night before we interviewed Hadil in the fall of 2008, her husband, whom she had not seen for two years, arrived in Halifax. This meant that one of the children had to share accommodations with the grandmother. Hadil explained:

> I think life in Canada is good if you have a job ... if you don't have a job, life is a problem ... to stay home take money from government is no good.... Yes, I wish to have a job but my English is not good, I prefer to work. If you work and you can do everything you want ... I have been three years here in this apartment.... When I receive money, I have to pay my rent, power and East Link phone and Internet. I have a cell phone. And the money is gone!

## Economic Independence and Integration

Adequate personal income is a key "indicator of successful settlement in Canada" (Abu-Laban et al. 1999: 159). Both financial security and economic independence form the bedrock of meaningful integration. Danso (2001) suggests that this is particularly pertinent to integration in a Western industrialized society like Canada. Suzane Lenon (2002) further adds that economic insecurity is a significant factor in shaping women's vulnerability to homelessness. In our study, low income, precarious jobs and underemployment were the primary causes of women's housing insecurity. The source of income for two of the women came from a combination of student loans and low paying jobs, two had casual work, one had part-time employment, one was receiving employment insurance, two were on social assistance, one was surviving with a small amount of money she received from her brother overseas, and another held a part-time job in the library of the university she attended, but she often did not have enough money to pay her share of the rent and electricity bills.

Although all the participants needed financial support, those who were eligible resisted asking for income assistance or were uncomfortable receiving it. They viewed income assistance as a dependency that limited their opportunities for upward mobility. They hoped to find employment and were working hard to meet the educational or training requirements to do so. However, the lack of recognition of their credentials, lack of Canadian experience, lack of local references, their racial background, their knowledge of English, their accents and issues with their immigration status were additional barriers and challenges. Asha explains:

> I have a lot of skills and experience. It's such a waste. This country could benefit from our skills. I also think employers make assumptions about immigrants. They stereotype us. All they know about Sudan is the fighting in Darfur and they don't think a person from Sudan could have the skills they are looking for. Mainstream Canadians have an advantage and it's hard to compete. Being an immigrant is disempowering because people only see the superficial things about you, they don't look past the colour of our skin or our accents.... So for me the issue is that there is unemployment associated with moving places ... you don't know where to go find a job, and you don't know where to go to apply for a job ... and how to really market yourself in the way this country is working.

Not having their professional qualifications recognized in Canada, even though they had years of experience in careers, meant that some participants needed to pursue further training in other areas to facilitate their market attachment in Halifax. Others needed language training before they could begin employment training. Kum was a teacher in her native Sri Lanka and Maldives Islands, and came to Canada in 2006 after her village was hit by a tsunami. She lived in a one-bedroom apartment and had not managed to find full-time employment. She had several contracts over the years and, at the time of the interview, she was working as a casual worker at a local hospital but did not earn enough to cover all her expenses including health care services, dental work and counselling.

> Nobody guided me.... I struggle a lot.... I found one place by myself as a filing clerk.... Something pretty temporary.... They told me "it is a very short work time, only for two weeks." So I prayed.... The company renovation took place,

so I got work while that was going on, so at least for four or five months I worked. After that, I applied for EI and whatever I earn I got part of that. That is the terrible part, you know. I want to pay my everything [it is not enough] ... there is very terrible days because I know wherever I go they asked Canadian credentials so, I thought I can study something, so I studied in NSCC and got the graduation too ... I got the Service Canada sponsorship ... I was very grateful ... now I have very casual work only for myself is not enough.

### Housing, Mental Health and Integration

According to the World Health Organization (1999), precarious employment is a source of stress due to lack of income, meaningful work, uncertain prospects for the future and its potential to undermine social support networks. In our study, barriers to economic self-sufficiency; poverty; lack of affordable, suitable, adequate and safe housing; and family violence were underlying issues that influenced women's visible and hidden homelessness. Their living situation in turn had an impact on their physical bodies, their emotional and mental health. Research shows that the health advantage known as the "healthy immigrant effect," seemingly enjoyed by new immigrants, as reflected in the health screening during their application process to enter the country, appears to deteriorate with increasing duration of residence in Canada (Newbold 2010: 28). Post-migration social experiences, in particular the quality of living conditions during the resettlement process, have a significant impact on mental health (Simich 2010). Although most participants had suffered profoundly as a consequence of being physically and mentally abused, raped, terrorized, militarily attacked and separated from partners, family and friends, and demonstrated their suffering in this regard, they named their present housing situation and their income insecurity as the sources of their emotional and mental health situation and as barriers to their integration and inclusion into society.

**Linking Gender, Homelessness, Immigrant Settlement and Housing Policies and Programs.**

Migrants, regardless of their immigrant status or gender, are in need of settlement assistance upon their arrival in a new society. The kind of assistance, support and resources available, how these are obtained, who is eligible to benefit from them and over what duration they are offered play a crucial role in the integration of newcomers in their society. However, it has been well documented that immigrant women's experiences and settlement service needs do differ from men's, particularly given that, generally, it is women who in the settlement process become the main caregivers in their families; the ones who will delay their labour market attachment in order to support their family's integration process; and the ones who often face barriers to accessing settlement services (Yax-Fraser 2007).

A common barrier in accessing settlement services and programs for immigrant women raising children is access to affordable childcare. Two of the participants enrolled in an English as a second language (ESL) course could only attend part-time because they had to care for their children. Their wish was to attend full time but waiting lists were long for full-time enrolment, and childcare offered by immigrant settlement organizations was limited. One participant who was forced to quit after having her baby explained that ESL language schools and settlement agencies "don't have daycare for tiny babies." Another participant who had two pre-school children could only access the support of a volunteer tutor who came to her house once a week.

Settlement services are not offered or provided free of charge to all migrants. This creates barriers to settlement and integration for those who are not eligible. Tiffany, who was seeking asylum, and Kalikeka, a Canadian born abroad, for example, could not access settlement services funded by Citizenship and Immigration Canada (CIC) and this had an impact on their social and economic integration. Tiffany spoke little English and wanted to improve her language skills but could not afford a private tutor.

Kalikeka felt that her inability to access employment was related to her lack of knowledge of the Canadian system but could not access labour attachment programs designed to help newcomers secure employment:

> I think, being sixty and a newcomer ... white middle-class Canadian, educated.... I am competent, I am articulate, and therefore I am expected to be able to navigate the system to do everything. Just to walk into a job, to know exactly how to function in the society, and I don't. I really don't and so there is no support whatsoever.

Immigrant status also defines the pathways to housing supports migrants can access including public housing. Immigrant settlement agencies only assist newcomers that come under the Government Assistance Refugee (GAR) program in finding accommodation. The most settlement organizations can do to help landed immigrants find housing is to provide them with a list of contacts for information about the kind of housing available in Halifax Regional Municipality (HRM). Linda, her husband and their three-year-old son came to Canada from Congo under the GAR program in 2005 and moved into public housing in 2007. While Linda and her family were able to access affordable public housing, they were paying CIC the loan they received to cover their transportation cost to come to Canada while their only income was the small savings they had from the time her husband worked as a cleaner.

As it has been argued, the availability of not only affordable but suitable and adequate housing options to immigrants is important in defining their integration trajectories (Grant et al. 2000). Linda and her family were happy to access affordable housing but they found the premises "really dirty," undesirable and did not feel it was the right location for them. The long commute to their child's school was very inconvenient and created stress for Linda when she had an operation and could not walk. They missed their extended family, friends and ethno-cultural communities, supports that are vital in the integration of new immigrants (Yax-Fraser and Tastsoglou 2009). In Linda's country of origin, her relatives and friends would have offered to walk her child to school and to care for her baby so that she could attend language courses and find employment. Without those connections, "how can I prepare my future, it is difficult," she said. Linda's understanding of establishing a home in Halifax echoes the sentiments of most women in our study. Home for them was more than having a roof over their heads. It implied a set of social relations, and it represented a center of activities, a source of identity and a way of belonging to a culture.

Klodowsky suggests that an alternative reading of the experiences of migrant women's homelessness is needed because their experiences differ from migrant men and Canadian-born women experiencing homelessness (2006). Migrant women are confronted by multiple barriers to settling in a new country and cannot be equally served by the same women's emergency shelters, the same services for homeless women and the same federal government initiative against homelessness. The experiences of Jay and her three-year-old daughter, for instance, exemplify a specific difference. Jay, like most women in this study who were eligible, did not want to apply for income assistance in spite of her difficult financial situation. She was working hard to bring her husband, who was in a refugee camp in Kenya, to Canada and did not want to compromise her ability to sponsor him to immigrate. Because her nursing certification was not recognized in Canada, Jay enrolled in a caregiver certificate program. She worked twelve-hour shifts in exchange for her tuition and was left with little time to spend with her child. She lived in a two-bedroom apartment in a high-rise building. In addition to paying for rent, transportation and household expenses, she paid for daycare and babysitting services so she could have flexibility to work before and after regular daycare hours. Jay's experience suggests that homelessness can be all-encompassing at some points in time, and it also points to the diverse situations in which women find themselves and their distinct pathways into and out of homelessness.

The foregoing points to the dangers of relying on the visual, as invisibility has been at the core of migrant women's homelessness resulting in significant gaps between services based on dominant images of women's homelessness and the measures that would be required to respond to migrant women's needs in a more nuanced manner (Aubry et al. 2003; Klodawsky 2006). Consequently, this study underscores the need for diverse housing, policy and service initiatives in terms of both scale and rationale. In terms of scale, a homelessness initiative directed to migrant women will bring together the federal, provincial and municipal levels of government to incorporate improvements in the links between immigration, settlement and housing policies and programs. In regard to rationale, the settlement support that federal policy assumes is sufficient clearly requires expansion to take into consideration that integration goes beyond the settlement years. As well, settlement and integration policies should be developed in concert with other areas affecting immigrant settlement outcomes: employment; income support; affordable, suitable and adequate housing; health; transportation and education.

## Conclusion

The process of making home is vital to the successful integration of a newcomer into her new place of settlement, but what is crucial to this process of making home is having a dwelling place, a space one can territorialize and reconcile with notions of identity and security. Macgregor Wise asserts that when we territorialize, we mark and shape space in many ways to establish places of comfort (2000). In this chapter, we have outlined the multi-pronged nature of cultural effects such as the construction of the role of women in society, socioeconomic effects such as income and education, socio-demographic effects such as age and gender, and political and economic factors that produce and shape the participant's experience of gendered homelessness.

The experiences of the participants in this study exemplified that migrant women who are homeless cannot be seen as a homogeneous group, that their experiences and diverse situations have to be understood from a perspective that acknowledges time, space, class, race and cultural variations. The strength of the YWCA Housing Project was the integrated and individualized approach to services and supports. Using a holistic model, the researchers and project staff were able to better inform the participants about services appropriate to their individual needs, and help participants advocate for the services. The participants found that accessing multiple services from one organization was helpful, as they did not have to tell their stories over and over again.

The small size of the project allowed participants to have individualized support. This was helpful for participants who said that they felt respected and valued, and that their needs and concerns were heard. One participant said, "The strength of this project was that I was treated with respect. If Canada welcomes newcomers, it must ensure that it doesn't rob people of their dignity." In addition to its holistic nature, one of the strengths of the YWCA project was that it focused on women. The gender differences in women's experiences, strengths and needs, participants felt, were addressed through this project.

Settlement services play a critical role as enabling agents in providing all migrants, regardless of their immigration status, with the resources to facilitate integration and minimize social exclusion. We conclude that a gender analysis of services is warranted and that a holistic service approach that is client-centred and provides universal access to settlement and housing services regardless of immigrant status is needed. Our study also confirms the need for an immigrant women's centre to address the needs of immigrant women who are single mothers, women who experience family violence, single women, middle-aged women and women with children, to help them access free or subsidized childcare and support services in order to settle and integrate successfully into Canadian society, and into Atlantic Canada, more specifically.

We advocate for the development of a public housing policy that makes sense for newcomers and is sensitive to the support that can ensure that people will not fall between the cracks, or be taken advantage of by individuals who prey on the lack of knowledge of the newcomer (Gajardo 2010). As does Gajardo, we call for a national housing policy that incorporates the principle of Housing as a Right that will ensure that all people of Canada can access safe, secure and affordable housing. Access to affordable housing provides a springboard that influences the economic and social integration of newcomers, and this of particular concern given the Atlantic context.

### Notes

1. We understand the term immigrant to refer to individuals who have moved to Canada to live and have permanent residency status, and understand the term migrant to refer to individuals who have moved to Canada temporarily or do not have permanent status including temporary foreign workers, refugee claimants, international students and those who have no status at all.

2. The Canada Mortgage and Housing Corporation (CMHC) uses what it calls the National Occupancy Standard (NOS) to measure whether or not a dwelling has sufficient space for its inhabitants. This it calls "housing suitability" (Canada Mortgage and Housing Commission 1991). http://cmhc.beyond2020.com/ HiCODefinitions_EN.html#_Suitable_dwellings).

### References

Akbari, Ather H. 2009. *Socioeconomic and Demographic Profiles of Immigrants in Atlantic Canada (2001-2008)*. Report prepared for Atlantic Canada Opportunities Agency. http://www.atlantic.metropolis.net (accessed February 27, 2008).

Ardener, Shirley, ed. 1981. Ground Rules and Social Maps. London: Croom Helm.

Assanand, Shashi. 2004. *Homelessness: Immigrant Women and Domestic Violence*. British Columbia Institute Against Family Violence, Fall 2004 Newsletter.

Aubry, Tim, Fran Klodawsky, Elizabeth Hay and Sarah Birnie. 2003. *Panel Study on Persons Who Are Homeless in Ottawa: Phase 1 results.* Ottawa: Centre for Research on Community Services.

Ball, Jonathan D. C. 2002. *Home Made: A Snapshot of the MISA Settlement House Project.* Halifax: Metropolitan Immigrant Settlement Association.

Balley, Patrick and Michael Bulthius. 2004. The Changing Portrait of Homelessness. *Our Diverse Cities* 1: 119-23.

Brownridge, D. A. and S. S. Halli. 2002. Double Jeopardy? Violence Against Immigrant Women in Canada. *Violence and Victims* 17: 455-71.

Citizenship and Immigration Canada. 2002. *Performance Report.* Ottawa: Minister of Public Works and Government Services Canada.

Danso, Ransford. 2001. From "There" to "Here": An Investigation of the Initial Settlement Experiences of Ethiopian and Somali Refugees in Toronto. *GeoJournal* 55: 3-14.

Dempsey, Colleen and Soojin Yu. 2004. Refugees to Canada: Who Are They and How Are They Faring? *Canadian Issues* March: 5-9.

Fairless, Daemon. 2004. Mind the Gap. *The Coast.* May 13-20.

Fleury, Dominique. 2007. *A Study of Poverty and Working Poverty among Recent Immigrants to Canada.* Final Report. Human Resources and Social Development Canada. Catalogue No.: HS28-121/2007E.

Gajardo, Carolina. 2010. A Road to Home: Working with Homeless Immigrants and Refugees. *Canadian Issues/Thèmes Canadiens* Fall: 104-105. http://canada.metropolis.net/publications/aec_citc_fall2010_e.pdf (accessed February 27, 2012).

Grant, Miriam R. and Ransford K. Danso. 2000. Access to Housing as an Adaptive Strategy for Immigrant Groups: Africans in Calgary. *Canadian Ethnic Studies* 32 (3): 19-43. http://search.proquest.com.ezproxy.library.yorku.ca/docview/215638032accountd=15182 (accessed February 27, 2012).

Haan, Michael. 2010. "Residential Crowding in Canada" in Newcomers' Experiences of Housing and Homelessness in Canada. *Canadian Issues.* The Metropolis Project. Fall: 16-21. http://canada.metropolis.net/publications/aec_citc_fall2010_e.pdf (accessed February 27, 2012).

Halifax Regional Municipality (HRM). March 2004. *Municipal Land Use Policy and Housing Affordability.* Halifax: Halifax Regional Municipality.

Kappel Ramji Consulting Group. 2002. Common Occurrence: The Impact of Homelessness on Women's Health. *Phase II: Community Based Action Research Final Report.* Toronto: Sistering: A Woman's Place. http://www.sistering.org/advocacyandissues/commonoccurrence.php (accessed April 22, 2012).

Klodawsky, Fran. 2006. Landscapes on the Margins: Gender and Homelessness in Canada. *Gender, Place and Culture* 13 (4): 361-81.

Lenon, Suzanne. 2002. Living on the Edge: Women, Poverty and Homelessness in Canada. In *Violence Against Women: New Canadian Perspectives,* ed. Katherine M. J. McKenna and June Larkin, 403-408. Toronto: Inanna Publications and Education Inc.

Li, Peter S. 2003. Deconstructing Canada's Discourse of Immigrant Integration. *Journal of International Migration and Integration* 4 (3): 315-33.

Ling, Trixie.2008. The Reality of Housing Insecurity: A CPJ Backgrounder on Housing and Homelessness. *Citizens for Public Justice.* http://www.cpj.ca/files/docs/PJ-Backgrounder-on-Housing-and-Homelessness3.pdf (accessed February 27, 2012).

Macgregor Wise, J. 2000. Home: Territory and Identity. *Cultural Studies* 14 (2): 295-310.

Magat, Ilan N. 1999. Israeli and Japanese immigrants to Canada: Home, Belonging, and the Territorialization of Identity. *Ethos* 27 (2): 119-44.

Mohanty, Chandra T. 2003. Geneologies of Community, Home, Nation. In *Feminism Without Borders: Decolonizing Theory, Practising Solidarity.* NY: Duke University Press.

Neal, Rusty. 2004. *Voices: Women, Poverty and Homelessness in Canada.* Ottawa: The National Anti-Poverty Organization.

Newbold, K. Bruce. 2010. Linking Immigrant Settlement, Health, Housing and Homelessness in Canada. *Canadian Issues.* The Metropolis Project. Fall: 28-31. http://canada.metropolis.net/publications/aec_citc_fall2010_e.pdf (accessed February 27, 2012).

Novac, Sylvia. 1996. *A Place to Call One's Own: New Voices of Dislocation and Dispossession.* Ottawa: Status of Women Canada.

National Homelessness Initiative (NHI). 2003. Call for Expression of Interest on Immigration Issues Related to Homelessness in Canada. Ottawa: National Homelessness Secretariat. http://www.homelessness.gc.ca/research/eoifall2003/eoifall2003_print_e.asp (accessed October 2008).

Passaro, Joanne. 1996. *The Unequal Homeless: Men on the Streets, Women in Their Place.* New York: Routledge.

Picot, Garnett. 2004. The Deteriorating Economic Welfare of Canadian Immigrants. *Canadian Journal of Urban Research* 13 (1): 25-45.

Silver, Jim. 2008. *Public Housing Risks and Alternatives: Uniake Square in North End Halifax*. Canadian Centre for Policy Alternatives-Manitoba/ Halifax. http://www.policyalternatives.ca/sites/default/files/uploads/ publications/Nova_Scotia_Pubs/2008/Public_Housing_Risks_and_Alternatives.pdf (accessed February 27, 2012).

Simich, Laura. 2010. Refugee Mental Health and the Meaning of Home. Canadian Issues. Newcomers' Experiences of Housing and Homelessness in Canada. The Metropolis Project. Fall: 68-72. http://canada. metropolis.net/publications/aec_citc_fall2010_e.pdf (accessed February 27, 2012).

Teixeira, Carlos and Barry Halliday. 2010. Newcomers' Experiences of Housing and Homelessness in Canada. *Canadian Issues*. Newcomers' Experiences of Housing and Homelessness in Canada. *The Metropolis Project*. Fall: 3-7. http://canada.metropolis.net/publications/aec_citc_ fall2010_e.pdf (accessed February 27, 2012).

Thurston, Wilfreda E., Barbara Clow, David Este, Tess Gordey, Margaret Haworth-Brockman, Liza McCoy, Rachel Rapaport Beck, Christine Saulnier and Jana Smith. 2006. *Immigrant Women, Family Violence and Pathways Out of Homelessness*. Final Report PMC. http://www.homelesshub.ca/ResourceFiles/NRP_EN_Immigrant_Women_Family_Violence_and_Pathways.pdf (accessed March 14, 2012).

Tota, Kasia. 2004. *Homelessness in HRM: A Portrait of Streets and Shelters*. Halifax: Halifax Regional Municipality.

Watson, Sophie. 1988. *Accommodating Inequality*. Sydney: Allen Unwin.

Watson, Sophie and Helen Austenberry. 1986. *Housing and Homelessness: A Feminist Perspective*. New York: Routledge.

Wayland, Sarah. 2006. *Unsettled: Legal and Policy Barriers for Newcomers to Canada – Final Report*. Ottawa: Community Foundations of Canada and Law Commission of Canada.

Yax-Fraser, Maria Joséfa. 2007. *A Balancing Act: The Cultural Choices and Processes of Cross-Cultural Mothering*. Unpublished Master's Thesis. Dalhousie University.

Yax-Fraser, Maria Joséfa and Evangelia Tastsoglou. 2008. *Attraction, Promotion and Retention of Immigrants in Atlantic Canada: A Synthesis of Existing Research and Recommendations*. Citizenship and Immigration Canada.

5

# Women, Immigration and Violence: Focusing on Atlantic Canada

*Evangelia Tastsoglou*
*Barbara Cottrell*
*Peruvemba Jaya*

This chapter derives from a study[1] that examined the various forms of violence that immigrant women of diverse ethno-cultural backgrounds experience in their daily lives in Atlantic Canada. It assessed the impact of this violence on the women's lives, these women's coping mechanisms and their experiences with social services. More specifically, starting with a broad framework on violence, we explored violence in the family, in the workplace and in the public arena, from the immigrant women's own perspectives. The study also explored the ways in which immigrant women interface with and are constructed by social institutions such as settlement, social, criminal justice, employment and education services when it comes to issues of violence; the ways that immigrant women may be victimized in the respective settings, particularly in the context of institutional and systemic factors pertaining to gender, class and race/ethnicity; and the individual and collective strategies that immigrant women resort to in order to cope with, or resolve, violence in their daily lives and in the longer-term.

This chapter reviews our key findings on violence in the lives of immigrant women, its impact on them and other family members, and its consequences for adaptation. We also discuss women's strategies for coping with/resolving the violence and their identification of service needs. The narratives of immigrant women illustrate their resilience and agency, and the complex intertwining of violence with integration, in particular how the former (violence) may act as a powerful barrier to the latter (integration). Furthermore, our findings underscore the need for culturally appropriate intervention services in support of immigrant women and families in crisis, not only as a measure to deal with violence but also as an integration strategy for immigrant women.

## Conceptual and Theoretical Framework

To capture the entire spectrum of what immigrant women perceive and experience as violence, a broad definition of "violence" was used which included (a) violence related to cultural practices that may be illegal or socially unacceptable, (b) domestic violence; (c) workplace abuse (including exploitation or abuse of live-in care-givers) and (d) violence related to public services (such as culturally inappropriate treatment by service providers).

The term "immigrant women" was also used broadly to include foreign-born women living in Canada: citizens and permanent residents, refugee women, women refugee claimants; women on work permits (including live-in caregivers) and international students; as well as any other undocumented foreign-born women. We sought to interview a broad spectrum of immigrant women who had one or more of the following characteristics: belonged to a racialized group, did not speak English (or French in French-speaking areas) well, or spoke English (or French in French-speaking areas) as a second language.

The term "racialized" refers to those systematically discriminated against on the basis of a social, and historically variable, construction of Otherness. Otherness is related to and can be explained as a discourse of power (Foucault 1977; Said 1978, 1983,

1993). The identity of self is not only existent because of the presence of the Other, but there is a hierarchical relationship between the two. Racialization is understood as the socio-historical process by which race as Otherness is being constructed in juxtaposition to a normative self in specific societies. "Race" as a social construction, then, is socially and historically variable, a relational category, an outcome and expression of power relations as well as a mechanism reinforcing such relations (Tastsoglou 2001; Bolaria and Li 1988). Omi and Winant (1986) define the racialization process as "the extension of racial meaning to a previously racially un-classified relationship, social practice or group" (64).

As is widely documented in the literature, along with racialization, immigrant women face problems of sexism and class discrimination (cf. Agnew 1996, 1993; Boyd 1999, 1990; Calliste 1996, 1989; Das Gupta 1996; Dhruvarajan 2000; Ng 1993, 1990 and 1989; Preston and Man 1999; Preston et al. 2003; Ralston 1996; Tastsoglou and Preston 2005; Tastsoglou and Miedema 2005). These forms of social division and their powerful intersections translate in the labour market into underemployment and de-skilling (cf. Man 2004), employment ghettoization, lack of recognition of foreign credentials and experience (cf. Basran and Zong 1998), lower incomes and downward mobility, unemployment for many highly skilled labourers, social isolation and attendant health issues (cf. Weerasinghe 2000). These are all forceful barriers to immigrant women's integration into Canadian society as well as to the practice of citizenship and sense of belonging.

In addition, scholars have documented barriers, often amounting to violence, to immigrant women's integration and citizenship within the state and state institutions. Lowry and Nyers (2003) discuss violence by state authorities and the isolation, discrimination and outright violence that refugee women especially experience (Lee 2000), including cases of deportation of migrant and refugee women by Canadian authorities (even in the middle of high-risk pregnancies) while, in other cases, women are being singled out for differential treatment, for instance, because of their special social insurance numbers. Alaggia, Regehr and

Rishchynski's 2009 study explores the barriers, many relating to immigration laws, policies and legal processes, that immigrant women face in reporting and seeking services for domestic violence. Furthermore, sponsored women and live-in caregivers may be particularly vulnerable but unlikely to report because of their dependent status (Oxman-Martinez et al. 2005). Other scholars have discussed the issues faced by specific groups. For instance, Bullock and Jafri (2000) talk about the misrepresentations and stereotypical images of Muslim women in the media and the fixation on the hijab, thus representing them as "alien" and "scary" outsiders rather than showing the women as multi-dimensional human beings.

While the literature on domestic violence informs us that its root causes are structural and include poverty, unemployment, economic disparity, racism and a patriarchal social structure (Barnes 2001; Michalski 2004; Friedman 1985; Drakich and Guberman 1988; Miedema 1999; Kim and Emery 2003; Donnelly et al. 2005), a number of empirical studies in specific communities articulate the links between such factors as patriarchy (in its specific expressions in various cultural traditions), racism and spousal abuse (Hassouneh-Phillips 2001; Ahmad et al. 2004; Van Hightower, Gordon and DeMoss 2000; Hyman 2004; Musisi and Mukta 1992). However, there is a dearth of data to make comparisons of the rates, experiences and consequences of domestic violence that immigrant women experience (Cohen and Maclean 2004).

Miedema (1999) and Miedema and Wachholz (2000, 2002) are among the few scholars who have studied violence against immigrant women in Atlantic Canada. In her 1999 study, Miedema, focusing on New Brunswick, identified the interplay of cultural norms and structural oppression as barriers to accessing services. In a more recent study focusing on immigrant women and violence in Halifax, Cottrell, Tastsoglou and Moncayo (2009) identified culturally-based gender relations colliding and adapting to gendered structures and practices in the new society post-migration as factors that can not only produce a great deal of strain and conflict, but can also spawn and perpetuate intimate partner violence. Additionally, a social structure of economic disparity and inequality based on immigrant status, ethnicity and gender compounded the problem.

There is recognition in the literature that specific "risk factors" are conducive to violence as well, such as social isolation, relational distance, centralization of authority and unequal gender relations (Michalski 2004; Drakich and Guberman 1988). Immigrant women may suffer additional vulnerability to "intimate partner violence" (IPV) due to factors relating to their immigrant status, such as: their legal status and associated insecurity as well as lack of information regarding their rights and services available (Raj and Silverman 2003; Sharma 2001; Miedema 1999; Miedema and Wachholz 2002); culturally specific forms of, and norms around, violence (Baba and Murray 2003; Hassouneh-Phillips 2001); increased isolation as a result of lack of family and social-support networks in a new society (Menjivar and Salcido 2002; Raj and Silverman 2003); cultural and language barriers to seeking help (Shirwadkar 2004; Law Reform Commission of Nova Scotia 1993; Miedema and Wachholz 2002; Tiede 2001, Torres et al. 2000; Wong 2000); lack of sensitivity on the part of workers in the criminal justice system, which renders access to intervention and services more difficult (Miedema and Wachholz 2000, 2002; Raj and Silverman 2003; Eliasson and Lundy 1999; Erez, Hartley and Copps 2003); alienation of immigrant women from services because of their embarrassment by their poverty, unemployment and other related problems (Agnew 2003); as well as changing gender relations post-migration that may constitute a source of strain and conflict in certain families (Hyman et al. 2004; Oxman-Martinez, Abdool and Loiselle-Leonard 2000; Hightower, Gorton and DeMoss 2000). Furthermore, abuse of women can take place at the hands of their adolescent children, as Cottrell and VanderPlaat's 2005 study demonstrates, as a result of various integration stressors.

A little-discussed consequence of immigrant women not seeking outside intervention and services when abused is the so-called "hidden" or "invisible homelessness" (i.e., women stay-ing in their own home but living in fear and in an unsafe home environment) (Novac et al. 1996; Lenon 2000; see also chapter in this volume by Yax-Fraser and Cottrell). Most women will try to exhaust social and family networks before they search for outside shelter. Lack of knowledge about rights and options connected with immigrant status and economic insecurity are often not only factors that increase immigrant women's susceptibility to this "invisible homelessness," but also to their vulnerability when it comes to violence.

The feminist literature is ambivalent on "home" and "fam-ily" and their significance for women. There are feminists who view "home" as a place of oppression for women (Kibria 1990; Pessar and Mahler 2003) and others who view "home" as a "haven" from the world outside, particularly for immigrant and racialized women who experience exclusion and racism outside the home (Tastsoglou 1997). This research highlights the tension and contradiction around the meaning of "home" for immigrant women. Disproportionately found in the "family class" immigra-tion category, immigrant women are often isolated and oppressed within the home/family especially in cases of domestic violence. Yet, at the same time, they appear to view home/family as a source of strength and support in the migration and settlement process, and are reluctant to give up on the concept of home/family, even when there is violence. Furthermore, these women who do not have a safe home at all are expected, at the same time, by policy-makers and society at large, to settle as immigrants and make a "home away from home" for themselves in Atlantic Canada. In an effort to resolve this contradiction, this chapter addresses the question of what it would take for immigrant women to feel safe enough to make Atlantic Canada their home.

## Methodological Considerations and Participant Profile

Our study utilized qualitative methodologies aimed at maximiz-ing diverse immigrant women's participation and encouraging community input into the research and interpretation of findings. Immigrant women and service providers in five Atlantic Canadian cities participated: Charlottetown, Halifax, Moncton, St. John's and Sydney.[2] Participatory research workshops were conducted in each site at the beginning of the project to help develop the interview guides. Five workshops were also conducted at the end of the project in order to provide opportunities for the local participants to read and give feedback on the interpretation of findings.

A diverse selection of immigrant women was interviewed in 2006 in order to enable us to capture the experiences of women from many ethno-cultural groups. For example, to address the dimension of "race" in the experience of violence, and facilitate a broader comparison between racialized women versus other immigrant women, attempts were made to include about half of the participants from each category. In total, forty-three in-depth interviews with immigrant women and fifty-one interviews with service providers were conducted. The interviews were transcribed and coded for analysis using the qualitative software program, NU*DIST.

Participants came from thirty-one countries spanning four continents. The majority of participants described their current place of residence as a small town (n=twenty seven), and stated they lived in a predominantly English speaking area (n=thirty six) where they themselves spoke English (n=thirty two). The majority of these women held high levels of education including college/university degrees (n=twenty five); however, despite this level of education, the majority of the women were not employed (n=twenty three). Of those who were employed (n=eighteen), the majority were working full time (n=ten). The positions held by the employed participants ranged from professional to managerial and self-employed in the private sector to front-line worker in the social services sector. Thirteen participants were married, nine were separated, eight were divorced, and seven were single. The majority of the participants described their current household structure as being comprised of one, two or three (n=twenty eight) family members.

## The Contours of Violence

Our research revealed that the participants had primarily experienced three kinds of violence: (a) domestic violence, (b) racism and discrimination in the workplace, and (c) institutional abuse and targeting of minorities by authorities. Of the three, domestic violence was the most prevalent, and took similar forms to that experienced by non-immigrant women.

The majority of immigrant women we interviewed said they had experienced some form of violence in their own home. However, other places were also implicated, such as their workplaces, neighbourhoods, schools and other public institutions. Many of the participants had experienced more than one form of violence in their lives. The most frequent forms of violence experienced by the participants were physical and emotional violence, as well as discrimination. The majority of participants said the violence they had experienced occurred in Canada, but many had experienced violence both in Canada and in their country of origin. While only a few women reported a marked increase in the levels of discrimination and violence that they experienced in Canada post-September 11, 2001, the majority of participants had observed an increased singling out and hardening of attitudes toward Muslims in particular. IW9, from the Middle East, describes the physical violence she went through, starting from her country of origin and continuing in Canada:

> I had an arranged marriage, I was fifteen at the time. He was thirty three.... Within two weeks I was married and the abuse started on the first night of the honeymoon. It was a very horrifying time.... [The abuse started] in my country. And that night he wanted, of course, to have intercourse, and I was very scared ... the whole arrangement was by force, so there was no love, nothing like that and he didn't help at all. I was very scared so he started hitting me. He broke a chair on me, and I got so scared I went to the balcony of the hotel we were staying in and I told him that if he came out I would scream and I would jump.... I run away three times.

I begged him to divorce me, I begged my mom, because she was the main decision-maker in my life, to help me. I tried to explain to them, that, you know, he is a bad man. But no one wanted to help.

In most cases, the violence the women had experienced at home was perpetrated by their spouses (n=twenty three) or another family member. IW13, another woman from the Middle East, stated:

It was me who brought up my husbands' children when they were little. He was calling me dirty names like "you animal." When the kids abused me and did the same thing as he was doing to me, and I started to defend myself, he would say, this is Canada and the law is with the kids, the most important thing in Canada is the children, and no one will listen to me because I am the step-mom. Every day the children were threatening me and saying they would call the police if I didn't listen to them.

In addition to these more obvious forms of violence, the participants also described a number of incidents outside the home which decreased their ability to feel at home in Canada. The perpetrators included: their boss, co-workers, military (soldier and rebels), strangers, clients from work, potential employers, neighbours and even a social worker. Moreover, the whole process of immigration to Canada itself was also experienced as violent by some women (systemic violence). Also, some of the participants experienced violence committed by employees working at different companies and organizations such as a moving company; the airport; a landlord; the shelter; housing authority; school/ university; government; loan board at a small business; and an organization that helps people find jobs.

Although the violence continued for varied lengths of time, ranging from one day to the extreme of forty years, there was one consistent finding when it came to the women who experienced violence within their marriage: it started near the beginning and continued throughout the entire length of their marriage. A woman from Lebanon stated that the violence worsened as she started standing up for her rights:

> ...it started at the beginning, but it got worse at the end. The reason it got worse was that I started standing up for my rights and I was accused as a person who had changed and become Canadianized ... but I had never changed, I just was able to speak out and ask for my life. (IW1)

The majority of participants said that the problem of violence in their lives had been resolved. The resolutions included: separation; divorce; death of spouse; quitting their jobs; leaving the school or site of violence; getting fired, and leaving their country of origin and coming to Canada. IW-27, an immigrant woman from Iran, stated:

> So when the escalation started my son was involved with it. He watched me be beaten up. And that was the last straw. Maybe, and I'm thinking in the back of my head, if my son had not watched it, maybe I would have still stayed in the relationship. Maybe. But you see that was the time when I finally realized, after that, up to that point I stayed in the relationship because of the kids. The kids need both a mother and a father. But, finally, I left because of the kids.

Three participants felt there had been changes since 9/11 (2001) in the violence or abuse they had experienced. Interestingly, in one woman's case, the change was positive because after 9/11, people started to take action on her request to confiscate her husbands' weapons and advised her to speak to the Crown about safety issues. For another immigrant woman from Iran, however, people were more openly racist after 9/11:

> Then when I tell them I am half Muslim, their eyes just open up.... It's ridiculous. It's a good thing I don't look Arabic.... I have a lot of friends that do look Arabic and people look at them and say.... because they think, he's a terrorist. My best friend, he looks like one of those guys who like to blow up things. But he is Catholic. (IW7)

Many of the participants had not experienced any changes in violence against them personally since 9/11. However, the majority of participants made general comments about the changes they had seen, focusing on an increased singling out and hardening of attitudes toward Muslims in particular. One participant knew of people who could not get work because they were Muslim. One woman's supervisor was shocked that she wore a hijab to work. Another said that three buses would not stop to pick her up when she wore hijab. One participant had considered buying coloured contact lenses and replacing her hijab with a hat.

### The Effects of Violence on Survivors and Others

The violence affected the women in different ways. Some were physically sick, suffering from headaches and from high blood pressure. Some had sleep and eating problems, and felt degraded, afraid and depressed. Some said they "cried all the time," were touchy, or even admitted feeling "paranoid." An immigrant woman from Germany said:

> It was pretty bad. At the time I was in that marriage I realized that I had depression, I had blood pressure problems, I started to ignore certain health symptoms like, emotionally, I ignored myself but I always kind of detached myself from my feelings because I would realize in what kind of dilemma I was in. (IW31)

A number of the participants responded that the violence made them feel old and ugly, good for nothing, self-hating and suicidal. A woman from the Middle East said she felt:

> Really low. I mean when your husband, the man who is supposed to respect you and love you and you know all that ... call you a whore and a slut and beat you ... you just lose yourself. You know, you look in the mirror, you believe you are old, you are ugly, you are good for nothing. You lose your identity, basically. There is no you. (IW9)

The majority of participants said they became withdrawn or aggressive, fearful and reclusive. Nevertheless, other participants identified positive changes in their behaviour because of the violence (or in spite of it). In an ultimate act of resistance demonstrating their agency, they learned how to start fighting back instead of being passive, how not to be a victim and how to respond to violence without being violent themselves. One woman underwent training in peace and conflict resolution to get her through the violence. Women who were abused by their children said they learned how to avoid punishing their children and learned "how to speak to them." One participant said that although she still had negative feelings of resentment and was now always aware that the men in her life could abuse her, she had developed an increased sense of understanding and connectedness to other women. Another participant stated that in the beginning she felt weak and depressed but, once she started to legally fight against her violence, she felt stronger and more courageous. An immigrant woman from Congo discussed her experience:

> Many people when they have a problem cannot sleep; spend a lot of time in bed, that doesn't help mentally. Personally, when I feel weak and what I did during the war, I did a lot of things, I did volunteer work. This gave me the opportunity to see more difficult situations and that minimized my own difficulties ... what I do is I begin to take on bigger challenges.... I had the courage to do my Masters, I had the courage to go out during the winter to take my courses and all that made me overcome what was boiling inside me and the frustration, I changed the way of seeing things, and these are things that are helping me today. (IW20)

It was not only the victims who were hurt by the violence. Their family members were affected both directly—that is, they were also being abused by the perpetrator—and indirectly because they knew what their mothers, daughters or wives were experiencing. The violence particularly impacted the women's children. The women spoke of their children being afraid of men, having nightmares, and being scared to go outside and talk to other people. They told us of children losing weight and developing eating disorders. Two women said their sons witnessed the violence and became violent themselves. An immigrant woman from the Middle East reported:

> He did it in front of the children and the truth is my children are the ones who called the police on him, it was not me.... One of the children was really bothered by that. [H]e always wanted me to sleep beside him every night and when his father left the house he said that he was scared his father would hurt or kill me. (IW30)

After she left her abusive partner, this woman saw a difference in her children. She said, "They excelled at school, C. excelled at gymnastics ... like the girls got scholarships.... M. stopped asking to come sleep beside me, he was a more relaxed child."

## Effects of Violence on Adaptation

The majority of participants stated that the domestic violence they experienced had made it more difficult for them to adapt to living in Canada. It affected their ability to find employment, limited their associations and made them more reclusive.

Job-related dimensions of violence included problems with looking for and finding work, and not having their qualifications accepted by the government while, at the same time, not being eligible for student loans to go back to school because of their professional qualifications. Furthermore, they spoke of experiencing racist comments, being subjected to stereotyping, and of feeling like they were the subject of everyone's mockery. All of the above impacted the women's ability to adapt to life in Canada.

Their experiences of domestic violence made it difficult for some women to make a home away from home for themselves in Atlantic Canada because they had lost trust in others, particularly Canadian men, in themselves and in Canadian institutions. This made it difficult for them to make contacts. One woman said she'd lost faith in Canadian law. A European woman from the Netherlands discussed how not being able to trust people had made it hard for her to adapt in Canadian society:

> It's quite different.... When I came initially here I obviously trusted people more than I do now. I didn't really speak out and I kept a lot to myself so ... obviously it is harder to settle in if you just don't have anything to hide and you know it's easier to make contact. So I have been by myself quite a lot. But now you are in such a different position. I mean obviously now I have to find a place to live and go out myself and rebuild pretty much my life so that when I don't know when I will be able to stay here or have to go back, you know, that's pretty scary. I really find that hard now and I'm really frustrated. (IW5)

By contrast, some participants were able to re-construct the violence they had experienced and give it a positive meaning. For these women, coming to Canada was construed to mean escaping violence in their countries of origin, and settling in a country with resources that enabled them to live their own lives in freedom and be able to get involved in the community in spite of abusive husbands. For one participant, being treated well by the local settlement organization and her family doctor counteracted the negative consequences of violence in her life. Another participant was able to overcome the violence she had experienced because she had Canadian friends from her own culture who supported her.

For a number of women, the negative experiences made adapting to Canada difficult but, eventually, they were able to transform the hardships into opportunities and positive outcomes. One woman said that the racism she experienced left her feeling inferior and she had to try very hard to overcome such feelings. Another woman felt the violence she had experienced made her more resilient. A woman from Lebanon discussed the negative effects of the violence she experienced and how eventually they became opportunities for her to change her life for the better in Canada:

...back then, I didn't have a chance to adapt to a new society because I wasn't allowed to ... I was just a prisoner in my home and even when I was out, then like a couple of years or something, of course he wanted me to work with him, so I was to work endless hours in the business, even when I got the children, I worked every day in the business. So really I had no social life. And then, after I left, it was a different story.... I love it ... when I first left, I went to a shelter ... the workers there are angels. You know, they help so much. They did whatever they could. (IW9)

## The Intersection of Gender, Violence and Immigration

The consensus among the participants was that being an immigrant and coming from a non-mainstream ethno-cultural background made the experience of violence and the way they were treated different for them than for other women. Not knowing either of the official languages, not knowing their rights and the laws of Canada, and being Black, were some of the concrete grounds provided. Our findings in this regard confirm those of other research (cf. Raj and Silverman 2003; Sharma 2001; Miedema 1999; Miedema and Wachholz 2002; Cottrell, Tastsoglou and Moncayo 2009).

Participants were asked if they sought support, and if they did, who they turned to, whether they felt supported and how. Some of the participants did not turn to any source of help. The reasons given were often similar to the reasons mainstream Canadian women keep their experiences of abuse secret, such as believing that their experiences were not serious enough to warrant going to a shelter, being ashamed to reveal the abuse, or being afraid of what their spouses might do to them if they found out they had talked about the abuse.

However, many of the reasons for not seeking help were connected with their being immigrants. As other research has shown (Raj and Silverman 2003; Sharma 2001, Miedema 1999; Miedema and Wachholz 2002), not knowing about their rights and the services available weighed heavily on their decision not to seek help: they did not know what service providers would or could do, or what services were being offered.

Immigrant women said that they were afraid that they would be deported if they reported the violence; and they were afraid of the police based on previous experience with police in their country of origin. One woman said she was afraid her husband would kill her if he lost his right to stay in Canada. One woman thought one could see a doctor only for health issues related to the body. Another said she did not know enough about counselling. Consistent with other research (Shirwadkar 2004; Law Reform Commission of Nova Scotia 1993; Miedema and Wachholz 2002; Tiede 2001; Torres et al. 2000), language and cultural barriers prevented a number of women from telling anyone about the violence. As Raj and Silverman (2003) found as well, isolation caused by the physical distance from friends, family and networks was the reason many women did not share their secret.

To be sure, some participants were fully aware that their experience of violence was the same as for any other women. A Hispanic woman stated:

> I always think that there is an element of universality to the experiences that women go through. And that is one of the things that frustrate me when people say oh you from Mexico and your cultural things are different.... Although different things are culturally accepted in different countries I think that men are very similar and, well, at least in Canada and in Mexico, men are very similar. We do things differently but I just feel like the things that women go through here and in Mexico are very similar. And women there might be poor and might not have access to different services but you know the same things happen there and here. I just don't feel like my nationality has any bearing. (IW7)

In conclusion, although we acknowledge the significance of exacerbating the risk factors for immigrant women experiencing violence in Canada, it is important not to universalize about immigrant women, as the circumstances of immigration, socio-economic status, information about and knowledge of Canada and cultures of origin do mitigate and differentiate the experience of violence and the response to it.

## Coping and Social Support Mechanisms

Our participants had a number of suggestions for what would help immigrant women feel safe enough to seek support. In putting them forth, they were also identifying the gaps and problems in support and services they had experienced. They felt that service providers were neither sufficiently knowledgeable about nor sensitive to their cultures and recommended training in these areas. At the same time, however, because of the need for confidentiality, a number of women expressed their preference that the service provider not necessarily be someone from their own community. A Hungarian Christian woman from Romania stated:

> First of all I would like to know well and trust the person from whom I am asking for help. Confidentiality is also important to me. And, definitely, the person should be knowledgeable about my culture but not someone from my country. I would trust maybe more another immigrant woman who experienced similar situations and not necessarily a professional counsellor. (IW24)

Still, a number of women said that they would rather speak with counsellors, preferably female counsellors, of their own cultural origins.

The fact that they did not turn to anyone for help because they were not familiar with Canadian systems was stressed by a number of women, a finding that is also congruent with other research. The women themselves said that they needed more opportunities to integrate into Canadian society and learn about their rights and how things are done here and, consequently, they would like to see increased promotion of services and outreach from various organizations. They also pointed out that women needed translators who would talk to them in their own languages. They had a number of concrete suggestions, such as, an information manual to help them find a place to get help; an association that would provide immigrant women with legal assistance, a home, counsellors and job-seeking resources, and a general women's group/association where women could go to share and talk about their lives. Such resources would go a long way in assisting with both accessing help to deal with violence as well as integration. A woman from Mexico argued:

> An association ... listen, an association for immigrants. I would've loved to have an association ... not the Association of New Canadians—an association for helping women. Like they can give you Legal Aid. They can help ... you can go to the house ... get out of your house temporarily, right, for a couple of weeks or something ... somebody who can tell you, don't worry; he's just threatening you. They can provide you with counsellors so you can speak with ... they can help you financially. (IW4)

Many of the women did seek help. Like mainstream Canadian women, they talked with friends, family members, their bosses and teachers. Some turned to their church, their doctor or their sponsors and other volunteers. Many sought support from government and NGO services including the police, shelters, counsellors and support groups.

Several participants said that friends provided concrete help by teaching them English, opening their houses to them or offering food and furniture. Friends encouraged them to go to outreach programs or the police. One woman said she could get emotional support from her friend because the friend could speak her language and understand her situation. Experience with friends however was not always positive but sometimes idiosyncratic and subject to social conventions. One participant said that friends sometimes cannot handle the situation, another said friends think they have to "take sides" or do not take the situation seriously.

A few participants were helped by family members who supported them when they left their husbands, sent encouraging messages, or gave advice on how to minimize stress, but family members were also not always understanding. A number of participants said they told family members but did not receive any help or support. IW9, originally from the Middle East, stated:

> ...my second cousin, she lived here and she used to work at the business with my ex-husband and with her husband. I was here for like three years, I didn't have children at that time, and I asked her for help. I remember I was fresh beaten and I was crying and I was begging her, I said I would do anything for you, I'll clean the house for you, just get me out, and I promise I won't tell anybody that you helped me. She said well, I have to ask my husband. But anyway, she told me she can't help me.

Work environments were often helpful, though occasionally problematic in terms of dealing with the situation professionally. One woman was supported by her work supervisor; however, others had stories like the woman whose ESL teacher said she would help her but ended up telling the whole class her story even though she promised to keep her situation confidential. Another participant said she told the director at her workplace about her problem but no action was taken.

Churches provided some women with assistance. One woman said her church helped her by giving her information that led to her moving out of the house and getting away from the violence. One participant said that the church had not provided her with any helpful assistance other than the suggestion to pray through her trouble.

Relevant professionals were often helpful though not systematically so. Experiences with doctors, for example, were mixed. One woman said the doctor did not believe her story. Immigration sponsors and volunteers were helpful in finding furniture and addressing all kinds of practical needs as well as making useful connections. A support group had turned out very helpful in another case. Experiences with counsellors were equally mixed. An immigrant woman from Congo, who was abused by her children, said she was helped by a counselling service because:

> I attended sessions where they taught us how to talk to our children and how to listen to them, that gave me good examples. There is a difference in the culture between my country and Canada. In my country we used to punish them until the children understand. (IW1)

A number of participants said they turned to the police. While some had very positive experiences, others did not. One participant did not because the police did not explain to her what was happening and she was afraid that she was being charged. Another woman felt that the police officer was disturbed that she had to speak through a translator and she felt that the officer was not "on her side." Lawyers were also named as both helpful and unhelpful in providing assistance and protection. One woman felt supported because her lawyer wanted to learn about her values and faith in order to help her, another, however, said the government lawyer was very rude to her, mocked her and talked to her as if she were a child.

The majority of participants who used shelters named them as very helpful places where they felt believed, cared for and safe, and one woman said that it was especially meaningful that the shelter respected her religion and bought Halal (appropriately slaughtered) meat for her. The major problem women had with the shelters was inadequate follow-up after they left. While it may be that some Canadian-born women have that problem, it appears to be especially severe for immigrant women because of the isolation that they experience.

The women named numerous government and other service organizations that helped them by providing opportunities, financial aid, advice and contact information, teaching computer skills, assisting with résumés, providing interpreters free of charge, facilitating language learning and providing medical care.

One said the agency she turned to provided the opportunity for her to talk with people her own age. A Zimbabwean woman said the Black Business Initiative and the Black Educators Association "have been, very helpful...all those guys are just amazing. You know, the opportunities that they are providing me, I'm so grateful." (IW8)

However, one third of the women told us that the government and other services they approached for assistance were not helpful to them because they did not receive the financial aid or accommodation they applied for, or they felt uncomfortable with the workers. A participant said food bank workers thought she did not need their services because of the way she was dressed and the jewellery she wore. One felt the employment counsellor sided with the employer.

An African woman from Liberia described how immigration authorities were not helpful to her:

> [O]ur stories were ... documented with them, so they should have known that this person went through this kind of problem and as soon as they arrive in Canada, there would be a counsellor. [W]e had to start everything all by ourselves so it was, and still is, hard. Even though we have the immigrant settlement finding a house for us, getting us settled down that was not all what we expected from the Immigration of Canada. [C]oming from a war country there are a lot of things, a lot of experiences we went through, so we felt that we would have people, and we would have some counselling services.... (IW22)

Some of the participants believed that being an immigrant was the reason they did not receive adequate or appropriate help and protection. When these women were asked specifically in what ways being an immigrant was the reason, responses ranged from being looked at differently because of one's immigrant status; stereotyping immigrants as not understanding; lack of services, in particular of services for immigrants with a violent past; lack of services that are sensitive to immigrants' problems; and lack of information and knowledge about services, rules and rights. An immigrant woman from Africa stated:

> There are not too many resources here in [name of province], maybe it is badly organized, there are not services with active and sensitive people to our problems, to our culture ... if I would have experienced my problem in another province such as Ontario, I would have received a better service. Because here is not as multicultural, or maybe I was an isolated case, they did not have a similar case before, you understand.... (IW17)

Four participants believed that not speaking English well was the obstacle for not receiving adequate help and protection. A Hungarian woman from Romania stated:

> I could not communicate in any of the official languages. Using an interpreter would not work for me and I think other immigrant women think the same way. I do not feel comfortable to talk about my private life in front of a stranger or someone from my culture. People not always respect the confidentiality terms. On the other hand, I wasn't really aware of these services. (IW24)

## Conclusion

In this chapter, we have discussed the experience of violence and desirable intervention/support from the perspective of immigrant women from Atlantic Canada. Violence has a grave impact on immigrant women's and families' ability to make Atlantic Canada a "home away from home" for themselves. It is necessary therefore to work toward eradicating violence not only because it is a human rights issue affecting not just individuals and entire societies, but also because violence presents a serious impediment toward successful settlement and integration. Domestic violence in particular results in women struggling not just to make a "home away from home" in Atlantic Canada, but to simply secure a "home." The chapter also discussed how women exercise their agency through strategies of coping with/resolving the violence as well as through identification of unmet service needs. It is this identification that offers us a glimpse into the problems and issues that immigrant women are confronted with in their struggle to survive the violence.

Starting from the premise of advancing women's equality and promoting diversity, we conclude with some final recommendations, where we have tried to synthesize such experiences and views with mainstream values, and practical constraints of policy makers and service providers in Canada. While some of the issues with regard to violence are faced by Canadian born women too, immigrant women do face challenges in terms of access to resources and support, due to culturally specific and systemic aspects of being racialized and seen as the "other." As a result, access to social networks and social capital often becomes problematic for immigrant women, as is also the case in other immigrant-receiving societies (McMichael and Manderson 2004).

Policy changes could mean better services for immigrant women who experience violence. In particular, an integrated approach to immigrant women, involving collaboration between provincial governments, settlement and multicultural NGOs, law enforcement agencies and immigrant women's organizations, would ensure continuity and a seamless web of services. In addition, we recommend increased support and funding for a number of non-governmental agencies that work with very limited resources. We also call for the provision of culturally appropriate and needed services for diverse immigrant women.

More specifically, we recommend that the federal, provincial and municipal governments launch major education campaigns about immigrants for the general public as well as for those who provide services to immigrants. Pre-immigration policies should be created to educate prospective immigrants to Canada about their rights and responsibilities as citizens. Public education and outreach must be culturally sensitive and available to immigrants, in multiple languages, venues and in all ethnic communities in Canada. Justice personnel, including the police, should be provided with cultural sensitivity and anti-racism education, and the government should fully fund prevention and intervention programs and services to immigrant women, including hard-to-reach women in Atlantic Canada.

Initiatives to encourage and value diversity in the workplace, specifically among service providers in the NGO sector, social services and CIC are important. The government should ensure fair evaluation of credentials, and re-invest in training programs for immigrant women. Finally, we recommend increased efforts to improve working conditions and human rights for immigrants, including the most marginalized. Such initiatives are particularly important for Atlantic Canadian communities, not only as measures to combat violence, but also as integration strategies in a region of low immigrant densities and immigrant retention rates, ostensibly trying to increase immigrant attraction and retention. Our research underscores the links between integration and violence against women in families, workplaces and the entire private-public continuum.

Although our approach focuses on Atlantic Canada, it has national relevance. Following Erving Goffman (1967, 1986), we believe that mainstream society can learn a great deal about itself from the study of the margins. As "the occasionally precarious and the constantly precarious form a single continuum" (1963: 127), it is a focus on the latter and an understanding of the continuum that can shed light on the former. The ethno-cultural and diversity landscape of Atlantic Canada and its attendant service-providing infrastructure is part of a continuum in multicultural Canada. The lower the immigrant concentrations, the greater the isolation of immigrant families and women; the lower the level and frequency of engagement with diversity on the part of service providers, the lower the support of immigrant families and women when it comes to both violence and integration. As a result, this study has the potential to inform the work of policy makers and service providers not only in Canadian communities with fewer immigrants, but also in those with more dense immigrant populations.

## Notes

1. An initial pilot project within the "Gender, Migration and Diversity / Immigrant Women" domain of the Atlantic Metropolis Centre (2005) gave rise to a major study, funded by Status of Women Canada, Policy Research Fund (Barbara Cottrell, Peruvemba Jaya and Evangelia Tastsoglou. 2006. *Navigating Anti-Violence Work in Atlantic Canada in a Culturally Sensitive Way,* Status of Women Canada, Policy Research Fund. October 2006. Unpublished, Final Report, 110 pages).

2. Halifax was chosen as the largest metropolitan area in Atlantic Canada with the largest immigrant population; Moncton was chosen for its linguistic and cultural differences, with a special focus on Francophone immigrant women or immigrant women who live among predominantly French-speaking populations; Charlottetown and Sydney were chosen as they offered the opportunity for a comparison of rural (Canadian) versus urban (Canadian) immigrant women's experiences; and St. John's for Newfoundland and Labrador, representing a unique culture and a different historical trajectory than the other Atlantic provinces.

## References

Agnew, Vijay. 1993. Feminism and South Asian Immigrant Women in Canada. In *Ethnicity, Identity, Migration: The South Asian Context,* ed. M. Israel and N.K. Wagle, 142-64. Toronto: University of Toronto Press.

———. 1996. *Resisting Discrimination: Women from Asia, Africa and the Caribbean and the Women's Movement in Canada.* Toronto: University of Toronto Press.

———. 2003. *Gender, Migration and Citizenship Resources Project.* Status of Women Canada. http://www.cwhn.ca/en/node/2506 (accessed September 11, 2010).

Ahmad, Farah, S. Riaz, Paula Barata and Donna E. Stewart. 2004. Patriarchal Beliefs and Perceptions of Abuse Among South Asian Immigrant Women. *Violence Against Women* 10 (3): 262-82.

Alaggia, Ramona, Cheryl Regehr and Giselle Rishchynski. 2009. Intimate Partner Violence and Immigration Laws in Canada: How Far Have We Come. *International Journal of Law and Psychiatry* 3 (6): 335-41.

Baba, Yoko and Susan B. Murray. 2003. Spousal Abuse: Vietnamese Children's Reports of Parental Violence. *Journal of Sociology and Social Welfare* 30 (3): 97-122.

Barnes, Brittny McCarthy. 2001.Family Violence Knows No Cultural Boundaries. *Journal of Family and Consumer Sciences* 93 (1): 11-14.

Basran, Gurcharn S. and Li Zong. 1998. Devaluation of Foreign Credentials as Perceived By Visible Minority Professional Immigrants. *Canadian Ethnic Studies* 30 (3): 496-510.

Bolaria, B. Sing, and Peter S. Li. 1988. *Racial Oppression in Canada*, 2nd ed. Toronto: Garamond.

Boyd, Monica. 1990. Immigrant Women: Language, Socioeconomic Inequalities and Policy Issues. In *Ethnic Demography: Canadian Immigrant, Racial and Cultural Variations,* ed. S. Halli, F. Trovato and L. Driedger, 275-96. Ottawa: Carleton University Press.

———. 1999. Integrating Gender, Language, and Race. In *Immigrant Canada: Demographic, Eeconomic, and Social Challenges*, ed. S. Halli and L. Driedger, 282-306. Toronto: University of Toronto Press.

Bullock, Katherine H. and Gul J. Jafri. 2000. Media (Mis)representations: Muslim Women in the Canadian Nation. *Canadian Woman Studies* 20 (2): 35-41.

Calliste, Agnes. 1989. Canada's Immigration Policy and Domestics From the Caribbean: The Second Domestic Scheme. In *Race, Class and Gender: Bonds and Barriers*, Society of Socialist Studies, ed. J. Vors et al. 33-165. Winnipeg: Between the Lines.

———. 1996. Anti-Racism Organizing and Resistance in Nursing: African Canadian Women. *Canadian Review of Sociology and Anthropology* 33 (3): 361-90.

Cohen, Marsh M. and Heather Maclean 2004. Violence against Canadian Women. *BMC Women's Health* 200, 4 (Suppl. 1): S22

Cottrell, Barbara, Evangelia Tastsoglou and Carmen Celina Moncayo. 2009. Violence in Immigrant Families in Halifax. In *Racialized Migrant Women in Canada. Essays on Health,Violence and Equity*, ed. Vijay Agnew, 70-94. Toronto: University of Toronto Press.

Cottrell, Barbara and Madine VanderPlaat. 2011. My Kids Want to Eat Pork: Parent-Teen Conflicts in Immigrant Families. In *Immigrant Women in Atlantic Canada: Challenges, Negotiations, Re-constructions*, ed. Evangelia Tastsoglou and Peruvemba Jaya, 267-96. Toronto: Canadian Scholars' Press/Women's Press.

Das Gupta, Tania. 1996. *Racism and Paid Work*. Toronto: Garamond Press.

Donnelly, Denise A., K. J. Cook, D. Van Ausdal and L. Foley. 2005. White Privilege, Color Blindness, and Services to Battered Women. *Violence Against Women* 11 (1): 6-37.

Drakich, Janice and Connie Guberman. 1988. Violence in the Family. In *Family Matters. Sociology and Contemporary Canadian Families*, ed. Karen Anderson, 201-35. Scarborough, ON: Nelson Canada

Eliasson, Mona and Colleen Lundy. 1999. Organizing to Stop Violence Against Women in Canada and Sweden. In *Women's Organizing and Public Policy in Canada and Sweden*, ed. Linda Briskin and Mona Eliasson, 280-309. Montreal: McGill-Queen's University Press.

Erez, Edna, Carolyn C. Hartley and Carolyn Copps. 2003. Battered Immigrant Women and the Legal System: A Therapeutic Jurisprudence Perspective. *Western Criminology Review* 4 (2): 155-69.

Foucault, Michel. 1977. *Discipline and Punish: The Birth of the Prison*. New York: Pantheon Books.

Friedman, Lisa. 1985. Wife Assault. In *No Safe Place: Violence Against Women and Children*, ed. Connie Guberman and Margie Wolfe. Georgetown, ON: Women's Press.

Goffman, Erving. 1963. *Stigma*. Englewood Cliffs, NJ: Prentice Hall.

———. 1967. *Interaction Ritual*. New York: Pantheon.

Hassouneh-Phillips, Dena Saadat. 2001. Marriage is Half of Faith and the Rest is Fear Allah. *Violence Against Women* 7 (8): 927-46.

Hyman, Ilene, S. Guruge, R. Mason, J. Gould, N. Stuckless, T. Tang, H. Teffera and G. Mekonnen. 2004. Post-Migration Changes in Gender Relations Among Ethiopian Couples Living in Canada. *Canadian Journal of Nursing Research* 36 (4): 74-89.

Kibria, Nazli. 1990. Power, Patriarchy, and Gender Conflict in the Vietnamese Immigrant Community. *Gender and Society* 4 (1): 9-24

Kim, Jae-Yop and Clifton Emery. 2003. Marital Power, Conflict, Norm Consensus, and Marital Violence in a Nationally Representative Sample of Korean Couples. *Journal of Interpersonal Violence* 18 (2): 197-219.

Law Reform Commission of Nova Scotia. 1993. *A Discussion Paper: Violence in a Domestic Context*. Nova Scotia: Law Reform Commission of Nova Scotia.

Lee, Alice. 2000. Working with Refugee Women. *Canadian Woman Studies* 20 (3): 105-107.

Lenon, Suzanne. 2000. Living on the Edge: Women, Poverty and Home-lessness in Canada. *Canadian Woman Studies* 20 (3): 123-26.

Lowry, Michelle and Peter Nyers. 2003. *No One is Illegal: The Fight for Refugee and Migrant Rights in Canada* (Roundtable Report). *Refuge* 21 (3): 66-73.

Man, Guida. 2004. Gender, Work and Migration: Deskilling Chinese Immigrant Women in Canada. *Women's Studies International Forum* 27 (2): 135-48.

McMichael, Celia and Lenore Manderson. 2004. Somali Women and Well-Being: Social Networks and Social Capital among Immigrant Women in Australia. *Human Organization* 63 (1): 88-99.

Menjivar, Cecilia and Olivia Salcido. 2002. Immigrant Women and Domestic Violence: Common Experiences in Different Countries. *Gender and Society* 16 (6): 898-920.

Merali, Noorfarah. 2006. South Asian Immigration to Canada through Arranged Marriages. *Canadian Issues, Immigration and Families* Spring: 36-41.

Michalski, Joséph H. 2004. Making Sociological Sense out of Trends in Intimate Partner Violence. *Violence Against Women* 10 (6): 652-75.

Miedema, Baukje. 1999. *Barriers and Strategies: How to Improve Services for Abused Immigrant Women in New Brunswick.* Research Paper Series 1. Fredericton: University of New Brunswick.

Miedema, Baukje and Sandra Wachholz. 2000. Risk, Fear, Harm: Immigrant Women's Perception of the 'Policing Solution' to Woman Abuse. *Crime, Law and Social Change* 34: 3-8.

——— 2002. *A Complex Web: Access to Justice for Abused Immigrant Women in New Brunswick.* Status of Women Canada. http://www.swccfc.gc.ca/pubs/pubspr/complexweb/index_e.html (accessed July 30, 2011).

Musisi, Nakanyike and Fakiha Mukta. 1992. *Exploratory Research: Wife Assault in Metropolitan Toronto's African Immigrant and Refugee Community.* Toronto: Canadian African Newcomer Aid Centre of Toronto.

Ng, Roxana. 1989. Sexism, Racism, Nationalism. In *Race, Class, Gender: Bonds and Barriers, Society for Socialist Studies,* ed. J. Vorst et al. 10-25. Winnipeg: Between the Lines.

————. 1990. Immigrant Women and Institutionalized Racism. In *Changing Patterns*, ed. S. Burt, L. Code and L. Dorne), 184-203. Toronto: McLelland and Stewart.

————. 1993. Racism, Sexism and Nation-Building in Canada. In *Race, Identity and Representation in Education*, ed. W. Chrichlow and C. McCarthy, 50-59. New York: Routledge.

Novac, Sylvia, Joyce Brown and Carmen Bourbonnais. 1996. *No Room of Her Own: A Literature Review on Women and Homelessness*. Ottawa: Canadian Mortgage and Housing Corporation.

Omi, Michael and Howard Winant. 1986. *Racial Formation in the United States: From the 1960s to the 1980s*. New York: Routledge and Kegan Paul.

Oxman-Martinez, Jacqueline, Shelly N. Abdool and Margot Loiselle-Leonard. 2000. Immigration, Women and Health in Canada. *Canadian Journal of Public Health* 91 (5): 394-95.

Oxman-Martinez, Jacqueline, Jill Hanley, Lucyna Lach, Nazilla Khanlou, Swarna Weerasinghe and Vijay Agnew. 2005. Intersection of Canadian Policy Parameters Affecting Women with Precarious Immigration Status: A Baseline for Understanding Barriers to Health. *Journal of Immigrant Health* 7 (4): 247-58

Pessar, Patrica R. and Sarah J. Mahler. 2003. Transnational Migration: Bringing Gender. In *International Migration Review* 37 (3): 812-46.

Preston, Valerie and Guida Man.1999. Employment Experiences of Chinese Immigrant Women: An Exploration of Diversity. *Canadian Woman Studies/Cahiers de la femme* 19: 115-22.

Preston, Valerie, L. L. and S. Wang. 2003. Immigrants' Economic Status in Toronto: Stories of Triumph and Disappointment. In *The World in a City*, ed. Paul Anisef and Michael Lanphier, 192-232. Toronto: University of Toronto Press.

Raj, Anita and Jay G. Silverman. 2003. Immigrant South Asian Women at Greater Risk For Injury from Intimate Partner Violence. *American Journal of Public Health* 93 (3): 435-36.

Ralston, Helen. 1996. *The Lived Experience of South Asian Immigrant Women in Atlantic Canada*. Lewiston / Queenston / Lampeter: The Edwin Mellen Press.

Said, Edward W. 1978. *Orientalism*. New York: Vintage Books.

———. 1983. *The World, the Text, and the Critic*. Cambridge, MA: Harvard University Press.

———. 1993. *Culture and Imperialism*. New York: Vintage Books.

Shirwadkar, Swati. 2004. Canadian Domestic Violence Policy and Indian Immigrant Women. *Violence Against Women* 10 (8): 860-79.

Tastsoglou, Evangelia. 1997. The Margin at the Centre: Greek Immigrant Women in Ontario. *Canadian Ethnic Studies* 29 (1): 119-60.

———. 2001. *Re-Appraising Immigration and Identities: A Synthesis and Directions for Future Research*. Commissioned by the Department of Canadian Heritage. http://www.canada.metropolis.net/events/ethnocultural/publications/Tastsoglou-E.doc (accessed July 20, 2011).

Tastsoglou, Evangelia and Baukje Miedema. 2005. Working Much Harder and Always Having to Prove Yourself: Immigrant Women's Labour Force Experiences in the Canadian Maritimes. In *Gender Realities: Local and Global*, special volume of *Advances in Gender Research* 9, ed. Marcia Texler Segal and Vasilikie Demos, 201-33.

Tastsoglou, Evangelia and Valerie Preston. 2005. Gender, Immigration and Employment Integration: Where We Are and What We Still Need to Know. *Atlantis: A Women's Studies Journal* 30 (1): 25-37.

Tiede, Lydia Brashear. 2001. Battered Immigrant Women and Immigration Remedies: Are the Standards too High? *Human Rights: Journal of the Section of Individual Rights and Responsibilities* 28 (1): 21-22.

Torres, Sara, J. Campbell, D. W. Campbell, J. Ryan, C. King, P. Price, R. Y. Stallings, Y. Rebecca, S. C. Fuchs and M. Laude. 2000. Abuse During and Before Pregnancy: Prevalence and Cultural Correlates. *Violence and Victims* 15 (3): 303-21.

Van Hightower, Nikki R., Joe Gorton and Casey Lee DeMoss. 2000. Predictive Models of Domestic Violence and Fear of Intimate Partners Among Migrant and Seasonal Farm Worker Women. *Journal of Family Violence* 15 (2): 137-54.

Weerasinghe, Swarna, PI. 2000. *Equitable Access to Healthcare, Health Promotion, and Disease Prevention for Recent Immigrant Women Living in Nova Scotia, Canada: Report on Phase I*. Maritime Centre of Excellence for Women's Health. Halifax: Dalhousie University Press.

Wong, Madeleine. 2000. Ghanaian Women in Toronto's Labour Market: Negotiating Gendered Roles and Transnational Household Strategies. *Canadian Ethnic Studies* 32 (2): 45-76.

# Section 3

# Immigration in Small Communities

# 6

## Why Do Immigrants Want to Come Here?
## A Case Study of Immigration in Colchester County[1]

*J. David Flint*

### Introduction

Colchester County is located just north of Halifax County and stretches from Cobequid Bay in the southwest to the Northumberland Strait in the north. Almost half the county's 49,305 residents are concentrated in the Truro-Bible Hill area. The rest of the population is scattered widely in many small villages and rural areas. The landscape ranges from rolling agricultural land in the south to forested mountains and seashore in the north. The manufacturing sector is the largest employer in the region, followed by retail sales and health and social welfare occupations. Only about 6 per cent of the workforce is employed in the traditional rural occupations of farming, forestry and fishing.

Colchester County's population has grown slightly in the last decade, but it has also aged. The county's birth rate is declining, and the number of younger working-aged people has fallen in both relative and absolute terms, a trend that is expected to continue in the future (Canmac 2003). An aging population coupled with a shrinking younger work force challenges the county's plans for economic growth. One way to meet the challenge is to encourage immigrants to settle in the region. This is an attractive option since, besides supplementing the work force, immigrants often contribute new skills, ideas, resources and investment capital. But Colchester County has a very small immigrant population (1,610, or 3.3 per cent of the total population) and the number of immigrants coming to Colchester County is declining. Only about 15 per cent of these immigrants arrived in the decade between 1991 and 2001, the lowest influx of immigrants during any ten-year period since 1951-1961. Yet many of the immigrants who do live in the County enjoy successful careers, make significant contributions to their communities, and seem relatively satisfied with life in the region. This research project was undertaken to find out more about these people.

The vast majority of Canada's immigrants settle in Toronto, Vancouver, or Montreal (Statistics Canada 2003). Most of Nova Scotia's immigrants settle in the Halifax area (Akbari and Dar 2005), but every year a handful choose to start a new life in Colchester County. What factors attract them to Colchester County, and what factors keep them there? There are relatively few contemporary studies of immigrants in Canada's rural regions and most of them focus on the issues of "attraction" and "retention." Some classify rural immigrants according to their immigration category, their professional skills or their country of origin, but none that I am aware of classifies or "types" them with reference to their personal hopes and expectations.

My study begins with the assumption that *different kinds* of people are attracted to Colchester County for *different reasons*: immigrants arrive here with a variety of hopes and expectations. Following this logic it can be imagined that the people most likely to remain—and those upon whom recruitment efforts should be focused—are those whose hopes and expectations are realistic and most closely match conditions on the ground. Life in rural and small-town Nova Scotia is not for everyone. If rural communities hope to attract—and retain—more immigrants, it would be useful to know what sorts of people to be looking for, and where and how they might be found. With this in mind I have developed a typology of immigrants to facilitate recognition of people most likely to adapt to life in this region.

## About the Respondents

I selected the thirty interviewees to reflect the wide range of immigrants who have settled in Colchester County—sixteen women and fourteen men. Fifteen had settled in or near the town of Truro and fifteen lived in more rural parts of the county in the vicinities of Tatamagouche and Stewiacke. The youngest were in their early 20s and the oldest in their mid-60s. They were born in fifteen different countries on five continents: thirteen in Europe, eight in Asia, four in South America, three in North America and two in Africa. "Country of birth" does not tell the whole story because the majority of the respondents were experienced world travellers; indeed, eleven of them had immigrated to Canada from a country of residence other than their country of birth.

Eleven of the people I talked to had immigrated to Canada as part of a married couple. Six (five women and one man) had come to Colchester County because they had married or become engaged to a Canadian who lived there. All but one of the married couples had children. Only four of the thirty immigrants came to Canada as single persons, and one of these was sponsored by a child who had immigrated earlier.

These were well-educated people. All had completed high school, and all but three had some post-secondary education. Twelve had bachelor degrees, and three had graduate degrees. Seven others had college diplomas or some other form of technical certification, and four had attended university or college but had not received a diploma. Prior to coming to Canada they were engaged in a variety of occupations. One was a senior business manager and five had had occupations related to business, finance or administration. Four had been in retail sales and service, and four worked in social services or education. There were four health professionals, including two physicians. Three respondents had been employed in the natural or applied sciences, and five had been farmers. Three had worked in the skilled trades, and one in the arts. Only one had not held a paying job immediately before coming to Canada. Altogether, six individuals had owned their own businesses, and two couples had operated farms (See summary of respondents' profiles at end-of-chapter table on "Key Characteristics of the Respondents").

### Why They Chose Colchester County: The Importance of Family and Friendship Ties

Nine of the respondents had not planned to settle in Colchester County when they arrived in Canada. Three had initially located in Toronto, two in Hamilton, one in Vancouver, one in New Brunswick, and three in Halifax. Of these nine, two were attracted to the Truro area because their spouses' parents lived there. The other seven came primarily because of better job opportunities, but five of them had relatives living in the area. Of the twenty-one persons who immigrated directly to Colchester County, six were attracted to the region because they had relatives living there. Eight had become interested in the area because friends from their home countries were already residing there. Five came to be with their fiancés or partners. One couple came because they were sponsored as refugees by a local church.

Putting the direct and indirect immigrants together, twenty-eight of the thirty respondents became aware of Colchester County or considered Colchester County as an immigration destination because they had a close personal connection with at least one County resident before they arrived. Five were joining spouses or partners. Eleven had personal relatives in the area. Two had spouses with relatives nearby. Eight had friends from their home countries in the area. The refugee couple had been located in a refugee camp and brought to Colchester County by a local church group.

In the case of Colchester County, the importance of family and friendship ties is evident, suggesting that future immigrants might be recruited through contacts with immigrants presently living there. Of course, most respondents didn't decide to live in Colchester County simply because a friend or relative lived there, or because they had been offered a job. They were also drawn by the promise of a better quality of life for themselves and their children. They were most likely to mention the area's rural character as an important factor in their decision and often remarked on the strong sense of community that existed in the small towns and villages.

## The Immigration Process

Twenty-four of the respondents offered criticisms of the Canadian immigration system. The most common complaint was that the immigration process took such a long time, putting applicants' lives "on hold" while they awaited a decision. On average, respondents had to wait about a year and a half after submitting their application to receive landing papers, though several had waited more than three years. Applicants sponsored by family members or fiancés experienced the shortest waiting times and were usually able to enter Canada and obtain temporary work visas while they were waiting.

Respondents also criticized the complexity of the immigration process. Only one (a fiancé) was fortunate enough to be processed within Canada on "compassionate" grounds. The rest had to apply through the visa office outside of Canada. This was of course problematic for those who were already residing in Canada when they made their applications, but it was also a problem for some of those who made their applications while still residing in their home countries. In recent years Canada has "rationalized" its immigration services by consolidating them. Canada now maintains relatively few visa offices abroad that are authorized to process immigration applications. There are only five authorized offices in western Europe (in London, Berlin, Vienna, Paris and Rome) so an applicant from the Netherlands must go through the office in Berlin, while an applicant from Norway must apply in London. Similarly, an applicant from Japan must apply in Manila, and all applicants from the United States must work through the visa office in Buffalo.

As a result, most potential immigrants are obliged to make their applications by mail and some respondents encountered serious difficulties with this system. Several reported that Canadian visa offices had lost or mislaid important documents; in one case a cashier's cheque for a substantial immigration fee was deposited but not credited to the applicant. Other respondents reported that receipt of their application (and fee payments) was not formally acknowledged. It is quite impossible to contact an official in a visa office by telephone since each office is equipped with a voice mail system that only offers a menu of recorded messages. Therefore applicants are obliged to communicate by mail or fax, and some respondents reported that their letters and faxes were not answered in a timely fashion—if they were answered at all.

## Finding Employment

Twenty-two respondents were engaged in paid work: eighteen had full-time jobs and four had part-time jobs. Two others were looking for work, and one was a full-time homemaker. The remaining five had not yet been granted work visas but all five were working nonetheless—without pay—in businesses they had set up themselves. Three owned retail businesses, and one couple had purchased a farm. None of the respondents were receiving support from employment insurance or social assistance.

Fourteen of the people I talked to (including the five without work visas) were self-employed, and twelve of them had arrived in Colchester County with the intention of setting up businesses. Six (three couples) had purchased farms and six (including two couples) had purchased or set up retail businesses. The other two were women who had turned to part-time self-employment when they were unable to find work in the professions for which they had been trained.

Nine of the respondents had found jobs in their areas of expertise. Most of these were professionals, including two physicians, two engineers, an educator and a natural scientist. Four others were employed in entry-level jobs, two in factories and two part-time in supermarkets.

## Investment Does Not Guarantee Landed Status

Most people talked about the difficulties immigrants face as they try to establish a livelihood in Canada. Almost half had addressed the problem by creating their own businesses, and twelve had invested substantial sums, often their life savings. Yet as the five oldest entrepreneurs discovered, investing a substantial sum in a business, even in an economically depressed rural area, does not guarantee landed status or even a work visa. Age is also a factor. The other business owners had immigrated in their thirties, and none of them had experienced difficulties getting a work visa once they had submitted a business plan. For them the greatest difficulty was generating enough money from the business to support themselves.

## Difficulties Establishing Credentials[2]

Despite their training and experience, nearly all of the professionals I talked to had had difficulty finding work in their field, and this was usually due to problems with credentials. Most had not anticipated how little recognition they would get for their training and experience abroad. The health professionals (two male physicians, a midwife and a female continuing care worker) had the most difficulty with credential recognition. Both physicians had to obtain Canadian medical credentials before they were allowed to practice, and this was time-consuming, expensive and difficult. The examination and assessment process can take a year or two and during this time the physician must find alternative employment to support their family. The midwife and the continuing care worker were unable to find work in their professions even though their skills are in high demand in Nova Scotia because their credentials and training were not recognized in this province.

Finding work was not quite as hard for the two engineers I spoke with, though the civil engineer had difficulty obtaining professional certification. He landed in Ontario with twenty years of experience in his native country but certification required one year of work experience in Canada plus a series of professional examinations. He explained:

> I applied for my professional engineering license but in order to get it I needed a minimum of one year Canadian experience. And that became the real stumbling block—what they call supervised training. I must have applied to 80 or 90 consulting engineers but it was a chicken and egg problem because they said I needed the license to work for them, but I needed experience to get the license!

This dilemma brought him to Nova Scotia. He had relatives in Halifax with friends in the engineering profession who recommended him for a job opening in Colchester County.

The other engineer had also landed in Ontario. He quickly found a job as an industrial engineer, but not in his area of expertise. After a year of job searching across Canada he finally found a suitable position in Truro: "I came to Truro because of the job. That's the only reason an immigrant would think of moving here."

## Difficulties Related to Language, Cultural Difference and Visible Minority Status

Ninety-eight per cent of the Colchester County population learned English as a mother tongue, and only 2.2 per cent are classified as "visible minority." In areas where there is little cultural diversity, employers may be reluctant to hire someone who is "different." Several reports have also indicated that immigrants with obvious cultural differences may have more difficulty finding employment in Canada's rural areas than in its more cosmopolitan urban centres (Baldacchino 2006; House of Commons 2005; Silvius 2005). White Anglophone immigrants may have the easiest time finding work in Colchester County, but this hypothesis cannot be tested in this study. Eight of the thirty respondents were indeed white Anglophones, but only one of them had looked for employment in Colchester County. The rest were self-employed.

Most of the respondents of both sexes who did not come from English-speaking countries—or who could otherwise be perceived as "different"—reported difficulties finding work in Canada. However within this group most of the males had arrived in Colchester County with a job in hand. Only two men from this group had been obliged to look for work after they had arrived, but seven women had either searched for a job or were still searching.[3] Of these nine who had looked for work, five women and one man felt that either their own difficulties with English or their "foreign" accents had been a barrier to finding employment. Several women also reported what they saw as the reluctance of employers to hire them because of their racial or ethnic "differences." Recent studies (Chicha 2010; Tastsoglou and Preston 2005) have shown how prejudices based on race, ethnicity and language difficulties intersect with gender discrimination to create special problems for immigrant women trying to enter the Canadian labour market.

Married women from non-English-speaking countries with perceptible ethnic or racial differences had the greatest difficulty finding work in Colchester County. If they found jobs at all, they were entry-level positions that did not reflect the women's educational or work experiences. About half of these women had immigrated with their husbands to Canada, and had located in Colchester County because their husbands had found work there. Most of the rest had married Canadians who already lived and worked in the area. Christina Ho provides an explanation of this phenomenon in her paper on Chinese women immigrants to Australia (Ho 2006). While married immigrant women may have had well-established careers in the home country, the challenges of re-negotiating work and care in a new setting often drives latent gender role expectations to the surface. The husband emerges as bread-winner, the wife as caretaker. This was generally the case for the married couples with children in my study whose first language was not English. In each case the family had moved to Colchester County because the husband had found work there. While the husband focused on performing well at his new job, the wife focused on maintaining the household and helping the family adapt to life in a new country. Unable to rely on the support that had made it possible for a mother to pursue a career in the home country, such as that of extended family, friends or paid help; unfamiliar with services available in the new country; and hampered by language difficulties and credential problems; none of these women had succeeded in returning to their former careers.

## A Welcoming Community?

> The Colchester Regional Development Agency recognizes that in order to be able to attract skills and investment we need to attract, embrace and welcome newcomers. We also recognize that we need to become a *Welcoming Community* that is able to create a welcome environment for new residents (Colchester Regional Development Agency 2004).

When asked if they had felt welcomed into the community, about half of the interviewees responded positively. Eleven of the positive respondents had some important things in common: they had settled in a rural area and they had started their own businesses or farms. This group of eleven included seven of the eight white Anglophones interviewed plus three immigrants from northern Europe and one from the Middle East. The three other positive respondents lived in Truro: one was a physician, one had recently married a Canadian, and one had come to join family in Truro.

The people who did not feel they had really been welcomed into the community tended to be those with greater cultural differences. Most of them qualified their statements by saying that Colchester County residents had certainly been "friendly," but not really "welcoming":

When we first arrived, a neighbour brought over cookies. That was nice. And generally we have very good neighbours. I will go over for coffee. But they only go so far, and that's the point.

Some of the negative responses were more critical:

They are friendly, but they don't mix with you very freely. That's difficult for me. Maybe they think our culture is different, our thinking is different, maybe that's why they don't want to meet foreign people. They are friendly, but not to invite you over for dinner. When nobody opens up to you, you feel shy about opening to them. In our country, people want to know *everything* about you (laughs)! Here, nobody really cares what you are doing. They don't want to interfere with your privacy. We've lived in this apartment for almost two years, and we don't know anyone in this building!

One summed up "welcoming" as a two-way process:

I would say that when I initially came here, it was just okay, but I think the acceptance level is better now. If, as an immigrant, I start expecting that the day I come here there will be people waiting for me with open arms, I am living in a fool's paradise. But if I come with an open mind I will find people with an open mind who are ready to experiment with me. And if I'm ready to experiment with them, if we're both ready to accept each other....

But for immigrants who are unfamiliar with North American culture and who may have language difficulties, making friends with local people is not enough. The region's institutions— political, economic, legal, educational and religious—must be welcoming as well. And this was the major problem for many of the people I spoke with. When they arrived they simply did not know how to find a decent job, how to get a driver's licence, where to go to improve their English skills, how to enroll themselves or their children in an educational program and so forth. They did not understand how the political and legal systems worked, or how the health system worked. In Canada's urban centres there is usually a number to call, a central switchboard for new immigrants, a settlement house or welcome centre that will answer their questions or direct them to someone who can. But in Colchester County immigrants must deal directly with each of these institutions—assuming they are even aware of their existence or location—and few if any of these institutions are equipped to respond to the questions that immigrants have, particularly if there are language difficulties.

## Integration: Becoming Part of the Community

### Cultural adjustment and culture shock

For most of the North Americans and Western Europeans interviewed, cultural adjustment was a positive experience. Many had moved to Colchester County to get away from the hustle and bustle of urban areas and they were charmed by the slower pace of life in Colchester County, the friendliness of strangers on the street, the neighbourliness that they had experienced in their communities and the low incidence of crime. Some mentioned frustrations when searching for goods and services and a few noted problems navigating the local and regional bureaucratic structures, but overall, "cultural adaptation" was more a case of easing into a lifestyle that was simpler and less chaotic.

Immigrants from more distant countries found the cultural adaptation process more challenging. The most commonly cited challenge was getting used to the "stand-offishness" of Colchester County residents, who were described as polite and friendly but also as emotionally cool and not really interested in getting to know people with different cultural legacies. A few respondents seemed distressed by North American cultural norms in general. They found children to be disrespectful, disobedient and sexually precocious and they found young women to be immodest. One couple was dismayed by what they saw as an addiction to comfort and convenience: "They drive to their mailboxes to pick up the mail. And everything is packaged for convenience—like microwave popcorn. Convenience will be the death of us all!"

I expected that people would complain about the unavailability of traditional "ethnic" foods, but this didn't seem to be a problem. Most people seemed very happy with the variety of food available, particularly the fresh meat and produce from local farmers. Those who missed foods from "home" had found convenient sources in Halifax or other urban areas.

When I asked people how they were adapting to the local culture, several jokingly responded with "What culture?" They were referring to "high culture," symphony orchestras, art museums, live theatre and so forth, very little of which is available in Colchester County. This was something they had not expected to find in the immediate area, and most satisfied their needs with occasional trips to Halifax.

### Integration into the community

There are many ways to measure the extent to which newcomers have become members of the community. Have they made friends? Have they become part of a social network? Have they established a satisfactory livelihood? Are they members of local civic, voluntary, social or recreational associations? If they are religious, have they found a suitable place to worship? Are their children well established and comfortable in the local schools?

### Making friends

Eight of the respondents said they had made many friends in their new community. All of them had immigrated from northern Europe or North America, all lived in rural areas, and all but one had started their own businesses. Only one spoke English as a second language, but he spoke it very well. The rest of the respondents said they had not made many friends. Some said they were too busy trying to establish a livelihood, some blamed language or cultural differences, some said they were "shy," and some cited the aloofness of the natives. There were differences of opinion as to what constituted a "friend," and some of the respondents who claimed few friends made a careful distinction between "real friends" and "acquaintances."

Business networks

Becoming integrated into a community means becoming part of a social network, and those respondents who claimed the most friends were typically involved in multiple formal and informal social networks. This was particularly the case for those who had started businesses. One such couple said they were members of "eight or ten" business-related civic organizations, and that the husband had been immediately asked to preside over one of them because of his expertise. The professionals and farmers also found many of their social contacts in the context of work, through collegial friendship networks and professional organizations.

Religious networks

Most of the respondents were members of religious congregations, and this gave many of them access to social networks. As one professional put it, "One thing I have learned is that this society works through the churches." The interviewees represented at least eight religious denominations; they were Christians, Hindus and Buddhists. Most had found congregations in the Colchester area though a few went to services in Halifax.

While most respondents were pleased with the social opportunities that membership in religious organizations provided, several Roman Catholics expressed disappointment. At home, the local parish had been the nexus of their social life, but this was not found to be the case in Colchester County.

Voluntary, charitable, social and sports organizations

Most of the people I talked to were affiliated with voluntary or social organizations, a good strategy for making friends and connecting with the community. Several female respondents had also become volunteers with the hope of improving their English and office skills in order to find paid employment. At least four women attended meetings of the International Ladies Group of Colchester County, a social group that welcomes newcomers to the area, and several respondents of both sexes volunteered in other organizations dedicated to helping new arrivals, including the Multicultural Association, The Colchester Immigration Partnership, the Colchester Adult Learning Association (which offers ESL courses), the Truro and Area Newcomers Club, and the International Students Association at the Nova Scotia Agricultural College. While voluntary and social organizations provided a valuable connection to the community, mostly for women with language difficulties and cultural differences, men with these problems sometimes made the connection through sports. Several of the men had been welcomed into local teams as players or coaches.

### Integration of children into the community

Most of the respondents had school-aged children, and most of these children were not born in Canada. Though a few parents reported that their children were occasionally homesick, all said that they had adapted well to their new home, often more easily than their parents. A few parents were concerned that their children were not learning as much in school as they would have in their home country:

> The school system here is really slow. I'm not happy with it. Not tough enough. Our son was in the second class when we came over, but right away he was the best in math. We think that the kids here need more pressure to push them in the first and second years.

Other parents preferred the Canadian approach to education:

> When he came here, he found school easier. Here they are behind. But I think the schools here are okay. He has lots of projects and he has to learn to do research by himself. [Back home] the teachers just come and read, and the students just take notes.

Several parents noted that having children had helped them make friends in the community by connecting them with a network of parents in the context of school and recreational activities.

## Why We Like It Here

Despite the difficulties of adjusting to life in Colchester County, the majority of the respondents (sixteen) said they were "very satisfied" with their new life. Ten said they were "content" with life here. Four were clearly "not satisfied" and were seriously considering leaving the area. Overall, seven respondents said they had either considered leaving at one time or another or would consider leaving if they found a better livelihood opportunity elsewhere, but the remaining nineteen said they had no intention of ever leaving the area.

When I asked the respondents what they liked most about Colchester County, all but one praised one or more of the county's rural qualities. The most common response was that Colchester County gave them the feeling of being surrounded by open space with access to the natural environment without being completely cut off from the amenities of civilization. They also stressed the advantages of living in a small community. Life was quiet and safe. There was less crime, less pollution and life could be lived at a slower pace. Though many of the people I talked with had not found Colchester natives to be especially "welcoming," they nevertheless appreciated their values, ethics and decency toward others:

> I love the people—that's number one—and the simple life-
> style. I mean, they're busy, but they care about relationships,
> about what's going on. They're not glued to a television set,
> or worried about traffic, or having a siege mentality like you
> have in the city where you just try to get home every day.

People with younger children characterized the region with its natural environment and slower pace as an ideal place to bring up a family. Some other advantages mentioned by more than one respondent were low real estate prices (especially for farm land), access to higher education and quality adult education courses, and the availability of farm-fresh produce.

When I asked the respondents whether other people from their home country would be attracted to Colchester County, all but two said yes. Furthermore, thirteen of them said that relatives, close friends, or former business associates had in fact expressed a serious interest in coming to join them in the region—though some of these friends and relatives had been discouraged by the difficulties the respondents themselves had faced during the immigration process.

## A Typology of Immigrants

According to the Nova Scotia Immigration Strategy, retention of immigrants is a key issue (Nova Scotia Office of Immigration 2005). A major premise of my research is that if retention is the goal, attention should be paid to the characteristics of those immigrants who *have* remained, as well as to the problems that have led to the departure of others. A further premise is that immigrants who have been attracted to and have remained in Colchester County will have special characteristics that suit them to life in the region, but that this group will contain different *types* of successful immigrants with different sets of characteristics. It follows that if Colchester County wishes to recruit and retain immigrants it would be helpful to know what types of immigrants are most likely to settle permanently in the region. For this reason I have developed a typology of recent immigrants based on characteristics of the people I interviewed.

The German sociologist Max Weber developed the concept of "ideal types" as a way of grappling with the infinite variability of human subjects in the course of social analysis. An ideal typology is a set of categories sociologists can use to sort people into different "types." These types are "ideal" rather than "real" because no real human being would fit perfectly into any of them. In most cases people will have characteristics tying them to several of the types, but they usually fit best into one category. In the following analysis I assign each respondent to one type only, but I note the considerable overlap.

The "visionaries": Realizing the dream

The "visionaries" (fourteen respondents) came to Colchester County to realize a dream. Most of the people I talked to were hoping to realize one dream or another, but the visionaries came to this area primarily because it seemed the very best place in the world to do this. They were idealistic but practical. They had searched carefully for the ideal spot and had planned their lives and saved their money in order to make their dream come true. Almost half of the respondents were primarily visionaries.

The visionaries believed they had found a relatively unspoiled rural or small-town environment surrounded by natural beauty and a small population of natives with the traditional rural values of hard work, self-sufficiency, thrift and community spirit. They were prepared—and often eager—to sacrifice luxury and convenience for a simpler life. The visionaries I talked to were all from northern Europe or the United States. The lifestyle they envisioned would at one time have been possible for them in their native countries, but increasing land costs and cultural changes in these countries had led them to look for a less-developed region that bore some resemblance to their own country in previous times. Nearly all of the visionaries had integrated comfortably into their adopted communities, though it was more difficult for those who spoke English as a second language. All were small businesspersons, farmers or professionals, and as such they were viewed by the natives as contributors to the local economy.

The "relatives": Family ties

The majority of the people I interviewed (18) had family ties in the region. Some had relatives living in or near Colchester County while others had come to join fiancés. They had learned about Colchester County from their relatives, and none would have otherwise thought of living in the area. But for eight respondents (seven women and one man), the *primary* reason for coming was to be with a family member and for this reason I have typed these eight as "relatives." In all but one case they came to join a future spouse or partner. As a rule they had difficulty finding a place for themselves in the community. They felt isolated, had difficulty finding work or forming close friendships, and their social circle was often limited to the friends of the person they had come to join. All eight had the additional problem of English as a second language.

### The "professionals": Professional opportunities

Six of the respondents were employed as professionals: two physicians, two engineers and two academics. Five had settled in Colchester County primarily because of an employment opportunity though none had planned to live in Nova Scotia when they immigrated. In each case they had searched across Canada for work in their field and had found the best opportunity in Truro. Typically this was because employers here faced a shortage of professionals and were more open to hiring people with minimal Canadian experience. Unlike the "visionaries," the professionals had not come to the area for the natural or social environment, but they liked the rural setting and the slower pace of life. While their social networks were smaller than those of the visionaries, they had been able to make connections with the community through associations with professional colleagues. The wives of male professionals experienced greater social isolation. They had difficulty finding work themselves, and the work they found was typically "entry level" and did not reflect their prior training or experience. Without a job, and speaking English as a second language, they found it hard to forge friendships in their new community.

### The "entrepreneurs": Business opportunities

Nearly half (fourteen) of the respondents were self-employed "entrepreneurs," but only one had located in the area primarily because it offered the most attractive entrepreneurial opportunity. An experienced businessman, he came to Nova Scotia because some of his relatives were settled in the Halifax area. After searching throughout the province for a retail business he could afford to buy, he found the best opportunity in one of Colchester County's small villages. He expressed satisfaction with life in his new community, but said he would readily move if a better business opportunity came up elsewhere in the future.

Skilled workers

Aside from the professionals and farmers, ten of the immigrants I talked to could be classified as "skilled workers," people with training and experience in office work, the trades or the service occupations. All of them were women, and all but one was married. None had come to the region specifically to find work in their area of expertise, and so I have not "typed" any of them into the "skilled workers" category. Research has shown that there is a great need for skilled workers in Colchester County (Canmac 2003) so it is significant that none of the people I talked to (aside from the professionals and one farmer) had been landed on the basis of their skills. It is also significant that only two of these women were able to find employment commensurate with their training and experience.

Refugees

Very few refugees find their way to Colchester County. I was only able to find one refugee couple to interview. They had left an extremely difficult and dangerous situation in their home country and were grateful to have escaped to a situation where their lives were not in danger and there was a roof over their heads and food to eat. Yet despite support from the Canadian government and a local church sponsor, life in Colchester County was difficult for them. There were no other people from their home country in the area, and cultural and language differences and lack of appropriate skills or recognized credentials made it difficult to find work that paid a living wage.

## Conclusions and Recommendations

The typology reflects immigrant motivations. Those who came to realize visions or to pursue professional careers had the easiest time adapting to conditions in Colchester County and were most strongly committed to staying in the region. This is related to the fact that the livelihoods they chose and the lifestyles they pursued connected them with multiple social networks. Those coming primarily to join family members or as refugees had the most difficulty adapting. Most were skilled workers but because of language difficulties and ethnic discrimination they had difficulty finding work that reflected their skills. They had limited access to social networks and felt isolated from the community. It is significant that none of the respondents came to Colchester County specifically to take advantage of the region's need for skilled workers.

The problem for immigration facilitators is twofold: how to recruit the types of immigrants most likely to adapt to conditions in the region, and how to alleviate the problems that immigrants encounter once they have arrived. In terms of recruitment, the typology provides a means of assessing the adaptability of immigrants to existing conditions in Colchester County based on their reasons for coming. A most important finding is that virtually all the respondents learned about and were attracted to Colchester County through relationships with friends or family members already living in the region. This suggests that immigrants themselves may be a valuable resource for recruiting future immigrants, an idea that is supported by the fact that almost half the people I talked to mentioned relatives or friends who were interested in coming to the area. The research also indicates that while skilled, non-professional workers are needed in Colchester County, this type of immigrant has not been attracted to the region. It appears that skilled workers could be recruited readily through contacts with the County's existing immigrant community, provided that skilled employment was offered and visas were made available.

In terms of retention, different types of immigrants have different needs to be met if they are to adapt to conditions in Colchester County. Visionaries, professionals and entrepreneurs had the easiest time adapting. This is likely because they had greater financial resources, their livelihood activities involved them in more social networks, and they were perceived to contribute economic and social benefits and valuable skill sets to the community. The main obstacles were bureaucratic. The visionaries and entrepreneurs had taken substantial financial risks to set up businesses and while they were welcomed by their communities, Citizenship and Immigration seemed to regard them with suspicion without appreciating the contributions they were making. Immigrating professionals had problems establishing credentials in Canada. This worked to the advantage of Colchester County employers who were able to recruit recently arrived immigrant professionals from Canada's urban centres by recognizing their credentials.

Persons with English language deficiencies or marked ethnic or racial differences, refugees, skilled non-professional workers and women encountered different problems and had a harder time adapting to life in Colchester County. They had problems finding work commensurate with their skills and experience, problems engaging with social networks and problems adjusting to cultural differences. These problems underline Colchester County's need to become a more "welcoming community," a community that is not only friendly but also equipped to be helpful. A local "switchboard" could be established where immigrants could call for referrals to agencies, organizations or individuals who could help them solve these problems. A local employment counselling and referral service specifically designed for immigrants could match them with appropriate jobs and provide references for employers. An excellent ESL program in Truro introduces immigrants to a social network and provides practical and emotional support as well as teaching English, but its resources are very limited. Greater efforts must be made to reach out to immigrant women, particularly those in more remote areas of the County. The value of immigrants themselves as consultants and advisors on the immigration and settlement processes should be recognized and utilized more effectively.

Colchester County is justly renowned for developing progressive policies and programs to attract immigrants and to assist them in adjusting to rural and small-town life in Nova Scotia and these recommendations are meant as suggestions for the further

## KEY CHARACTERISTICS OF THE RESPONDENTS

| R# | age | sex | "visible minority" | English 1st lang. | educ. level | marital status | married a Canadian | children at home | place of birth | emigrated from | relative in area | friend in area | occupation | owns business | "ideal type" |
|---|---|---|---|---|---|---|---|---|---|---|---|---|---|---|---|
| 1 | 51 | F | no | yes | some u. | m | no | no | Poland | USA | no | yes | retail | yes | visionary |
| 2 | 40 | M | no | no | college | m | no | yes | Germany | Germany | no | yes | butcher | yes | visionary |
| 3 | 40 | F | no | no | college | m | no | yes | Germany | Germany | yes | yes | retail | yes | visionary |
| 4 | 36 | M | no | yes | college | m | no | yes | England | England | no | yes | farmer | yes | visionary |
| 5 | 36 | F | no | yes | college | m | no | yes | England | England | no | yes | farmer | yes | visionary |
| 6 | 33 | M | yes | yes | some u. | m | no | yes | England | England | no | yes | farmer | yes | visionary |
| 7 | 33 | F | yes | yes | h.s. | m | no | yes | Liberia | Ghana | no | yes | factory work | no | refugee |
| 8 | 30 | M | no | yes | h.s. | m | no | yes | Liberia | Ghana | yes | yes | factory work | no | refugee |
| 9 | 30 | M | no | yes | B.A. | c. law (com. law) | yes | no | Colombia | Colombia | yes | no | teacher | no | relative |
| 10 | 33 | M | yes | no | B.A. | s | n/a | yes | Poland | Australia | yes | no | teacher | no | profession |
| 11 | 40 | M | yes | no | some u. | s | n/a | n/a | Lebanon | Sierra Leone | yes | no | café owner | yes | entrepren. |
| 12 | 39 | F | no | no | B.A. | m | no | no | Germany | Germany | no | yes | farmer | yes | visionary |
| 13 | 61 | M | no | no | college | m | no | no | Germany | Germany | no | yes | farmer | yes | visionary |
| 14 | 59 | F | no | yes | h.s. | m | no | no | England | England | yes | yes | farmer | yes | visionary |
| 15 | 45 | M | no | no | M.D. | m | no | yes | Surinam | England | no | yes | physician | no | visionary |
| 16 | 45 | F | no | no | college | m | no | yes | Germany | England | no | yes | sales | yes | visionary |
| 17 | 43 | M | no | no | college | m | no | yes | Germany | England | yes | yes | farmer | yes | visionary |
| 18 | 70 | F | yes | no | college | widow | no | no | Holland | Holland | yes | no | farmer | yes | visionary |
| 19 | 30 | F | yes | no | B.A. | fiancée engaged to | yes | no | Mexico | Mexico | yes | no | p/t sales | no | relative |
| 20 | 43 | F | no | no | B.A. | m | no | no | Colombia | Colombia | yes | yes | unemployed | no | relative |
| 21 | 48 | M | yes | yes | B.A. | m | yes | yes | USA | USA | yes | yes | retail | yes | visionary |
| 22 | 28 | F | no | no | B.S | m | yes | yes | Ukraine | Russia | yes | no | unemployed | no | relative |
| 23 | 51 | F | no | no | some u. | m | yes | yes | Ecuador | USA | yes | yes | homemaker | no | relative |
| 24 | 42 | F | no | no | B.A. | m | yes | yes | Japan | USA | yes | yes | translator | no | relative |
| 25 | 48 | M | yes | no | M.D. | m | no | yes | India | India | no | yes | physician | no | profession |
| 26 | 33 | M | yes | no | B.A. | m | no | yes | India | India | no | no | engineer | no | profession |
| 27 | 33 | F | yes | no | B.A. | m | no | yes | India | India | no | no | relative | no | relative |
| 28 | 34 | F | yes | no | M.S. | s | n/a | no | India | India | no | no | biologist | no | profession |
| 29 | 41 | F | yes | yes | h.s. | m | yes | yes | Philippines | Singapore | yes | yes | seamstress | no | relative |
| 30 | 55 | M | yes | yes | B.Eng. | m | no | yes | India | India | yes | yes | engineer | no | profession |

expansion and enhancement of these policies and programs rather than as a critique.

**Notes**

1. This chapter is adapted from *Atlantic Metropolis Centre Working Paper* No. 07-2007.

2. The issue of foreign credential recognition is dealt with extensively in the Spring 2007 edition of *Canadian Issues* published by the Association for Canadian Studies. See, for example, Guo (2007) and Grant (2007).

3. The difficulties experienced by recent women immigrants to Nova Scotia are well-documented (Nova Scotia Advisory Council on Women 2004).

**References**

Akbari, Ather H. and Atul A. Dar. 2005. *Socioeconomic and Demographic Profiles of Immigrants to Nova Scotia.* Unpublished report prepared for the Atlantic Canada Opportunities Agency.

Baldacchino, Godfrey. 2006. *Coming To, and Settling On, Prince Edward Island: Stories and Voices.* Unpublished report prepared for the Population Secretariat, Prince Edward Island, and the University of Prince Edward Island.

Canmac Economics Ltd. 2003. *Economic Sector Strategy for the Colchester Region.* Unpublished report prepared for the Colchester Regional Development Agency.

Chicha, Marie-Thérèse. 2010. The Deskilling of Highly Qualified Immigrant Women in Montreal: A Matter of Degree? *Our Diverse Cities 7* (Spring).

Colchester Regional Development Agency. 2004. *The Colchester Immigration Partnership Initiative: Becoming a Welcoming Community.* Unpublished report.

Guo, Shibao. 2007. Tracing the Roots of Non-recognition of Foreign Credentials. *Canadian Issues* (Spring).

Ho, Christina. 2006. Migration as Feminisation? Chinese Women's Experiences of Work and Family in Australia. *Journal of Ethnic and Migration Studies* 32 (3).

House of Commons. 2005. Standing Committee on Citizenship and Immigration Evidence: Wednesday, April 20, 2005. 38th Parliament, 1st Session.

Nova Scotia Advisory Council on Women. 2004. Immigrant Women and a Framework for Immigration to Nova Scotia. http://women.gov.ns.ca/pubs2004_05/immigration%20brief%20oct%2019-04.pdf (accessed June 30, 2007).

Nova Scotia Office of Immigration. 2005. *Nova Scotia's Immigration Strategy.* Halifax: Communications Nova Scotia.

Silvius, Ray. 2005. Issues in Rural Immigration: Lessons, Challenges and Responses. *Manitoba Rural Immigration Community Case Studies Working Paper.* Brandon, Manitoba: Rural Development Institute, Brandon University.

Statistics Canada. 2003. *Longitudinal Survey of Immigrants to Canada: Process, Progress and Prospects.* Cat. No. 89-611-XIE. Ottawa: Industry Canada.

Tastsoglou, Evangelia and Valerie Preston. 2005. Gender, Immigration and Labour Market Integration: Where We Are and What We Still Need to Know. *Atlantis* 30 (1).

7

# Community Support for the Leisure and Well-being of Immigrant Families in Small Atlantic Canadian Communities

*Susan Tirone*
*Karen Gallant*
*Anne-Marie Sullivan*
*Charlene Shannon*
*Brenda Robertson*

## Introduction

Since the middle of the first decade of the 21st century, Atlantic Canada has begun to attract and retain more immigrants (Akbari 2011). This new trend is the result of lower out-migration from the region, increased international immigration and an increase in movement of immigrants who initially settled in other regions of Canada and then moved to the Atlantic region (Akbari 2011). This is in stark contrast to previous immigration trends that saw many new immigrants arrive in this region and leave shortly thereafter for larger urban centres. Policy initiatives support and stimulate the contribution immigrants make to the economic vitality of the region. However, less priority is given to policy and programs that address the social needs of new immigrants.

This chapter reports on the findings of a study that explored initiatives, made by small communities in Atlantic Canada, to support the social well-being of new immigrants. Beyond understanding how immigrants are supported when they arrive and through the time it takes for them to establish meaningful relationships in their new communities, our goal is to understand how welcoming services and supports contribute to immigrants' sense of well-being. Well-being is a complex concept, constructed from the meanings and evaluations people ascribe to the experiences they have in several life spheres such as family, friendship networks, work and leisure experiences (Mininni, Manuti, Scardigno and Rubino 2010). As leisure researchers, we are particularly interested in understanding the nature of the supports provided by leisure, recreation and social support providers in small communities in Atlantic Canada for new immigrants and how those supports contribute to the immigrants' well-being.

Canada relies on immigrants for a variety of reasons, not the least of which is to sustain population. Statistics Canada projects that by 2026, the time when the number of deaths in Canada will surpass the number of births, population growth will be dependent solely on immigration (Bollman, Beshiri and Clemenson 2007). Many small communities are particularly interested in attracting immigrants to address problems associated with aging populations, out-migration and population decline. For example, in October 2010 the province of Nova Scotia announced plans to invest $260,000 in efforts to attract foreign farmers to rural areas of the province. Nova Scotia policy makers hope immigrants will fill jobs currently held by aging farmers who do not have family members willing to take over family farms (Kaur 2010). Historically, however, immigrants arriving in smaller centres tended to remain in those centres only temporarily before moving on to larger metropolitan areas (Akbari, Lynch, Rankaduwa and McDonald 2008; Akbari and Sun 2006; Bruce 2007; Wilkinson and Kalischuk 2009). There is evidence that one of the reasons immigrants relocate to larger urban centres is their desire to be in cities where they can be in close geographic proximity to other members of their ethnic communities in order to receive cultur-ally relevant social support (Houle 2007). Consequently, we were interested in understanding how small communities in Atlantic Canada support the social well-being of new immigrants and how supportive communities may influence immigrants' decisions to remain in small communities long-term.

Many immigrants experience a sense of social well-being when they are able to develop supportive social networks and friendships and when they are able to access relevant services and resources (Spicer 2008; Walseth 2006). Social networks may contribute to immigrants' ability to resolve issues and problems that affect personal as well as community well-being such as pov-erty, poor health, unemployment and crime reduction (Heinonen et al. 2005; Putnam 1995). Leisure activity is known to provide an opportunity for people to develop supportive friendships and it has the potential to contribute positively to immigrants' sense of happiness and well-being (Spiers and Walker 2009). Participation in civic leisure activities such as concerts, festivals, sporting events and clubs is known to facilitate the development of social networks and friendships, and enhances one's ability to find places or "information grounds" where they may gain and share information, which further enhances social and economic well-being (Fisher, Durrance and Hinton 2004). Leisure is also a complex concept often defined as activity or experience that is freely chosen, and which provides opportunities to use an individual's particular skills in interesting ways (Kelly 1996). Leisure also has the capacity to enhance family and community cohesiveness (Conference Board of Canada 2005; Orthner and Mancini 1990), and it serves as a healthy outlet for coping with stressful events (Iwasaki and Mannell 2000). Leisure experiences such as sport participation can aid new immigrants in acquiring language proficiency, build social capital, provide opportunities for healthy and physically active lives and foster positive youth development (Doherty and Taylor 2007). Further, recreation and leisure involvement may promote the sharing of diverse cultural traditions that dominant groups would not otherwise know such as culturally diverse music, dance and food traditions (Ontario Council for Agencies Serving Immigrants (OCASI) June 2005; Tirone and Pedlar 2005).

We also recognize that immigrants may experience leisure as problematic when they are unable to access the leisure goods and activities they prefer such as ethnic foods and ethnic social groups. For example, some immigrants encounter difficulties when they attempt to participate in leisure activities due to poverty, discrimination, language barriers and the absence of activities they prefer (Frisby, Alexander and Taylor 2010; Tirone 1999, 2000). Other challenges are related to service providers' lack of knowledge and understanding of the interest new Canadians may have in joining local activities, and how to inform and shape the activities in ways that make it possible for newcomers to enjoy them. In addition, new Canadians may be disadvantaged by not understanding how to access information networks with which dominant groups are readily familiar (Livingston, Tirone, Smith and Miller 2008).

Leisure is the aspect of well-being we focus on in this chapter. We recognize the potential difficulty of program and service provision in small communities where only small numbers of immigrants settle and reside long term. In these places immigrants may not have social support from other immigrants who understand and appreciate the values and cultural practices of diverse ethnic groups. Furthermore, small communities may not have the capacity to provide the volunteers and other resources that would benefit new immigrants, nor a sufficient number of immigrants necessary to support such efforts. For example, in small communities there may be limited numbers of people available to fill volunteer positions specifically aimed at supporting immigrants.

Here we provide an overview of the efforts of twenty-four Atlantic Canadian communities with populations between 5,000 and 12,000. We chose to study communities of this size because they are the medium-sized communities in the region, they experience challenges due to out-migration and aging populations, they are the communities that support essential industries such as the farming and resource-based economy of the region, and they are interested in attracting immigrants. We identified efforts made by these communities to address the needs of new immigrants through programs, services and policies related to social well-being and leisure as suggested by their point of contact information. Point of contact information is publicly available information on community websites and/or web pages identified using keyword searches as well as through phone calls to munici-pal government offices.

## Approach to Collecting Our Data

In 2008, we compiled community profiles of nine communities in Newfoundland and Labrador, and over the winter of 2010-2011, profiles were created for six communities in Nova Scotia, six communities in New Brunswick, and three communities in PEI. In PEI, only one community fell within the population range we targeted, so we selected two additional communities, one larger and one smaller, to provide a more representative illustration of community services available to immigrants in that province. Each community profile included an overview of the community demographics and the measures taken by each community to as-sist immigrants in settling in the community, developing language proficiency, finding jobs, developing social support networks, establishing themselves as members of the community and enjoy-ing community recreation activities. Community profiles were compiled using two data sources: (a) point of first contact informa-tion, and (b) data from the 2006 Canada Census. A review of each community's website was conducted, with particular emphasis on identifying recreation and leisure facilities and resources as well as supports and programs intended to nurture cultural diversity and attract or retain immigrants. Community groups, festivals and ongoing events that were not specifically intended for immigrants but contributed to the overall well-being of community members were also of interest. Following this website review, searches were conducted using keywords such as "immigrant" and "newcomer," and any additional resources or programs for immigrants were noted. Finally, a phone call was made to the general information phone line or recreation department (if the department's number was noted on the website) in each community to inquire about programs and services for immigrants or aimed specifically at cultivating diversity. Table 7.1 provides an overview of the immigrant populations in profiled communities.

| Province Community | Pop | # immigr-ants[2] | % immigr-ants | Countries of origin; most prevalent[1] |
|---|---|---|---|---|
| **New Brunswick** | | | | |
| Grand Falls | 5650 | 135 | 2.4 | U.S., U.K., India, Netherlands, El Salvador |
| Oromocto | 8402 | 375 | 4.5 | Germany, U.K., U.S., Netherlands |
| Rothesay | 11,637 | 685 | 5.9 | U.K., U.S., South Korea, Italy, Philippines, Russia |
| Sackville | 5411 | 280 | 5.2 | U.S., U.K., India, Netherlands |
| Shediac | 4801 | 145 | 3.0 | U.S., Germany, U.K., Philippines, France, Belgium |
| Woodstock | 5113 | 105 | 2.1 | U.S., U.K., Netherlands |
| **Newfoundland & Labrador** | | | | |
| Bay Roberts | 5414 | 30 | .56 | U.K., Philippines, U.S. |
| Carbonear | 4723 | 70 | 1.5 | U.K., U.S., Germany, Sri Lanka, Ireland |
| Clarenville | 5274 | 95 | 1.8 | U.K., U.S., Pakistan, Sri Lanka, Iran, Greece, Ireland |
| Deer Lake | 4827 | 40 | .83 | U.K., Egypt, Ireland |

TABLE 7.1. DEMOGRAPHIC OVERVIEW OF PROFILED COMMUNITIES

| Gander | 9951 | 205 | 2.1 | U.K., U.S., Germany, Netherlands, South Africa, Iraq, Ireland |
|---|---|---|---|---|
| Happy V - Goose Bay | 7572 | 160 | 2.1 | U.K., Philippines, U.S., Germany, Egypt |
| Portugal Cove- St. Phillip's | 6575 | 230 | 3.5 | U.K., U.S., Italy, Germany, Switzerland |
| Stephenville | 6588 | 55 | .83 | U.K., U.S. |
| Torbay | 6281 | 55 | .88 | U.K., U.S., Italy |
| **Nova Scotia** | | | | |
| Amherst | 9505 | 230 | 2.4 | U.K., U.S., Netherlands, Iraq, Germany |
| Bridgewater | 7944 | 310 | 3.9 | U.K., U.S., Colombia, Lebanon, Germany |
| Kentville | 5818 | 255 | 4.4 | U.K., Germany, U.S., Jamaica, Netherlands |
| N. Glasgow | 9455 | 285 | 3.0 | U.K., U.S., Italy |
| Truro | 11,765 | 565 | 4.8 | U.K., U.S., India, Netherlands, China |
| Yarmouth | 7162 | 205 | 2.9 | U.S., U.K., Vietnam, Egypt |
| **Prince Edward Island** | | | | |
| Kensington | 1485 | 30 | 2.0 | U.K. |
| Stratford | 7083 | 390 | 5.5 | U.K., U.S., Belgium, Jamaica, Japan, Netherlands, Germany |
| Summerside | 14,500 | 460 | 3.2 | U.S., U.K., Serbia, Netherlands, South Africa |
| (Statistics Canada, 2010) | | | | |

## Community Profiles

Communities from each of the Atlantic Provinces are discussed in this section of the chapter starting with those explored in Newfoundland and Labrador (NL). In Newfoundland and Labrador researchers were able to identify only communities that had specifically developed activities of interest to immigrants or people from diverse cultural traditions. For instance, just two communities identified that they had a special event that reflected their multiculturalism and none of the communities had ongoing initiatives designed to welcome immigrants. However, in Newfoundland and Labrador most immigrants originated in countries that were similar in many ways to Canada (Sullivan, Ring and Harris 2009) and only a few communities had activities inspired by the cultural practices of people who had immigrated to the community (e.g., social events and festivals such as St. Patrick's Day dances in Portugal Cove-St. Phillip's and events featuring dances from multiple cultures on Canada Day in Carbonear). As is the case throughout Atlantic Canada, many immigrants in Newfoundland and Labrador were from the United Kingdom and the United States (Sullivan, Ring and Harris 2009), and special efforts to welcome them may not have been perceived as necessary since traditional practices of the host communities are similar to those of the new immigrant newcomers (Sullivan, Ring and Harris 2009).

In other parts of Atlantic Canada we found that some small communities had made considerable efforts to welcome immigrants and to help them become engaged in civic activities. For example, in Stratford, PEI, a community of just more than 7,000 people in close proximity to Charlottetown, the largest urban centre in the province, there was evidence of considerable effort to attract and welcome immigrants. At the policy level, the community had an active diversity and inclusion committee, had documented their plans to foster inclusion, and held memberships in provincial and national umbrella organizations that supported these efforts. Practical efforts included the provision of cultural and leisure activities reflecting and celebrating diversity, such as arts exhibits, culinary demonstrations featuring ethnic cuisine (i.e., "Flavours of the World" at the Canada Day celebration), and recreation facilities appealing to people who identify with sports such as cricket, which is not widely available in many Canadian communities. In turn, Stratford, a municipality adjacent to Charlottetown, is recognized as the fastest-growing community in PEI and its immigrant population, at 5.44 per cent, is higher than in Prince Edward Island overall (3.57 per cent) (Canada Census Community Profiles 2006). It is also notable that many of the supports available to immigrants in Stratford reflected a province-wide effort to attract and retain immigrants and are located in the nearby town of Charlottetown. For example, the PEI Association for Newcomers to Canada—an organization offering settlement services, employment and language training, social events and programs, and related supports—was active province-wide, and some of the events noted previously were jointly hosted by this group.

While Stratford represented an example of a small community in close proximity to an urban centre with more extensive services and supports, the community of Truro, Nova Scotia, with a population of fewer than 12,000, is a regional centre and service hub for surrounding rural areas. We found that the town's website featured information for newcomers quite prominently on a "New to the Area" page on the "Residents" section of the site. This page was devoted primarily to housing, education and cost of living information for newcomers, although there was also a link to general public information about parks and recreation. The town had an Affirmative Action Committee and a Diversity Management Coordinator. A newcomer's club open to all women new to the area, including immigrants, met regularly. The local economic development agency had been successful in attracting funding to provide settlement and related services. While a regional guide for newcomers included a section on recreation, services for immigrants appeared to be led by economic agencies.

Yarmouth, a town of 7,162, is the largest community in south-west Nova Scotia. Like Truro, Yarmouth acts as a central service hub for the region. The Yarmouth library housed a staff position, the Immigrant Information Navigator, who provided settlement guidance, designed programs for immigrants, promoted multi-culturalism and immigration, and helped to further the social integration of immigrants. The region had an active newcomers group that offered social support and events for immigrants. The multicultural association was active and planned a large multicul-tural festival annually and held fundraising and social events. The town's recreation department had been supportive of these orga-nizations' efforts to create a supportive and inclusive environment for newcomers by, for example, offering programs in cooperation with these groups, including one called "Introduction to Winter." The provision of supports for immigrants through recreation pro-gramming in communities such as Yarmouth represents recogni-tion that support for immigrants extends beyond their economic contributions and includes supporting leisure lifestyles.

Rothesay, New Brunswick is a town of just under 12,000 in an urban adjacent location, about fifteen km outside Saint John, New Brunswick. Rothesay benefitted from its close proximity to Saint John, where there was an active newcomers' centre. The town shares a library with neighbouring town, Quispamsis. The library offered two simultaneous programs on Saturday morn-ings which focused on English language training: a conversation group for adults and a volunteer-led "Reading Buddies" program for children.

In the university town of Sackville, New Brunswick, arts and culture are a source of community pride. The town was given the Heritage Canada designation of "Cultural Capital of Canada" in 2008. True to this title, the town had undertaken several cultural initiatives, such as a public art project which involved the creation of public sculptures created by artists-in-residence from countries including Mexico, Germany, Belgium, Italy and France. The town's efforts to cultivate a variety of cultural and artistic op-portunities and events for residents seemed to have also created opportunities for the recognition and celebration of diversity. The town also seemed to benefit from its local university, which provided additional cultural opportunities such as summer language immersion camps for high school students.

## Discussion

Our findings indicate that small communities in Atlantic Canada are motivated to find ways to attract immigrants. However, program developers and policy makers in small communities have little guidance on which to base efforts to attract and welcome immigrants (Reitz and Banerjee 2007). Our study is a snapshot of community efforts to provide services and supports and in some cases these supports are specifically intended to address the needs of new immigrants. Clearly, more work needs to be done to fully understand how supports for new immigrants contribute to their well-being. However, we are able to make some initial observations based on the work completed so far.

People tend to immigrate to Canada to improve their job prospects and some immigrants are satisfied with the jobs they find in small communities (Bollman et al. 2007; Flint 2006). Yet, young immigrants and the children of immigrants have historically migrated in the same way as other Canadians, migrating to large urban centres in search of better jobs, to improve their education and to access other opportunities that are not as readily available in smaller centres (Houle 2007). As leisure researchers, we expect that quality of life issues (see also Natasha Hanson's chapter in this volume), social support and access to familiar traditional cultural practices likely play a part in some immigrants' choices to leave small communities and relocate to larger urban centres. However, the significance of these social supports tends to be obscured by the stronger emphasis on economic contributions. One observation is that the role of immigrants as contributors to the economic viability of small communities is prioritized in the public information we explored for this study. We noticed that when we contacted municipal governments to inquire about advertised initiatives that addressed the needs of new immigrants, we were often directed to departments of economic development. For example, when we contacted Summerside, PEI we were directed to the department responsible for economic development. In Summerside, social support for immigrants is fairly substantial but it is definitely an economic development initiative. We question how well the personal, social and leisure needs of immigrants are met by other communities when services are funded as economic development initiatives, especially for immigrants who come from countries with vastly different cultural values and traditions from the ones we know in Canada (see also the chapters by Dobrowolsky, Bryan and Barber, and by Ramos and Yoshida in this volume).

Related to this observation, social programs were often offered in small communities, but tended to be designed to give immigrants an opportunity to gain language fluency, and were mostly aimed at attracting and supporting family members who would be entering the workforce. Participation in community activities and acquiring language proficiency are important for all family members and we note that only in a few instances did communities provide social support programs that engaged all members of immigrant families.

A majority of the immigrants in Atlantic Canada are from the United States and from the United Kingdom (Statistics Canada 2010). Since their cultural practices are thought to be similar to those of Canadians, small communities may assume that social supports for these immigrants are unnecessary. We do not, however, know the settlement experiences of immigrants from the United States and United Kingdom, if they have traditional cultural practices that differ significantly from those of the communities where they settle, and if and how they find social supports in Atlantic Canada's small communities. We expect that as immigrants arrive in the region from parts of the world where traditional cultural practices are vastly different from the practices of Canadians, it is important for communities to create a welcoming environment and to support them in gaining language proficiency, developing social networks and becoming members of local communities.

Several of the small communities we included in this exploration are located in close proximity to larger, more urban areas. For example, Stratford, PEI, is located near the provincial capital of Charlottetown; Portugal Cove-St. Phillip's in Newfoundland and Labrador is located adjacent to St. John's, the provincial capital of that province; and Rothesay, New Brunswick is only a short distance from Saint John. In each of those cities there are universities that attract professional staff and faculty from around the world. Moreover, Sackville, New Brunswick is the location of Mount Allison University, which offers an extensive fine arts program and liberal arts education. Small communities that are located in close proximity to large urban areas and universities are unique in the context of this study because they may not need to provide extensive supports for immigrants; often, urban centres and institutions will provide many of the social and ethnic supports immigrants desire (Chiswick and Miller 2002). Those communities may attract immigrants who work in the larger urban centre. Communities that are located far from major urban areas may need to provide far more social supports in order to successfully attract immigrants and welcome them as members of the community. Yarmouth and Truro in Nova Scotia are examples of communities that have made efforts to create these supports.

While much of the immigration literature focuses on the primacy of jobs and how immigrants contribute to the Canadian economy, this study is different in that it focuses on efforts to provide social support and leisure opportunities for immigrants, which are strong contributors to overall well-being (Maninni et al. 2010). We recognize that many immigrants settle in places primarily based on the availability of jobs, but job satisfaction is only one aspect of well-being.

## Limitations of the Study

Our observations are based on profiles we compiled from small communities in Atlantic Canada from Census Canada data, and the types of information that people may be able to access on community websites and through phone calls to municipal government offices. We are not able to draw conclusions about what causes immigrants to settle quickly in a particular small community, or the kinds of services immigrants find most helpful in settling into a small community in Atlantic Canada. We also cannot discern what causes immigrants to leave the communities where they settle. We do support the continuation of research into several questions that arise out of our findings.

Our research suggests there are only a few examples of point of contact information that address the issue of the overall well-being of newcomers. What is more, immigrants need a certain degree of language proficiency to access the information we acquired for this study. We are not able to conclude how well the information we accessed reaches and informs the new immigrants it is designed to serve. We expect that many immigrants access informal networks through friends and relatives and these may provide the supports they need. Further research into the experience of immigrants is necessary in order to understand those informal supports and the role they play in the settlement experiences of newcomers.

We also recommend that research into the subjective experiences of immigrants in small communities in Atlantic Canada be conducted. In this context, subjective experiences refer to the meanings immigrants attach to their experiences. This type of study will contribute to our understanding of how immigrants access information, services, programs and other supports and their perceptions of how helpful those supports were. By learning about the subjective experiences of new immigrants we will gain a better understanding of how their expectations and aspirations unfold over time and how they are supported or hindered in reaching personal, family and career goals.

We expect it is important for agencies supporting cultural, spiritual, artistic and leisure interests to be funded adequately to address the needs of immigrants. We realize that many of these agencies may well be providing supports and the information they use to promote their services may not have been accessible through our study. To understand the role of social support and leisure in the well-being of new immigrants, we suggest that studies be developed to explore the type(s) of social activities or organizations that immigrants find most helpful. Which of these services contribute to the long-term retention of immigrants in small communities in Atlantic Canada? What role does the public and not-for-profit leisure delivery system have for supporting new immigrants in the settlement process?

**Notes**

1. For some communities with few immigrants, all the countries of origin are named, but for those with more immigrants of varied origin, only the most prevalent countries of origin are listed.

2. Statistics about the demographic characteristics of each community were compiled using the Canadian Census Analyser to access data from the 2006 Canada Census. Statistics Canada uses random rounding and data suppression to protect privacy of individuals in categories where there are few cases (Statistics Canada 2007). Data suppression means that the data will show "0" if there are very few individuals with a certain characteristic. Random rounding refers to the rounding of all figures so that all values end in "0" or "5." Whether a particular statistic is rounded up or down is random, with a higher probability of rounding in the direction with the smaller increment between the actual and rounded number. Because of random rounding and data suppression, the totals listed may not match the sum of individual categories (Statistics Canada 2007). Random rounding and data suppression mean that the data does not represent the actual number of cases, but rather provides a more general depiction or "profile" of the composition of a community.

## References

Akbari, Ather H. 2011. Labour Market Performance of Immigrants in Smaller Regions of Western Countries: Some Evidence from Atlantic Canada. *International Migration and Integration* 12: 133-54.

Akbari, Ather H. and Colin Sun. 2006. Immigrant Attraction and Retention: What Can Work and What is Being Done in Atlantic Canada? *Our Diverse Cities* 2: 129-33.

Akbari, Ather H., Scott Lynch, Wimal Rankaduwa and Ted McDonald. 2008. Immigrants in Atlantic Canada: A Socio-Demographic Profile. *Our Diverse Cities* 5: 8-10.

Bollman, Ray D., Roland Beshiri and Heather Clemenson. 2007. Immigrants to Rural Canada. *Our Diverse Cities* 3: 9-15.

Bruce, David. 2007. The Challenges of Immigration as a Rural Repopulation Strategy in Maritime Canada. *Our Diverse Cities* 3: 90-96.

Canada Census Community Profiles. 2006. Available from Statistics Canada Community Profiles website. http://www12.statcan.ca/census-recensement/2006/dp-pd/prof/92-591/index.cfm?Lang=E. (accessed July 11, 2011).

Chiswick, Barry R. and Paul W. Miller. 2002. Do Enclaves Matter in Immigrant Adjustment? *Discussion paper 449*. Bonn, Germany: Institute for the Study of Labor.

Conference Board of Canada. 2005. *Socio-Economic Benefits of Sport Participation in Canada*. Ottawa: Conference Board of Canada.

Doherty, Alison and Tracy Taylor. 2007. Sport and Physical Recreation in the Settlement of Immigrant Youth. *Leisure/Loisir* 31 (1): 27-55.

Eccles, Jacquelynne S. and Bonnie Barber. 1999. Student Council, Volunteering, Basketball, or Marching Band: What Kind of Extracurricular Involvement Matters? *Journal of Adolescent Research* 14:10-43.

Fisher, Karen E., Joan C. Durrance and Marian Bouch Hinton. 2004. Information Grounds and the Use of Need-Based Services by Immigrants in Queens, New York: A Context-Based, Outcome Evaluation Approach. *Journal of the American Society for Information Science and Technology* 55 (8): 754–66.

Flint, J. David. 2006. *Rural Immigrants Who Come to Stay: A Case Study of Recent Immigrants to Colchester County, Nova Scotia*. AMC Working Papers Series.

Frisby, Wendy, Ted Alexander and Janna Taylor. 2010. Play is Not a Frill: Poor Youth Facing the Past, Present, and Future of Public Recreation in Canada. In *Lost kids: Vulnerable Children and Youth in Canada, the U.S., and Australia, 1900 to the Present*, ed. M. Gleason, T. Myers, L. Paris and V. Strong-Boag, 215-29. Vancouver: UBC Press.

Heinonen, Tuula, Carol D. H. Harvey and Karen M. Fox. 2005. Leisure as Part of Cultural Retention of Finnish-Canadian Immigrants. *Leisure/ Loisir* 31:105-32.

Houle, Rene. 2007. Secondary Migration of New Immigrants to Canada. *Our Diverse Cities* 3:16-24.

Iwasaki, Yoshi and Roger C. Mannell. 2000. Hierarchical Dimensions of Leisure Stress Coping. *Leisure Sciences* 22:163-81.

Kaur, Harleen 2010. Nova Scotia Needs More Immigrant Farmers. *Canada Updates* October 21.

Kelly, John R. 1996. *Leisure*, 3rd ed. Boston, MA: Allyn & Bacon.

Livingston, Lori A., Susan C. Tirone, Emma L. Smith and Andrew J. Miller. (Forthcoming). Participation in Coaching by Canadian Immigrants: Individual and Sport System Accommodations Required. *International Journal of Sports Science and Coaching*.

Mininni, Giuseppe, Amelia Manuti, Rosa Scardigno and Rosella Rubino. 2010. Subjective Well-being Between Organizational Bonds and Cultural Contaminations. *World Futures* 66: 87-97.

Ontario Council for Agencies Serving Immigrants (OCASI). 2005. *OCASI Research on Inclusive Recreation Model for Immigrants and Refugee Youth: A Provisional Model – Abridged Version*. Toronto: OCASI.

Orthner, Dennis K and Jay A. Mancini. 1990. Leisure Impacts on Family Interaction and Cohesion. *Journal of Leisure Research* 22:125-37.

Putnam, Robert D. 1995. Bowling Alone: America's Declining Social Capital: An Interview with Robert Putnam. *Journal of Democracy* 6 (1): 65-78.

Reitz, Jeffrey G. and Rupa Banerjee. 2007. Racial Inequality, Social Cohesion, and Policy Issues in Canada. In *Belonging? Diversity, Recognition and Shared Citizenship in Canada*, ed. T. J. Banting, T. J. Courchene and F. L. Seidle, 489-545. Montreal: Institute for Research on Public Policy.

Spiers, Andrew and Gordon J. Walker. 2009. The Effects of Ethnicity and Leisure Satisfaction on Happiness, Peacefulness, and Quality of Life. *Leisure Sciences* 31:84-99.

Spicer, Neil. 2008. Places of Exclusion and Inclusion: Asylum-Seeker and Refugee Experiences of Neighbourhoods in the U.K.. *Journal of Ethnic and Migration Studies* 34:491-510.

Statistics Canada. 2007. *Data Quality, Sampling and Weighting, Confidentiality and Random Rounding.* http://www12.statcan.ca/census-recensement/2006/ref/dict/app-ann002-eng.cfm (accessed April 12, 2011).

Statistics Canada. 2010. *2006 Census of Canada Census Subdivision Profile Tables* [data file]. Available using the Canadian Census Analyser at http://dc1.chass.utoronto.ca/census/. Toronto, ON: University of Toronto.

Sullivan, Anne-Marie, Kathleen Ring and Savanna Harris. 2009. *Exploring the Meaning of Welcoming Communities for Immigrants in Newfoundland and Labrador.* St. John's: Harris Centre, Memorial University of Newfoundland.

Tirone, Susan. 1999-2000. Racism, Indifference and the Leisure Experiences of South Asian Canadian Teens. *Leisure/Loisir: The Journal of the Canadian Association of Leisure Studies* 24 (1): 89-114.

Tirone, Susan and Alison Pedlar. 2005. Leisure, Place and Diversity: The Experience of Ethnic Minority Young Adults. *Canadian Ethnic Studies* 37 (2): 32-48.

Walseth, Kristin 2006. Sport and Belonging. *International Review for the Sociology of Sport* 41 (3): 447-64.

Wilkinson, Lori and Alison Kalischuk. 2009. Recent Trends in Migration to Third-Tier Centres in the Prairies. *Our Diverse Cities* 6 (Spring): 18-25.

# 8

# Immigrant Adolescents' Journey to Belonging in New Brunswick: Making Friends with Local-born Peers

*Stacey Wilson-Forsberg*

*"Home" is where they accept you for who you are and they are willing and eager to listen to your story. A lot of people just don't; all of us, some of us, or most of us don't really care to listen to newcomers' stories. That happens. It would be hard for local people to get to know a stranger, and to be really close to a stranger, and, especially a stranger from across the world who knows little English. (Van Anh, Vietnam)[1]*

Adolescence (ages twelve to twenty) is an awkward time for migration to occur. While many immigrant adolescents adapt well to Canada and ultimately go on to live comfortable and fulfilled lives, research suggests that the difficulties faced by adolescents in moving to adulthood become compounded by the immigration experience. Immigrant adolescents must adjust to a new culture and, often, a new language, as well as to new surroundings, while simultaneously balancing the contradictory expectations of both family and peers (Anisef and Kilbride 2000; Beiser et al. 2005; Rajiva 2005). Making Atlantic Canada a "home away from home" for immigrant adolescents is a particularly crucial consideration given that these are the citizens of the future. Engaged and attentive citizens build the social networks and resources required to sustain the small cities and towns of the Atlantic Provinces and help to make them more receptive to change and diversity.

This chapter documents the everyday worlds of immigrant adolescents as they adjust to their new lives and gradually acquire a sense of belonging to a small city and rural town in the province of New Brunswick where there are no earlier non-European immigrant communities to which the young newcomers can affix themselves. Finding a sense of belonging to the receiving society involves connecting oneself to the surrounding environment, people and social institutions to become part of a larger structure (Wilson-Forsberg 2012). It also involves a feeling of interdependence that is maintained by supporting or being supported by others (McMillan and Chavis 1986; Sarason 1974). The chapter reveals that immigrant adolescents first and foremost draw upon their friendship networks to help them cope with the move to a new society. Networks of friends help them to find their way around, learn the unwritten rules and practices of a new culture, and become confident and settled.

### Immigrant Adolescents in New Brunswick

In the decades following the Second World War, New Brunswick attracted few immigrants and many of them quickly left the province for better economic opportunities and more generous immigrant adjustment programs elsewhere in Canada (Steel 2006). However, immigration to New Brunswick has increased in recent years, especially since the province signed its Provincial Nominee Agreement with Ottawa in 1999. The province also receives government-sponsored refugees each year, as well as temporary foreign workers and foreign students from around the world.[2]

Although all of the Atlantic Provinces now have immigration strategies in place, settlement in New Brunswick is unique. Newfoundland and Labrador, Nova Scotia and Prince Edward Island all have one metropolitan centre serving as the destination point for most of their immigrants, but immigrants destined for New Brunswick are dispersed among three cities and three small towns, dividing government-sponsored programs for their settlement and integration into smaller portions, and also dividing the social support networks of family and friends found in their own small ethnic communities. As Canada's only officially bilingual province, moreover, the protection of Francophone language, culture and identity puts New Brunswick in a distinctive position with respect to immigration in the Atlantic Provinces. Approximately 30 per cent of immigrants recruited to New Brunswick are Francophone.

The findings of the research summarized here are based on qualitative data collected through semi-structured interviews and focus groups over an eleven-month period in 2008-2009 with thirty-three immigrant adolescents and fifty-two other volunteer participants in Fredericton (population: 50,535) and Florenceville-Bristol (population: 1,500) (Table 8.1). Qualitative research cannot determine which variable best predicts an immigrant adolescent's sense of belonging to a community; however, qualitative research can collect people's feelings and perceptions about some of those variables. In describing their experiences adapting to the two communities, the teens gave me the privilege of listening to their beliefs, dreams and motivations. From their words, I came to have a better understanding of what "home" means to them.

By highlighting the integration process as it occurs at both the individual and community levels through the formation of friendships with local-born peers, the chapter shows the young immigrants and local residents interacting with one another, and the gradual changes that occur as a result of that interaction. It also reveals differences between a small urban setting and a rural setting with respect to the settlement and adaptation of the immigrant adolescents. Although Florenceville-Bristol does not have the formal programs for immigrant adolescents that a city the size of Fredericton is able to deliver, the citizens of Florenceville-Bristol compensate for this absence by generally being more involved in their settlement and integration than the citizens of Fredericton. Their ability to recognize the strengths and abilities of the immigrant adolescents (and immigrants in general), and to include them in activities and structures where they would have the best fit, assists the adolescents in finding a sense of belonging in the community.

At the time of data collection, Fredericton was home to approximately 350 immigrant adolescents. My case study of the community involved twenty adolescents who immigrated to Fredericton as dependants of provincially nominated or economic immigrant parents, the dependants of refugees, or as international students with the intention of applying for permanent residency in Canada. Together these teens formed a varied group representing an assortment of cultural, linguistic and socio-economic backgrounds from a variety of source countries, including Belgium, Colombia, Congo, Iran, Indonesia and Vietnam (Table 8.2). The thirteen immigrant adolescents (out of a total population of fourteen) interviewed in Florenceville-Bristol were from a relatively homogeneous group of middle-class or aspiring middle-class families. With the exception of two international students from South Korea, eleven were the adolescent children of economic or provincially nominated parents from Colombia, India, Mexico and Moldova. All but the two Korean teens had at least one parent working at the McCain Foods, Ltd. Global Technology Centre (Table 8.3).

### Fredericton: "How Am I Going to Make Friends with These Kids?"

The city of Fredericton demonstrated that immigrant adolescents' opportunities to come into contact with and befriend local-born peers are often limited. The process of making friends with the New Brunswick-born adolescents was difficult for most of the immigrant adolescents in Fredericton, and for those participants who were recent arrivals at the time of my interviews, that process was still far from complete. "Making friends? Well out of a scale of one to a million, I would say a million," said Callie (Liberia).

Part of the difficulty in making friends was related to immigrant adolescents and local adolescents not making the effort to get to know one another. On the topic of active engagement with immigrant adolescents, participants in Fredericton debated the question "who should reach out to whom?" or "where should that effort come from?" They acknowledged that the effort is "lop-sided" with immigrants expected to adjust, change and integrate into Fredericton, while local residents go on with their lives in their normal fashion. For the immigrant adolescents, integration was not a "two-way street requiring accommodation and adjustments, and rights and responsibilities, on the part of both newcomers and the host society" (Biles et al. 2008). They felt that the effort to fit in with their New Brunswick-born peers rested solely with them. They had to learn enough English to understand and be understood and then worked hard at fitting in and making friends. Yet, a small number of them were not socially savvy enough to connect with others and even after three years in the city they still did not have friends.

In an ideal situation, immigrant adolescents' attempts at learning about their new society and its institutions would be matched by attempts by their New Brunswick-born peers to learn more about them. My research findings suggest a sense of ambivalence and a lack of commitment on the part of established residents in Fredericton to reach out to immigrants to the same degree as they expect immigrants to adapt to the mainstream. According to the International Student Advisor at UNB: "The thing that is most difficult or unwelcoming about the cultural mix here is not as overt as someone yelling at you telling you to get out of their city, but rather more subtle in that most local community members don't notice you are here at all." Immigrant adolescents reported that they wanted to be noticed, not because they were different, but because they were normal teens with the same needs as any other teen in Fredericton. Most of the immigrant adolescent participants felt ignored and at times invisible at school and in the wider community. The teens wanted their peers to reach out and pull them into their groups and activities. Every one of the immigrant adolescent participants described how difficult it was to get to know people in Fredericton and to become involved in the community. They saw the flurry of activity around them, but did not understand how to take part in it.

This sense of ambivalence and lack of commitment may not have been intentional, but rather the result of an attempt by citizens of Fredericton to be polite and non-intrusive in the lives of immigrants to give them the chance to blend into the community. However, the citizens became so polite and non-intrusive that they crossed over the line of politeness or political consciousness to the point of ignoring immigrants altogether. By way of illustration, teachers questioned how much attention is too much when adolescents want nothing more than to blend in with their peers at school:

> Sometimes teachers want to make a big deal about a student being from a different culture. They welcome that student by attempting to celebrate that culture and certainly they mean well by this. When I want to be welcoming I try not to draw attention to that and it is not because I don't want to know about that student's culture but because I want the student to feel a part of the immediate culture of where they are now. I want that child to feel like he or she is as much a part of this culture as any other child in the classroom. (Philip Sexsmith, Fredericton, NB)

A similar argument holds for the additional language classrooms in the two Fredericton high schools. By providing the immigrant adolescents "sheltered" instruction in special classrooms, the English as an additional language (EAL) programs separated the immigrant adolescents from their English-speaking peers for almost the entire day. Because the immigrant adolescents who participated in my research were segregated in EAL classrooms, they had limited access to a network of peers beyond their immediate immigrant group and across immigrant groups. Research conducted by Carola Suárez-Orozco and colleagues (2008; 2010) in the United States reveals that, in many cases, immigrant youth have almost no meaningful contact with English-speaking peers. More than one-third of the immigrant students in these studies reported that they had little opportunity to interact with peers who were not from their country of origin, which clearly contributed to their linguistic isolation.

Another obstacle to making friends in Fredericton, according to my research findings, relates to finding common ground. Some of the immigrant adolescent participants claimed they were too different from their local peers: they had different cultural, or in some cases socio-economic, backgrounds; they looked different; they spoke another language; and they had different beliefs and values than their local peers. It was also apparent in my data that perceptions of differential treatment based on racialization defined the self-worth and aspirations of the refugee adolescents from West Africa who participated in the Fredericton case study. This circumstance made community resources and a network of social support that much more critical for them to achieve their full potential in life. Callie, for example, equated her inability to make friends with the colour of her skin:

> I meet people at school but a friend, a real friend who has the same interests as I do and is from my background, or at least understands my background, it is impossible. I don't mean to be racist, but really I'm the only black kid. I feel very different. Sometimes I walk into a room full of white kids and I wonder how I should act. I want to fit in but I also want to be myself. So I find it easier to make friends with people of my colour and from my background. I try to approach kids at school but I feel like my English is no good or it sounds mixed up and I just look different than they do. (Callie, Liberia)

It remains unclear in my data whether the exclusion described by Callie and the other racialized teens has less to do with their race and more to do with their families' low socioeconomic status. Whether associated with race or socioeconomic status, it was nevertheless evident that the non-white refugee adolescents of low socioeconomic status (who made up about half of the population sample in the Fredericton case study) were not making contact with their white, middle-class peers as relative equals. In his 1954 book *The Nature of Prejudice*, Gordon Allport proposed that, under certain conditions, bringing together individuals from opposing groups could reduce inter-group prejudice. Perhaps the most critical condition in the contact hypothesis is that both groups perceive equal status in a given situation (Cohen 1982; Riordan and Ruggiero 1980). If one party has advantages that the other does not, then this unbalances power (qtd. in Wilson-Forsberg 2013).

That most of these stories were told by girls is not coincidental. The girls who participated in the Fredericton case study found it far more challenging to meet people and make friends than the boys. The idea that immigrant girls often experience a more difficult adjustment to the receiving community is discussed in literature on immigrant integration and adolescent development. Girls tend to have more household responsibilities and experience more parental control than boys; they are also more likely to take on the role of cultural broker (i.e., parenting the parents) than their brothers (Van Ngo and Schleifer 2005; Rajiva 2005). Yet, my findings did not reveal a significant difference between girls and boys in this regard. The boys who participated in the case study of Fredericton talked about their parents as much as the girls and none of the adolescents described cultural or generational conflicts with their parents. The girls took their education more seriously and held higher grades in school than the boys, but it was not clear to me how much control parents had over their study habits.

However, my findings also suggest different gendered norms in terms of leisure activities and the networks around them. For instance, soccer played a critical role in the integration of immigrant boys in Fredericton. Team sports such as soccer offered a meeting place where social interactions with local peers were stimulated and where the immigrant adolescents could be noticed, respected and appreciated by peers despite their level of fluency in English or French. This finding is consistent with previous studies of athletics and minority youth indicating that minority youth have the opportunity to feel more accepted by their peers if they participate and excel at a particular sport (Weiss and Duncan 1992; Chan 1998, 1999). While all but one of the boys who participated in the case study played soccer, none of the girls were involved in team sports.

### Florenceville-Bristol: "My Best Friend Means Everything to Me"

The rural town of Florenceville-Bristol enabled a close consideration of the interactions taking place among the immigrant adolescents and their friends as well as the larger social dynamics occurring within the community. The difficulties associated with making friends in Fredericton were not central to my discussions with the immigrant adolescents in Florenceville-Bristol. Friendliness and curiosity on the part of the local adolescents in Florenceville-Bristol appear to have facilitated the development of close friendships with the immigrant adolescents. The lack of separate EAL classrooms in the town's two schools served to increase the extent and sources of contact between the two groups, providing the immigrant adolescents with a sense of membership in the school community. The immigrant adolescents described New Brunswick-born friends as enabling an emotional sense of belonging and acceptance, as well as providing tangible help with homework assignments, language translations, orientation to school and advice about university and potential careers. They were afforded a network of knowledgeable local peers who supported them in their adjustment to school and the wider community—it was precisely this network that many of their Fredericton counterparts were missing.

In Florenceville-Bristol, the immigrant adolescents stood out as newcomers. Local residents were curious about where they came from and why they were in the community. That sense of curiosity was particularly obvious in the schools where students appeared to be much more aware of the world than their counterparts in Fredericton. Learning about the source countries of their immigrant peers had been incorporated into the academic curriculum and, sometimes, if they received advance warning of new students coming from abroad, the teachers would prepare the local students for their arrival through the use of geography books, online articles and audiovisual materials. When interviewed, the staff and students in Florenceville-Bristol's schools had no problem describing the personality and strengths of each immigrant adolescent. By way of illustration, three of the newcomer teens were exceptionally musical. Even before they learned English, staff and students were able to recognize their musical talents and tap into them. Ale, who played the piano, clarinet and saxophone, was recruited by the school band soon after she arrived and was also invited to play the background music for the Carleton North High School graduation prom; and Eric, a singer, dancer and athlete, earned the nickname "South Korea's Justin Timberlake" from local peers who held him in high esteem. The immigrant adolescents said they were included in groups and activities at school and the wider community, and even more so once they learned enough English to be able to communicate. They also spent time at the homes of their New Brunswick-born friends and reciprocated with invitations to their houses.

In accordance with Allport's (1954) contact hypothesis, contact between the young newcomers and their local peers occurred on a more equal footing in Florenceville-Bristol than in Fredericton because all of the immigrant adolescent participants came from middle-class professional families. Florenceville-Bristol is largely a one-industry town with many adults employed by the various divisions of McCain Foods, Ltd. This employment situation increased the likelihood that the immigrant adolescents' families interacted with each other and with local families, hence facilitating an easier integration into the community. Furthermore, provincially nominated immigrant parents working as systems engineers and computer programmers at the McCain Global Technology Centre would ultimately develop close ties with other middle class educated professionals allowing the parents to gain access to a broad range of social resources and information channels. These proved useful to their adolescent children as they integrated into the community. The Florenceville-Bristol schools also enabled equal contact through their inspired efforts to communicate with and teach the immigrant adolescents, as well as their efforts to include them in a wide array of extracurricular activities. In his study of the integration of immigrant youth in Israel, Reuvin Kahane (1986) revealed that immigrant students integrated better into schools with less formal curricula and teaching methods because they provided a context in which young immigrants could meet local youth and adults on their own terms and on a relatively equal footing. The immigrant adolescents in Florenceville-Bristol may actually have benefitted from the deficiency of formal programs for their integration into the schools. In particular, further study is needed on the benefits and drawbacks of EAL classes for small numbers of immigrant students in middle and high schools.

Incidents of racism were not mentioned at all by the adolescent participants, though it is important to note that in the social construction of race almost all of the teens from Colombia and Mexico in this case study would be considered "Caucasian" or "white"; only those from India and South Korea would be viewed as members of a visible minority group. And yet, I found it curious that local residents still associated the immigrants in Florenceville-Bristol with being "non-white." As one local resident put it "we are white and considered rich and they are darker and give up a lot to come to this country; therefore we need to do everything we can as a community to help them adapt to their new surroundings" (Local Resident). "Whiteness," in this case, appears to be the hidden norm and exclusive standard by which all other members of our society are measured (James 2003). It generates "we" feelings among the members when they share common belief and experience (Lazos 1998). This social construction of whiteness also brings to mind the "typical" Atlantic Canadian community where those not born there "come from away" no matter the length of time they have resided in the community.

With respect to gender, the immigrant girls in Florenceville-Bristol spoke with just as much enthusiasm about their friends as the boys. While two of the research participants noted conflicting values between themselves and New Brunswick-born girls with respect to dating and underage drinking, the girls appeared to be fitting into the community as much as their male counterparts. Two points are worth noting with respect to gender. First, the girls in the immigrant adolescent population outnumbered the boys. Of the fourteen immigrant adolescents in the community, nine were girls. Second, the girls were more involved in their schools and the school sports teams, which appeared to be less competitive and more welcoming to the girls. It is not that the Florenceville-Bristol schools offered more activities for girls than the larger schools in Fredericton; rather, the Florenceville-Bristol schools were better at encouraging the girls to participate in the activities that were offered by recognizing their interests and talents.

### "Are We Home Yet?" The Four States of Belonging

Finding a sense of belonging to a community involves building confidence in one's own identity and connecting oneself to the surrounding environment, people and social institutions. Young people from other cultural backgrounds face the additional challenge of deciding about their ethnic identity. Some researchers suggest that adolescents move steadily from a stage of ethnic or "racial unawareness," to one of "exploration," to a final stage of an "achieved" sense of racial or ethnic identity (Marcia 1966). Others note that the process of identity formation is more accurately described as "spiraling" back to revisit previous stages, each time from a different vantage point (Parham 1989). Still others argue that identity formation is not simply a process by which one passes through a variety of stages on the way to achieving a stable identity. Rather it is a process that is fluid and contextually driven (Suárez-Orozco 2003).

Positive psycho-social outcomes for immigrant adolescents are expected to be related to a strong identification with both their ethnic group and the larger receiving society (LaFromboise et al. 1993; Phinney et al. 2001). The notion of immigrants bringing their culture and a fixed, stable identity with them, moreover, has been replaced by the postmodern conception of a continuous process of identity formation and weaving together elements of the old and new cultures. Thus, over time, young immigrants learn to become part of a new society, peer group and school, while continuing to develop a sense of belonging related to their home country, culture, language and religion (Simard 2007).

Finding a sense of belonging to Fredericton and Florenceville-Bristol was a lengthy process for the immigrant adolescents who participated in this research, but in the end almost all of the adolescents were able to make, or were in the process of making, connections with a variety of people in the two communities. The data suggests that for the thirty-three immigrant adolescents I interviewed, there were at least four states of belonging at that specific moment in time:

(1) Bicultural and well-adjusted

Eight immigrant adolescent participants who had been in the receiving community for more than three years at the time of their interviews appeared to be happy, well-adjusted teens. Having arrived when they were entering adolescence, they adopted a bicultural identity and appeared to be confident, comfortable and fulfilled by their new lives. The teachers who participated in the case studies of Fredericton and Florenceville-Bristol commented that they could see these students growing, finding their place in the school, and beginning to have a bicultural attitude whereby they celebrated their own selves, appreciating their cultural root, but learning to love their new culture as well. These adolescents spoke with poise; they appeared to possess a deep self-understanding, and were astute and observant of their surroundings. Although they admitted to being bored at times, they were generally happy and regarded themselves as valued members of their communities. Jaime, for example, arrived in Fredericton from Colombia when he was in grade six. He was in grade eleven when interviewed:

> It is hard to say that I belong, but I think for the most part
> I probably do. It is like anywhere; once you have been here
> long enough; once you make friends and find a space for

yourself in the community then you think "yes I belong here." (Jaime, Colombia)

Heena arrived in Florenceville in grade six and at the time of her interview was preparing to graduate from Carleton North High School and leave the town for university in Ontario:

> I have strong family values. I know who I am and what is expected of me. I want to become something important and be successful in life. Yes I come from an entirely different culture, but this town feels like home now. I can't go anywhere without wanting to go back home to Florenceville. (Heena, India)

As indicated by Heena, most of the immigrant adolescents would ultimately leave Florenceville-Bristol to attend university. Once they leave they are not likely to return; and more often than not, immigrant parents follow their grown children to other parts of Canada, according to my research findings. Fredericton, to the contrary, is more likely to retain its immigrant adolescents for a longer period of time by encouraging them to attend university or community college there or by presenting them with the opportunity to return after they migrate to other cities to pursue careers.

Two other participants, who appeared to fit this bicultural, well-adjusted state of belonging, arrived in the community more recently as older adolescents. Ale, for example, had been in Florenceville-Bristol for less than a year when interviewed. A grade eleven student, she was still developing fluency in English and could find plenty of things wrong with the small rural town, yet she simultaneously demonstrated the same confidence, comfort and contentment with her new life. The last example of a bicultural, well-adjusted immigrant adolescent is Stefan despite the fact that he had only been in Florenceville-Bristol for a matter of weeks when I interviewed him. Stefan's enthusiastic responses to the interview questions, however, may have reflected the early phase of what Adrian Furnam and Stephen Boschner (1982) describe in the literature as a U-shaped curve of adjustment in which immigrants initially feel optimism and joy, followed by confusion and frustration, which eventually becomes satisfaction and confidence.

(2) Torn between two cultures

Seven of the immigrant adolescents described being in a cultural dilemma where they too were in the process of constructing a bicultural identity for themselves, but they did not understand exactly what that identity was and what they should do with it. These immigrant adolescent participants had been in the community for less than three years when interviewed. The teens were beginning to feel comfortable in Fredericton and Florenceville-Bristol, but also missed "home" so they felt torn between two cultures and unsure if they belonged to either. They felt compelled to choose between embracing Canadian mainstream culture and the values and traditions of their home countries. Participant Van Anh actually had an acronym for it:

> I feel like a "TCK" kid, a "third culture kid," because when I go home to Vietnam I'm too Western and I don't fit with Vietnamese people, but I don't fit here either because I have had an entirely different life experience. (Van Anh, Vietnam)

The participants admitted to feeling unsure if a bicultural identity is "acceptable." By way of illustration, Jorge had been in Florenceville-Bristol for two years and while he blended in with his local peers with respect to dress, accent and shared interests, he still claimed to live between two cultures:

> Sometimes I do belong here, sometimes I don't. I think I belong to two different places. Is that okay? It feels weird, like I am living in half a culture. Maybe someday I will feel more comfortable living in two cultures, but as a teenager it just feels complicated. (Jorge, Colombia)

(3) Struggling but optimistic

Fourteen (almost half) of the participants who had been in the community for less than three years and still identified primarily with their home culture did not feel like they belonged to Fredericton or Florenceville-Bristol, and did not feel at home in the communities. However, they expressed optimism about their future in New Brunswick and confidence that the sense of belonging will come with time. The teens were aware that being in the province could offer them excellent opportunities and they were ready to "fulfill their dreams." Most of the immigrant adolescents who fit this category were refugees in Fredericton. They were not necessarily happy in their school or neighbourhood, but they felt safe and knew that if they persevered there was light at the end of the tunnel. Abo, for example, had a tough three years in Fredericton. Having "gotten in with a bad group of kids," and having found himself in more than one sticky situation with law enforcement, Abo learned the hard way that not all social networks are beneficial to him. When interviewed, he was spending more time alone exercising and writing, and he hoped to take acting classes. He seemed to be aware of who he was and where he needed to go:

> I want to be an actor. I want to be famous. But when I am famous I will still be the same person. I will appreciate what I have here, but I won't forget where I come from. I won't forget my family back home. I will visit them and give them money. I want to take advantage of all the opportunities here so I can make lots of money and send it to Sierra Leone where they can use it to buy artificial limbs for people. Because you know in Sierra Leone during the war they cut people's hands and arms off, and also they can use it to start a national soccer team. (Abo, Sierra Leone)

The immigrant adolescents who had recently arrived as the dependants of provincial nominees also fit in this category in Fredericton, but less so in Florenceville-Bristol where they appeared to be more content and at ease. Their parents made the decision to immigrate to Canada to take advantage of educational opportunities for their children and give them better lives. The adolescent children did not ask to come here and, while their parents have their best interests at heart, the adolescents had not necessarily "bought into their program yet." Heo, for example, understood why her family had come to Canada and planned to make the most of the experience:

> No I don't think I belong here, but maybe someday I will belong. My parents came here so that me and my brother can have better opportunities. It hasn't been easy though and now my parents and my brother are not sure if they want to stay here, but I think despite everything, I will stay because there will be more opportunities here for me. (Heo, South Korea)

(4) Lost in translation

Length of time in the communities did not seem to make a difference to the two immigrant adolescent participants who did not feel that they belonged, and were pessimistic about ever finding that sense of belonging. The teens were struggling to learn English, overcome culture shock and make friends in their new community. Mateo, for example, had been in Fredericton for three years when interviewed. He arrived in the community from Colombia via Florenceville-Bristol where his family resided. High grades in university and flawless English aside, I detected sadness in his words:

> No I don't belong here. Not at all. I don't have any friends here really. I haven't made friends with any of the local students and I haven't met any of the Latin Americans. I guess I haven't been committed to finding friends. I don't make friends easily. I don't know. I understand why my family can't go back to Colombia. I understand why New Brunswick is a better place to raise a family, and to have better opportunities, and I accept that but that doesn't mean I have to be happy about it. (Mateo, Colombia)

Mark had immigrated to Fredericton the previous year from English-Speaking Liberia. When asked to describe what a welcoming community meant to him he replied with a cracking voice "it means home." Claiming to have no friends and no prospect of meeting peers in his largely white middle school or in the low-income apartment complex where he resided, Mark wanted only to return to Africa. Referring to a group of Jehovah's Witnesses who frequent his apartment complex he noted, "at the apartment we met some church people who brought us to church. That's fine but I wanted to meet my neighbours. I want to make friends and feel at home here."

## Conclusion

The data suggest that for immigrant adolescents the development of friendships in a small urban community is quite different from that of a rural community. In Fredericton there is little purposeful contact between the immigrant adolescents and their New Brunswick-born peers, while informal and spontaneous efforts of friendly engaged citizens in Florenceville-Bristol appear to ease the development of friendships and intra-group relations. Despite this difference, the immigrant adolescents in both communities appeared to have undergone similar journeys to belonging resulting in, for the most part, relatively positive outcomes. It would be incorrect to state at this juncture that all of the immigrant adolescents who participated in the research were part of peer networks and were happy with their new lives. However, the majority were involved in activities in their schools and wider community. They were generally doing well in school, and each adolescent expressed a desire to pursue post-secondary education.

Immigrant adolescents in Fredericton comprised a more diverse group than their counterparts in Florenceville-Bristol due to the addition of refugees from West Africa to the population, all of whom were members of a racial minority group. Nevertheless, if I remove the ten refugees from the Fredericton sample, and compare only the ten economic immigrants (including the international students) with the thirteen economic immigrants in Florenceville-Bristol, my findings would remain the same. The five provincial nominees in Fredericton did not experience the same discrimination and economic hardship as the ten refugees, but they were equally lonely, friendless and unsure of their sense of belonging. The citizens of Fredericton were not only ambivalent toward refugees, they were ambivalent toward the economic immigrants as well and especially those from non-European source countries.

My findings in the two New Brunswick communities bring to mind Augie Fleras's line of reasoning that the key challenge in securing a welcoming, inclusive society is not about integrating minorities and migrants, but about ensuring they become equal citizens who are emotionally bonded to society and to other members of society through ties of mutual commitment, engagement and attachment (Fleras 2009). The immigrant adolescents who participated in my research had to adapt to their new environment, learn a new language and gradually take on the responsibilities, involvement and obligations that citizenship entails. And yet, their local-born peers also had to adapt, make concessions and fulfill their social responsibilities toward the immigrant adolescents. In Florenceville-Bristol this process of acculturation was balanced and reciprocal. In Fredericton it was not, as demonstrated by the seemingly formidable task of making friends. Generalizing theoretical findings from this sample to a wider immigrant population in the Atlantic Provinces or across Canada was not the aim of my research. However, the clear urban/rural contrast with respect to the dynamics of integration and citizenship in the New Brunswick data is a tentative starting point for future research on the "warmth of the welcome" in Atlantic Canada and beyond.

| TABLE 8.1 OVERVIEW OF PARTICIPANTS | |
|---|---|
| Category of Participants | Total |
| Immigrant Adolescents | 33 |
| New Brunswick-Born Adolescents | 10 |
| Immigrant Adults who stayed in community | 6 |
| Immigrant Adults who left community | 4 |
| Community Organization Members | 20 |
| Local Residents | 12 |
| Total in Sample | 85 |

| TABLE 8.2 PARTICIPANTS FREDERICTON | | | | |
|---|---|---|---|---|
| Sex | Age | Source Country | Mother Tongue | Official Language | Immigrant Classification |
| M | 14 | Congo | French/ Swahili | French/ English | Refugee |
| M | 12 | Congo | French/ Swahili | French/ English | Refugee |
| M | 12 | Liberia | English | English | Refugee |
| M | 13 | Colombia | Spanish | English | Refugee |
| M | 17 | Sierra Leone | English | English/ French | Refugee |
| M | 16 | Guatemala | Spanish | English | Refugee |
| F | 13 | Sierra Leone | English | English/ French | Refugee |
| F | 13 | Liberia | English | English | Refugee |
| F | 14 | Liberia | English | English | Refugee |
| M | 17 | Colombia | Spanish | English | Refugee |
| M | 19 | Colombia | Spanish | English | Pr. Nominee |
| F | 15 | Netherlands | Dutch | English | Pr. Nominee |
| F | 14 | Belgium | Dutch | French/ English | Pr. Nominee |
| F | 17 | Iran | Farsi | English | Pr. Nominee |
| F | 17 | South Korea | Korean | English | Pr. Nominee |
| F | 15 | Venezuela | Spanish | English/ French | Economic |
| F | 17 | Taiwan | Mandarin Chinese | English | Economic |
| M | 15 | Iran | Farsi | English | Student* |
| F | 20 | Vietnam | Vietnamese | English/ French | Student† |
| M | 18 | Indonesia | Indonesian | English | Student† |
| *(sibling guardian is a permanent resident) †(applying for permanent residency) | | | | |

| TABLE 8.3 PARTICIPANTS FLORENCEVILLE-BRISTOL | | | | | |
|---|---|---|---|---|---|
| Sex | Age | Source Country | Mother Tongue | Official Language | Immigrant Classification |
| M | 15 | Colombia | Spanish | English | Pr. Nominee |
| M | 17 | Colombia | Spanish | English | Pr. Nominee |
| M | 16 | Moldova | Russian | English | Pr. Nominee |
| M | 19 | South Korea | Korean | English | Student † |
| M | 20 | South Korea | Korean | English | Student† |
| F | 14 | Colombia | Spanish | English | Pr. Nominee |
| F | 14 | Colombia | Spanish | English | Pr. Nominee |
| F | 14 | Colombia | Spanish | English | Pr. Nominee |
| F | 13 | Colombia | Spanish | English | Pr. Nominee |
| F | 13 | Colombia | Spanish | English | Pr. Nominee |
| F | 17 | Colombia | Spanish | English | Pr. Nominee |
| F | 15 | Mexico | Spanish | English | Pr. Nominee |
| F | 18 | India | Hindi | English | Pr. Nominee |
| †(applying for permanent residency) | | | | | |

## Notes

1. Quotations from interviews undertaken with immigrant adolescents in 2008-2009 contain the participant's name or pseudonym and the country where he or she originated.

2. In 2006 its annual intake of immigrants doubled from the 600 to 800 of previous years to 1,646. Over half of these newcomers (967) were provincial nominees and their dependents (Citizenship and Immigration Canada 2008). In 2007 the number of immigrants decreased to 1,643—921 of whom were provincial nominees and their dependents. This number then increased to 1,845 immigrants in 2008—1,199 of whom were provincial nominees and their dependents. By 2009 there were 1,910 immigrants accepted into New Brunswick, 550 of whom were provincial nominees and their dependents, and in 2010, 2,125 immigrants entered the province, 770 of whom were provincial nominees and their dependents. New Brunswick also receives approximately 200 government-sponsored refugees each year (that number has remained more or less the same since 1985), and approximately 1,700 temporary foreign workers and 1,400 foreign students each year.

## References

Allport, Gordon. 1954. *The Nature of Prejudice*. Reading, MA: Addison-Wesley Pub. Co.

Biles, John, Meyer Burstein and James Frideres, eds. 2008. *Immigration and Integration in Canada in the Twenty-First Century*. Kingston, ON: School of Policy Studies, McGill-Queens University Press.

Chan, Stephen. 1998-1999. The Role of Supports on Minority Adolescents. *Poverty and Prejudice: Our Schools Our Children* Spring Quarter.

Cohen, Elizabeth, G. 1982. Expectation States and Interracial Interaction in School Settings. *Annual Review of Sociology* 8:209-35.

Fleras, Augie. 2009. *The Politics of Multiculturalism: Multicultural Governance in Comparative Perspective*. New York: Palgrave MacMillan.

Furnham, Adrian and Stephen Bochner. 1986. *Culture Shock: Psychological Reactions to Unfamiliar Environments*. London: Methuen.

James, Carl E. 2003. *Seeing Ourselves: Exploring Race, Ethnicity and Culture, 3rd ed.* Toronto: TEP.

LaFromboise, Teresa, Hardin L. K. Coleman and Jennifer Gerton. 1993. Psychological Impact of Biculturalism: Evidence and Theory. *Psychological Bulletin* 114 (33): 395-412.

Lazos, Sylvia R. 1998. Deconstructing Homo[genous] Americanus: The White Ethnic Immigrant Narrative and Its Exclusionary Effect. *Tulane Law Review* 72:1493-1596, 1505-43, 1594-96.

Marcia, James E. 1966. Development and Validation of Ego Identity Status. *Journal of Personality and Social Psychology* 3:551-58.

McMillan, David W. and David M. Chavis. 1986. Sense of Community: A Definition and Theory. *Journal of Community Psychology* 14:6-23.

Parham, Thomas. 1989. Cycles of Psychological Nigrescence. *The Counselling Psychologist* 17:187-226.

Phinney, Jean S., Gabriel Horenczyk, Karmela Liebkind and Paul Vedder. 2001. Ethnic Identity, Immigration, and Well-Being: An Interactional Perspective. *Journal of Social Issues* 57 (3): 493-510.

Rajiva, Mythili. 2005. Bridging the Generation Gap: Exploring the Differences Between Immigrant Parents and their Canadian-born Children. *Canadian Issues* (Spring): 25-28.

Riordan, Cornelius and James Ruggiero. 1980. Producing Equal-Status Interracial Interaction: A Replication. *Social Psychology Quarterly* 43:131-36.

Sarason, Seymour B. 1977. *Work, Aging, and Social Change: Professionals and the One-Life One Career Imperative.* New York: Free Press.

Simard, Myriam. 2007. Immigrant Integration Outside Montreal. *Our Diverse Cities* 3:109-14.

Steel, Heather. 2006. Where's the Policy? Immigration to New Brunswick, 1945-1971. *Acadiensis* 35 (2): 85-104.

Suárez-Orozco, Carola. 2003. Formulating Identity in a Globalized World. In *Globalization: Culture and Education in the New Millennium,* ed. Marcelo M. Suárez-Orozco and Desiree Qin-Hilliard, 173-202. Oakland, CA: University of California Press and Ross Institute.

Suárez-Orozco, Carola, Hee Jin Bang, Erin O'Connor, Francisco X. Gaytán, Juliana Pakes and Jean Rhodes. 2010. Academic Trajectories of Newcomer Immigrant Youth. *Developmental Psychology* 46 (3): 602-18.

Suárez-Orozco, Carola, Marcelo Suárez-Orozco and Irina Todorova. 2008. *Learning a New Land: Immigrant Students in American Society.* Cambridge: Belknap Press of Harvard University Press.

Van Ngo, Hieu and Barbara Schleifer. 2005. Immigrant Children and Youth in Focus. *Canadian Issues* (Spring): 29-33.

Weiss, Maureen R. and Susan C. Duncan. 1992. The Relation Between Physical Competence and Peer Acceptance in the Context of Children's Sport Participation. *Journal of Sport and Exercise Psychology* 14:61-99.

Wilson-Forsberg, Stacey. 2013. Budding Multiculturalism or Veiled Indifference? Inter-Group Contact Among Immigrant and Native-Born Adolescents in Small-Town Canada. *Journal of Intercultural Communication* 31.

# Section 4

# Building Belonging

# 9

## A "Stopover Place" at Best?
## Recent Trends in Immigrant Attraction
## and Retention on Prince Edward Island

*Godfrey Baldacchino*

### Introduction

*[M]any of those arriving under the [PEI PNP] program promptly decamped for elsewhere in Canada. (Curry and Moore 2011)*

Recent immigrants have not been drawn to Atlantic Canada in significant numbers, especially in the more rural and remote regions. The Atlantic region suffers from a series of vicious cycles that contours the migration experience, with no end in sight. While Canada absorbs 250,000 or so newcomers every year, the four Atlantic Provinces attract less than 3 per cent of these, even though these four provinces—New Brunswick, Newfoundland and Labrador, Nova Scotia and Prince Edward Island—comprise some 7 per cent of the national population. And so, while the 2006 Census reports that visible minorities now represent close to 75 per cent of immigrants to Canada as a whole, the proportion of visible minorities in the Atlantic Provinces remains abysmally low, with a mean of just 2.6 per cent of the total resident population of the region in 2006, and Nova Scotia reporting the highest proportion of 4.2 per cent thanks to its long-time African-Nova Scotian population. Moreover, the retention rate of those immigrants who do come to the region is equally poor, when compared to the rest of the country. Indeed, along with Saskatchewan, the four Atlantic Provinces have systematically had the lowest retention rates of immigrants by province in the country, ranging from 36 per cent (NL) to 62 per cent (NB) for immigrants moving into the country between 1991 and 2001 (Gilroy 2005: 19). While "hyper-diversity" (Biles et al. 2008: 3) may be what brands Canada as a whole, mono-culturalism rules largely undisturbed in Atlantic Canada, still marked by a relative lack of diversity.

Immigration inflows to this region have, however, changed substantially in recent years, thanks mainly to provincial nominee programs (PNPs). These federal-provincial agreements expedited immigration to Canada "for individuals and their families who meet provincial criteria in support of the following initiatives: (a) increased business and economic development; (b) increased supply of skilled workers; (c) increased population; and (d) the achievement of provincial demographic, social and cultural objectives" (PEI-PNP 2008). Largely as a consequence of the PNP, the annual immigrant inflow in Atlantic Canada rose from 3,025 registered landings in 2001, to 5,307 in 2006, and to 5,583 in 2007 (Tutton 2008). And yet, in spite of the influx, the evidence so far suggests that few of these newcomers choose to stay in the region, with the occasional exception of better retention rates achieved where PNP nominees belong to the skilled worker category. While "hyperdiversity" (Biles et al. 2008:3) may be what brands Canada as a whole, mono-culturalism rules largely undisturbed in Atlantic Canada, still marked by a relative lack of diversity.

Akbari (2008) provides some insights into this recent flow of (mainly PNP-facilitated) newcomers broken down by province in the Atlantic region. Prince Edward Island (PEI) was the province in the region with the largest percentage increase in the number of landed immigrants during the inter-census period (from 134 landings in 2001, to 585 landings in 2006, to 2,631 landings in 2010).[1]

And yet, ironically, it is the only province in Atlantic Canada that has seen its retention rate of landed immigrants actually fall by 7 per cent (from 60 per cent to 53 per cent) between 2001 and 2006; meanwhile, in the same period, NB, NL and NS registered modest increases in their mean immigrant retention rates, of 8 per cent, 4 per cent and 15 per cent, respectively.

The four Atlantic provinces of Canada share major and abiding concerns with their (still low overall) immigrant retention rates,[2] and their provincial governments in particular are likely to be well disposed to consider what mechanisms they may effectively deploy in order to improve these.[3] Yet, as the data presented in this paper suggests, PEI is behaving mainly as a temporary, transit station where immigrants deposit some of their funds before they proceed with their plans to settle more permanently elsewhere in the country; indeed, some PNP beneficiaries head straight to settle somewhere else, circumventing PEI altogether.

This chapter, based also on material from a larger study (Baldacchino et al. 2009), explores and fleshes out these issues by focusing mainly on the opinions and experiences of a sample of twenty-four Korean immigrant respondents. Their views question the double assumption that immigrants have a desire to settle on PEI, and that the local host communities also desire or have as much interest in supporting such settlement.

## Barriers to Migration to Prince Edward Island

Two sets of important characteristics are borne out by the observable trends in immigration to Atlantic Canada. First, that no large cities, no immigrant clusters, no perceived economic opportunities, lower wages and a shortage of health-related human resources and services all conspire to make Prince Edward Island—and the Atlantic region generally—less attractive to immigrants. According to Census data, the proportion of visible minorities in PEI's population has gone up marginally, from 0.9 per cent in 2001, to 1.3 per cent in 2006.[4] Second, a tightly-webbed "WACS" (White, Anglophone, Christian and Straight/Heterosexual) monoculture acts as a rather understated but nevertheless powerful socio-cultural barrier to successful immigrant integration (PEI Population Panel 1999; Baldacchino 2006: 74).

Policy analysts have identified two main barriers to successful immigrant integration: the inability of migrants to adapt to the host society, and systematic discrimination in the host society (Wang and Lo 2007). Both barriers are at work on PEI. The island's singular cultural mould—what has been described as "a strong cultural norm of sameness" (PEI Population Panel 1999: 56)—is a powerful source of bonding social capital and resourcefulness from which this small island community (population as of 2014 around 146,000) has benefited handsomely in the face of rampant globalization. Growing up in an ascribed network of relatives and friends, most Islanders walk through life in regular company of the same social cohort, with whom they inevitably connect and thus reinforce relationships. It is this same intensive social interaction—a "communal togetherness" which doubles as a "straitjacket of community surveillance" (Weale 1992: 9-10)—that can induce Islanders to seek escape and solace via self-imposed exile. For better or for worse, any immigrants to Prince Edward Island automatically do not belong to this intricate web of strong and durable social networks. Nor can they ever fully belong, though their children might, if they persevere: one has to be *born* on PEI to be an "Islander"; otherwise, immigrants will forever remain "CFAs": (come from aways) (e.g., Wright 2009a). Thus, what is a source of identity and community for self-professed Islanders acts to thwart diversity, and can even be perceived as a subtle (but unintentional) form of racism:

> This is what different immigrants have explained as finding bewildering, exasperating, cliquist, small-minded, petty, racist ... and invariably difficult to plug into. No wonder immigrants find themselves befriending other immigrants. The Islander versus "come from away" category is an important contemporary social divide on PEI (just like the red-blue partisan one) and contributes to a reservoir of mutual misunderstanding. (Baldacchino 2006: 74)

Islanders are badly equipped in the skills that would enable them to reach out to newcomers and help the latter integrate better in the host society: they lack "bridging social capital" (Woolcock and Narayan 2000). The condition becomes effectively—though not necessarily intentionally—exclusionary and discriminatory. *Globe and Mail* columnist John Ibbitson fails to appreciate the value of social solidarity; he is thus harsh and outspoken in his commentary on the outcome of this vicious cycle:

> The racial homogeneity is pronounced.... Immigrants shun these communities.... These communities, in turn, display little zeal to attract immigrants, reveling instead in their so-called cultural heritage, which is really a desiccated remnant of Canada's colonial past. (Ibbitson 2005: 34)

### A 28 Per Cent Retention Rate

It is no wonder, then, that so many immigrants landing in Charlottetown are no longer living on PEI within a few years of their arrival. (The size of the island, and the significant role of the PEI Association for Newcomers to Canada [PEIANC], the single settlement agency, makes tracing immigrants relatively easier than elsewhere in the country.) The rate of immigrant retention is still impacted by the type of immigrant—the rate of retention for PNP beneficiaries is lower than that for refugees (more about which below), and consistent with findings elsewhere in the region (see the chapter by Ramos and Yoshida in this volume). Nevertheless, the challenges of integration cut across country of origin, social class, education, income, gender and race.

For Provincial Nominees, now the largest group of immigrants to PEI,[5] a total of 143 individuals from forty-four different families were registered with the PEIANC as having landed on PEI between September 1 and December 31, 2006. By May 2009, only eleven of these families, comprising thirty-seven net individuals, were registered as still living on PEI (Wright 2009b).

For Refugee Class Immigrants, a total of twenty-eight families with ninety-three family members were registered as having landed on PEI between January 1, 2006 and June 30, 2007. Of this total, just nine of these families, with twenty-nine family members in all, were known to be still residing in PEI in May 2009 (ibid.).

These 236 arrivals represent just more than one-third of all immigrant arrivals to PEI between September 2006 and June 2007: as interpolated from annual figures available from official provincial statistics, around 684 immigrants landed on PEI within that nine-month time window. This makes the study population a 35 per cent sample of the whole immigrant population within that period.

The retention rate for PNP beneficiaries is marginally lower than that pertaining to refugee immigrants (25 per cent versus 32 per cent, if calculated per family; 26 per cent against 31 per cent if calculated per individual).

The mean gross retention rate for immigrants from these two immigration classes combined is 28 per cent (whether calculated by family or by net individuals): much lower than the 52.5 per cent quoted by Akbari (2008) for 2001-2006. Former PEI Minister responsible for Immigration, Richard Brown, was much closer to the facts when he declared that the immigrant retention rate in the province was "just 30 per cent" (CBC News 2008a).

Migration to the province is also a decidedly urban phenomenon—just like in the rest of the country. Of the twenty families in the targeted PNP and refugee population still living in the province in May 2009, all except three (85 per cent) were living in Charlottetown, the provincial capital and largest city.

## Korean Immigrants to PEI

Between late May and early July 2009, forty-three recent immigrants to PEI (twenty-four males; nineteen females) accepted an invitation to take part in a face-to-face interview where a semi-structured questionnaire was used to elicit comments, particularly about their settlement experience. Among these were twenty-four recent immigrants from South Korea (eighteen males; six females) who came to PEI as Provincial Nominees, under the investor class.[6] The rest of this chapter focuses on the responses of these Korean respondents. While the subsequent findings could have been different had recent immigrants of diverse ethnic backgrounds been targeted, these observations nevertheless constitute a rare example of a focused and systematic study of a nationally profiled immigrant group on PEI in recent decades.[7] Immigrants from South Korea now represent the second largest national category of PNP beneficiaries in Canada, and have become the second largest national category of immigrants to PEI in recent years (in both cases placing second, trailing only after the People's Republic of China). They have already been the targets of focused inquiry and research in other contexts.[8]

According to the 2001 Canadian Census, 101,715 respondents identified themselves as being of Korean heritage, a significant 56 per cent increase from the 1996 Census count. Like other immigrant groups, Koreans are heavily concentrated in a few select provinces. Again, according to the 2001 Canadian Census, 1.8 million new Korean immigrants entered Canada during the 1990s and nearly 90 per cent of these resided in Ontario and British Columbia. Korean immigrants comprised 2.8 per cent of the Canadian population, according to the 2006 Census.

Despite their typically advanced education and middle-class backgrounds (as noted below), most Korean immigrants to Canada are still at an early stage of economic adaptation, and they have generally not been able to fully utilize their human capital in Canada, largely because they experience difficulties in finding an occupation in the Canadian labour market commensurate with their education and training (Yoon 2006: 17-19).

While their educational credentials are very strong—most have graduate and even postgraduate degrees—their English language competency is relatively poor. One indirect indication of the extent of English language literacy amongst this group is provided by their language of choice in responding to the survey questionnaire, which was available in either English or Korean.

Only one of the twenty-four Korean respondents chose to utilize the English version of the questionnaire and to answer its questions by using the English language. The twenty-three other responses to the survey were made in Korean, and then translated, for the sake of analysis, from the Korean original into English by the project research assistant.

The twenty-four Korean immigrants had various comments to make; these comments can be grouped under four distinct yet interrelated headings. These are: the management of the Provincial Nominee Program (PNP) on PEI; educational opportunities, mainly for their children, on the Island; securing suitable employment or self-employment; and the intention to leave PEI and settle elsewhere in Canada.

### The Management of the PNP

In terms of volume, the first and most strident criticism and concern was that levelled at the overall management of the PNP by the PEI authorities. This study came in the wake of some controversial statements concerning the manner in which this Program—and especially its investor class stream, as regulated until September 2008—has been managed by the PEI Government, and how the immigrants' investments were being allocated (e.g., CBC News 2008b; *Huffington Post* 2012).

The investor stream of the PNP program was terminated in September 2008—but not before PEI had processed almost 2,000 immigrant applications in the previous four months. There have been political charges of corruption and calls for investigations (e.g., CBC News 2008c). Elected members of the legislative assembly and government officials allegedly applied and received program money. There were questions about the quality of the "companies" approved for investment. According to the Hon. Jason Kenney, Federal Minister responsible for Immigration:

> We had a situation where a lot of promoters, who were profiting from the program, were making promises they

couldn't keep, promises to the newcomers about processing times and what the requirements of the program are. (CBC News 2010)

While it is not the scope of this study to discuss the PNP in any detail, the interviewed Korean immigrants voiced considerable disappointment with regards to the PNP, and they expressed reservations and suspicions about the PEI government and those who may have been associated with the management of the PNP. This issue perhaps affected any readiness they may have had initially about settling on the island province. It may also have affected those PNP beneficiaries who have yet to make it to the Island. These are some of the Korean respondents' comments on this subject:

> [There is a need for] (a) sharing information about job/business as well as offering a training program; and (b) making PNP better and showing everything clear, especially deposit-related issue (Respondent #27).

> I don't understand why there is no deposit back from the PEI government to those immigrants who have been staying here for at least three years ... everyone knows it's hard to get a job here; that's why my husband decided to stay in Korea to keep his business. If my husband were here with us for the last few years without any job, how would we support ourselves? [...] Considering the [PNP] issue, I really mistrust the PEI government, and I think many immigrants have the same idea as me. (R#24)

> I have a deposit that I need to get back from the PEI government (R #23).

> The PEI government has to use the investment from immigrants for immigrants, by offering [them] a better job or business opportunity. I think that's the best way that may convince immigrants of considering settling down on PEI. (R#43)

> The immigration policy has [been] changed every year here by the PEI Government, which is ridiculous. The PEI Government should integrate all the revised immigration policy to make it a trustworthy policy. (R#20)

Clearly, Korean immigrants who arrived in Canada via the PEI PNP have concerns about the administration of the program, and especially about those aspects which concern them directly: the refund of their good faith deposit, and the missed opportunities for training, employment and induction into the PEI and Canadian world of business. Theirs is also an overall appeal for trust and transparency.

## Educational Opportunities

The second most commonly expressed concern by the respondents dealt with educational opportunities, especially with regard to the interviewees' children. Extraordinary educational achievement for Korean immigrants has often been credited to the common cultural influence of Confucianism that emphasizes education, family honour, discipline and respect for authority (Zhou and Kim 2008). Korean society is driven strongly by achievement status; and so much of this is seen as dependent on excellent, quality university-level education. According to the 2001 Census, more than 47 per cent of Korean immigrants to Canada were graduates (Kim 2008).

The Korean respondents to this study are themselves gifted with considerable tertiary-level education: Almost all respondents (twenty-two out of twenty-four) claimed to have an undergraduate or graduate university degree. Three respondents (three out of twenty-four) stated that they moved to Canada for a better education for their children:

> [I moved to Canada because of] better job opportunity and educational atmosphere for my children (R#28).

> [I moved to Canada] for a better life and my children's education (R#25).

[I came here] for a better education for my children. I like PEI, but I think the educational system here is not great (R#39).

Key educational challenges faced by Korean immigrants to PEI may relate to both choice and quality. Given its small scale, there is an absence of choice in the provision of higher education in the province, restricted as it is to one vocational college (Holland College) and one university (the University of Prince Edward Island). The latter, meanwhile, does not offer degrees leading to most professional qualifications (such as architecture, medicine, law or pharmacy).

## Economic Opportunities

The third most expressed concern by respondents, and closely aligned to the above, is their keen desire to secure satisfying employment or self-employment that is commensurate with their skills, experience and credentials. Some respondents (four out of twenty-four) expressed disappointment at the absence or quality of opportunities for appropriate employment on PEI:

Not enough job opportunity on PEI (R#21).

I am trying to get a job here (R#23).

[We] need more job opportunity and related information and training (R#31).

The PEI economy is seeking to lure immigrants to work in a few targeted, knowledge-intensive areas: these include aerospace, bioscience and video game development. This is clearly displayed, for example, in a professional eight-minute promotional video on the provincial government's immigration website (It's About Time 2007). Yet, many job opportunities in the private sector are related to agriculture, fisheries, food processing, forestry and tourism, all of which are seasonal industries and do not provide full-time employment. A 2006 study amongst recent immigrants to PEI had similarly identified the "absence of good, challenging, careerist, specialized, well[-]paying and preferably all-year-round jobs, or any job at all" as a key obstacle to immigrant attraction and retention (Baldacchino 2006: 49).

## Secondary Migration

The fourth and final key trend that emerged from the interviews was that most of the Korean immigrants to PEI (nineteen out of twenty-four) involved in this study were not planning to stay for long in the island province. Various sour experiences connected to their status as PNP beneficiaries may have exacerbated this decision (as already explained above)[9]; but most appeared to have planned to come to PEI for the short term anyway:

> I'm not sure about my future plans. I am still trying to figure out what I should do in the future. I guess I'll be here for about two years (R#40).

> I have been here for around one year, and I'm leaving next month (R#36).

> I haven't decided yet. I'm trying to dig more information now, but it will be to a bigger city in Canada (R#39).

> I want to get a job, or run my own business here to settle down, but it seems to be very hard. I will decide whether I leave or not after I try [harder] to stay here (R#37).

> [I plan to go to] Vancouver. I think there are many Korean connections [there] so it seems to have more job or business opportunities (R#38).

> There's not enough Korean connections here [on PEI], such as lack of Korean food or lack of Korean culture. Therefore, I'm planning to move to western Canada, probably Vancouver, which has more Korean connections. I have been on PEI almost two years so far, and probably I am leaving after one more year of staying. (R#31)

Vancouver: My husband will run his business there (R#25).

Toronto: My children used to study [there], so they're familiar with that city ... understanding and accepting diverse cultures would be the key to living in Toronto, as it's a big city with a lot of different people from many countries. (R#24)

Not enough job opportunity on PEI. Planning to leave [to Toronto] in one or two years (R#21).

I am planning to leave in a year (R#32).

Toronto: I think there will be better opportunities for my job and my children's education [there] (R#33).

Those few Korean immigrants who did not express any intention to leave were those waiting for their children to complete their current educational program on PEI—typically at high school—before they made longer-term plans (five out of twenty-four). Not a single one of the twenty-four Korean immigrants interviewed in this study expressed a clear intention or desire to remain settled on Prince Edward Island.

The educational progress of their children was a paramount consideration for the Korean immigrants in this study in determining where they choose to resettle. One said, "What we decide to do will depend on my children's further education plan. If my children go to a university in another city, we're moving there together" (R#22). Perhaps what follows below is the most elaborate and articulate comment provided on this subject:

I think many immigrants on PEI ... don't consider PEI a place to settle down. Many immigrants, including my family, are more likely to be considering PEI like an entrance, or just a stop-over place before they settle down in other cities in Canada.... Many Chinese people usually leave in a year, regardless of anything ... they even don't spend a lot of money for housing or any house wares ... I think Korean people stay here for at least two to three years. (R#24)

## Discussion: The Challenge of Belonging

PNP beneficiaries have been the vast majority of immigrants to PEI and have remained so until 2012. Many have—certainly until September 2008—opted to migrate to Canada via PEI mainly for strategic reasons relating to ease, speed and level of required financial investment.[10] They reported less benefit in taking any initiatives to integrate with the host PEI society, when their long-term plan is to leave for larger cities where they can connect with their relatives and friends in their own ethnic or national diaspora, partake in ethnic food, speak their native language, share in ethnic feasts and events and place their children in what they consider to be better schools. PEI is just a convenient stepping stone, a transit zone, a "stopover place"; a destination of circumstances, and not of intent (Hirsch 2011). The controversy surrounding the handling of the PNP by the PEI Government may have also sullied PEI's attraction to immigrants, even for stepping-stone purposes. Most attempts to connect with the host island society by these PNP beneficiaries seem to be driven primarily by instrumental purposes, foremost among which is the desire to exploit all avenues for gaining important information.

The Korean PNPs are strategic, selective and pragmatic in how they connect, if at all, with the services of the PEI settlement agency. They engage with the PEIANC mainly through its "English as an Additional Language" program. The immigrants' key driver here is understandable: achieving a level of language proficiency that would allow them to get back a $20,000 language deposit, part of the conditions attached to securing immigration into Canada as a provincial nominee.[11] There is also a good-faith deposit of $100,000 that would be repaid to the applicant only if s/he is still residing in the province of entry twelve months after having landed in Canada: a policy explicitly meant to encourage retention in the province of landing. And yet, indicative of the affluence and net worth of these PNP nominees, some of them do not even bother to come and spend any time at all in PEI (their province of landing) but go straightaway to settle in (mainly)

Toronto or Vancouver, voluntarily forfeiting their language deposit.[12] For these, far from being a home away from home, PEI is not even a "stop-over place."

Meanwhile, the PEIANC's programs of assistance—such as the Host Program[13]— appear to be premised on an understanding that it is the immigrant participant who is expected to assimilate and learn the host culture. There is no expectation of a frank cultural exchange on equal power terms between host volunteer and immigrant. It is worth asking whether such a principle needs to be interrogated. While Canada professes to be a tolerant multi-ethnic society, Host Program praxis appears more driven by integration and assimilation. It may also be worth asking here what motivates Host Program volunteers to offer their time, interest and friendship to immigrants. Are they interested in and open to a frank cultural exchange on equal, peer-to-peer terms where, for example, they can "trade" language acquisition or business acumen? Or do the volunteers rather see themselves in an inevitably unequal relationship, where they serve as surrogate parents or patronising benefactors to the immigrants, rather than their "friends"?[14] Are the immigrants themselves interested in moving away from such skewed power interactions and dependencies?

These characteristics of recent settlers to Prince Edward Island are readily borne out of, and corroborated by, the responses to a larger and different survey. In late 2005, a qualitative survey of recent settlers to PEI was undertaken with 320 respondents (Baldacchino 2006). According to these respondents, the most common challenge to attracting and retaining new immigrants on PEI—identified by 55 per cent (N=172)—relates to the difficulty of landing an appropriate job (or any job at all) and the associated challenge of foreign credential recognition. The second most commonly identified set of challenges—with 18 per cent of respondents (N=59) commenting—deals variously with the Island society as being racist, bigoted, discriminatory, conservative, exclusivist and/or cliquist with regards to those branded for life as "CFAs." Some respondent comments about this are barbed and even cruel in their concern: they manifest sadness, disappointment and frustration. Other comments are more guarded, clinical and even reflexive, attributing this phenomenon to a cultural condition of which Islanders—especially those who have never lived away—are as much victims as perpetrators. It seems that a *close society* cannot help being a *closed society*:

> The "come from away" problem is one that probably results in settlers not staying settled for very long. This should not be seen as a "fault" of native Islanders; it's a condition. They've grown from childhood with friends and family around them and therefore have had no need to develop whatever skills are required to seek out and make welcome new people with a view to forming friendships. That simply hasn't been necessary. It's also true that those settlers who have traveled the world a little have experiences and knowledge to which the majority of Islanders can't relate. Again, it's not a criticism, but it is a condition. (Respondent #040 2006 study)

> Conservative social attitudes and what seems to be a "closed" society to newcomers may make it difficult for settlers to feel that they fit in. If there were not some existing family ties to PEI, I think it would be quite challenging to make social contacts. Most people want to know how you may be related to them, or their neighbour, or someone they know, to figure out how you fit into the overall picture of PEI society—your place or role or "standing" somehow. (Respondent #217 2006 study).

The "CFA descriptor" is applied widely and casually. It may appear endearing, but it can be bitterly resented and, in some circumstances, portrays what could be an implicit racist naïveté, arguably more prevalent in the rural areas of the province. The Island simply takes care of its own; and, by extension, no one else. Being "from here" versus being "from away" seem to be fundamental criteria for social division, in both Island-based organizations as well as Island-wide generally—perhaps as important as social class, political party affiliation or ideology. Some respondents claimed that being a CFA was equivalent to being a member of a visible minority on PEI:

> It became fairly obvious that *who* you were (family name), *who* you knew, etc., are factors as to how successfully you can conduct life in general on PEI. This has not affected me to date (that I'm aware of) but I've seen it in operation. It is hard to miss since it is prevalent and blatant. The funny thing is, it's much the same everywhere since people are people wherever they are, but in a "PEItri" dish, it's more noticeable. (Respondent #031 2006 study, emphasis in original).

Partly as a reaction to these exclusivist tactics, a group of newcomers to PEI has set up the Islander by Choice Alliance, whose mandate includes "To create an Island-wide community of individuals interested in bridging the gap between those moving to Prince Edward Island from other places and those born and raised on Prince Edward Island" (Islander By Choice Alliance 2011). In a society of tightly networked members, it can be great when you fit in; but not so great when you do not (Baldacchino 2011).

## Conclusion

*The PEI Provincial Government recognizes the pivotal role that newcomers bring to our Island; their Island.—Hon. Minister Richard Brown (2008a: 1, emphasis in original).*

*There are valuable social and cultural benefits associated with diversification including improved quality and access to leisure, cuisine, arts, knowledge of global trends and issues and lifelong learning through the introduction of new cultural practices and norms.—Hon. Minister Richard Brown (2008b: 6).*

Such and similar statements speak to a healthy dose of politically-correct rhetoric, forthcoming from government, business organizations and civil society groups; they champion diversity, the need to grow the local population, the need to boost the labour force in order to maintain public services at a sustainable level, and the importance of attracting skill and talent. And yet, in spite of and in contrast to the tenet of such utterances, it would appear that most Prince Edward Islanders have no real appetite for immigration. At best, they are willing to extend their generosity and hospitality to support refugee class immigrants settling down. They are willing to welcome tourists, as long as they come with the intention to leave (Baldacchino 2012). But, they remain largely suspicious of newcomers, especially if they do not have the Irish-Scottish background that most Islanders—other than the First Nations Mi'kmaq and the descendants of French Acadians—claim as their own. Immigrants end up as curiosa, objects of voyeurism, exotic specimens that one encounters formally and rarely in international tea houses or cultural extravaganza, divvying the four "Ds" of multiculturalism—dance, diet, dialect and dress—that continue to emphasize difference, rather than integration (e.g., Zachariah 1999). When the PEI Provincial Government set up a Population Secretariat in 2003, its mandate seemed predicated more on local Islander retention and repatriation than on immigration proper.[15]

When Stephen Stewart, a PEI mussel grower, hired eleven workers from Sri Lanka in 2006, only to see them disappear to Ottawa after two weeks on the Island, he commented wryly to the press: "People in the community criticized us for bringing in foreign workers and said we got what we deserved" (Duplain 2006).

Canada may earn high marks as a country that looks kindly on immigration, but not all parts of Canada would qualify equally. One should thus not be surprised by the outcome of a national poll on attitudes to immigration commissioned for *Policy Options Journal* (Nanos 2008). Atlantic Canadians appear to be the least convinced that immigration is important to the future of the country, and the most important response to the country's workforce skill requirements; but, at the same time, they are the most convinced that immigration is important for family reunification. Immigration strikes a chord with Atlantic Canadians if it means bringing back home one's own.[16] These tendencies may be exacerbated on the Island province most of all.

## Notes

The research behind most of the material in this chapter is based on a pilot project kindly financed by the 2008-2009 Atlantic Metropolis Grant Competition, and has benefitted from the additional support of the University of Prince Edward Island (UPEI) and the Prince Edward Island Association for Newcomers to Canada (PEIANC). Lisa Chilton (UPEI) and student research assistants Shine-Ji Youn Chung and Benjamin Mathew Mathiang supported the research process and helped draft the study report. The significant input of Kevin J. Arsenault, Joey Seaman and Julie Houde (formerly at PEIANC) in data collection and respondent identification is also acknowledged. My thanks also to the trio of editors for insightful comments on earlier, and weaker, drafts. The usual disclaimers apply.

1. There were 992 landings reported for 2007, 1,483 for 2008, and 1,725 for 2009. Statistics Canada reported that the 2,631 international migrants who came to PEI in 2010 "represent the highest level on the current record keeping system (since 1971). At a rate of 18.2 per thousand, the province [i.e., PEI] posted the highest immigration rate in the country," significantly above the national mean of 7.5 per thousand (PEI Department of Finance and Municipal Affairs 2011).

2. Provincial Government of New Brunswick (2008); Provincial Government of Nova Scotia (2005); Provincial Government of Newfoundland and Labrador (2007).

3. For example, parallel research in all Atlantic Provinces has been undertaken to explore key challenges faced by internationally educated health professionals (Baldacchino and Saunders 2010). The PEI Provincial Government has also developed and published a newcomer guide (PEIANC 2010) and a population strategy to support the development of a "culturally diverse and prosperous province" (PEI Provincial Government 2010).

4. A full 1 per cent of these 1.3 per cent constitute First Nations peoples (Statistics Canada 2006). This statistic captures the sheer dearth of non-indigenous visible minorities on the island province at that time.

5. Out of 992 immigrants to PEI registered in 2007, 690 were Provincial Nominees; out of 1,483 immigrants to PEI in 2008, 813 were provincial nominees (Baldacchino 2010, Table 3). Some 5,000 PNP beneficiaries arrived on PEI between 2010 and 2012.

6. The rest were nine refugee class immigrants and ten additional PNP (but not Korean) beneficiaries.

7. There are only two other known examples of such studies: an older review of Lebanese immigrants (Weale 1981) and a more recent study of Chinese immigrants to PEI (Chiang 2008).

8. A session examining the influx of Korean immigrants in Moncton, NB, was organized at the 2008 Atlantic Metropolis Annual Spring Retreat: http://www.atlantic.metropolis.net/events/AMC_Symposium_2008_Agenda_ENG.pdf.

9. One of these concerned the obligation to prove continuous residence on PEI of at least 183 days in order to claim back a "good faith" deposit of $25,000 (Wright 2009c). Another concerned a change in the rules regarding the refund of a language proficiency deposit of $20,000 (CBC News 2009).

10. As one website proudly declares, "Successful applicants will receive a Prince Edward Island Provincial Nomination Certificate, which will *speed up* the Canada Immigration (Permanent Resident) Visa application process." (Canadavisa.com 2011, emphasis added.)

11. See CBC News (2009) for evidence of some of the frustration that can result when this language deposit is not recovered.

12. Information from Jane Mallard, Population Secretariat, PEI Provincial Government, April 21, 2010.

13. First introduced in 1985, the Host Program is designed to assist newcomers with integration into Canadian life. It seeks to help immigrants overcome the stress of moving to a new country by matching them with trained Canadian volunteer hosts, who become their "new Canadian friends." These volunteers help newcomers by being there for moral support, facilitating information about and access to social events, directing them to available services, practising English or French, or assisting to obtain contacts in their field of work. At the same time, the Host volunteer will learn about other cultures and other countries, thereby providing an important knowledge link concerning the benefits of immigration: http://www.cic.gc.ca/english/newcomers/host-newcomer.asp.

14. Such an attitude may be inspired by Christian charity. Given the importance of church-driven immigrant support on PEI, this point may call for further research.

15. "The Population Secretariat's mandate is to retain youth, repatriate former Islanders and attract and retain immigrants" (Government of Prince Edward Island 2008).

16. These differences are significant at 95 per cent confidence level. Na-

tional Sample Size=1,002. Poll was conducted in May 2008. Margin of error is ±3.1 per cent. Atlantic Canadians in sample=ninety seven.

## References

Akbari, Ather H. 2008. *Immigrant Inflows and their Retention Rise in Atlantic Canada*. Moncton and Halifax: Atlantic Metropolis Centre.

Baldacchino, Godfrey. 2006. *Recent Settlers to Prince Edward Island: Stories and Voices*. Charlottetown, University of Prince Edward Island for the Provincial Government. http://www.islandstudies.ca/sites/vre2. upei.ca.islandstudies.ca/files/u2/Settlers_to_PEI.pdf (accessed February 20, 2014).

————. 2011. Breaking into a Clannish Society: The Settlement and Integration Experience of Immigrants on Prince Edward Island. In *Integration and Inclusion of Newcomers and Minorities Across Canada*, ed. John Biles, Meyer Burstein, Jim Frideres, Erin Tolley and Robert Vineberg, 355-72. Montreal and Kingston: McGill-Queen's University Press.

————. 2012a. Chinese Newcomers to Prince Edward Island. Presentation at Atlantic Metropolis Workshop, Memorial University of Newfoundland, St John's, NL, September 29.

————. 2012b. Immigrants, Tourists and Others From Away: 'Come Visit, but Don't Overstay': the Welcoming Society of Prince Edward Island. *International Journal of Culture, Tourism and Hospitality Research* 6 (2): 145-53.

Baldacchino, Godfrey, Lisa Chilton, Shine-Ji Youn Chung and Benjamin Mathew Mathiang. 2009. *The Host Program and Immigrant Retention on Prince Edward Island*. http://vre2.upei.ca/islandstudies.ca/sites/vre2. upei.ca.islandstudies.ca/files/HOST-REPORT%20on%20Study-October-8-2009.pdf (accessed February 20, 2014).

Baldacchino, Godfrey and Patricia Saunders. 2010. *Internationally Educated Health Professionals in Nova Scotia and Prince Edward Island: Why They Come, Why They Stay and the Challenges They Face: A Follow-Up Study*. Charlottetown and Halifax: University of Prince Edward Island and Interdisciplinary PhD Program, Dalhousie University for IEHP Atlantic Connection. http://www.islandstudies.ca/sites/vre2.upei. ca.islandstudies.ca/files/IEHPI-Oct%202010-Final.pdf (accessed February 20, 2014).

Biles, John, Meyer Burnstein and Jim Friederes. 2008. Introduction. In *Immigration and Integration in Canada in the Twenty First Century*, ed. John Biles, Meyer Burnstein and Jim Friederes, 3-18. Montreal and Kingston: McGill-Queen's University Press.

Brown, Richard. 2008a. Foreword. In *Immigrant Entrepreneurs on Prince Edward Island*, ed. Godfrey Baldacchino and Crystal MacAndrew Fall. Charlottetown: the authors for the Population Secretariat, Provincial Government of Prince Edward Island. http://www.islandstudies.ca/ islandstudies.ca/sites/vre2.upei.ca.islandstudies.ca/files/Immigrant-Entrepreneurs-of-PEI-2008.pdf (accessed February 20, 2014).

Brown, Richard. 2008b. Interview in *Immigration: It's Our Future*. Charlottetown: Greater Charlottetown Chamber of Commerce. http:// www.charlottetownchamber.com/index.php?mact=Uploads,m0e6f6,getf ile,1&m0e6f6upload_id=65&m0e6f6returnid=107&page=107 (accessed February 20, 2014).

Canadavisa.com. 2011. *Prince Edward Island Provincial Nominee Program (PNP)*. Canada Immigration Lawyers. http://www.canadavisa. com/prince-edward-island-provincial-nominee-program.html (accessed February 20, 2014).

CBC News. 2008a. PEI Must Work to Retain Immigrants: Minister. July 28. http://www.cbc.ca/news/canada/prince-edward-island/p-e-i-must-work-to-retain-immigrants-minister-1.764812 (accessed February 20, 2014).

———. 2008b. PEI Auditor General Will Do Full Review of Immigrant Fund. October 2. http://www.cbc.ca/news/canada/prince-edward-island/p-e-i-auditor-general-will-do-full-review-of-immigrant-fund-1.769388 (accessed February 20, 2014).

———. 2008c. PEI's $400M Question: Was There Insider Dealing in the Provincial Nominee Program, or Is It Just Bad Optics? December 2. http://www.cbc.ca/news/canada/prince-edward-island/p-e-i-s-400m-question-1.698752 (accessed February 20, 2014).

———. 2009. Chinese Immigrant Protests Over Language-Proficiency Deposit. February 20. http://www.cbc.ca/news/canada/prince-edward-island/chinese-immigrant-protests-over-language-proficiency-depos-it-1.810806 (accessed February 20, 2014).

———. 2010. Kenney Reviews PEI's Immigration Program. June 25. Accessed November 2, 2012. http://www.cbc.ca/news/canada/prince-edward-island/kenney-reviews-p-e-i-s-immigration-program-1.913483 (accessed February 20, 2014).

Chiang, Hung-Min. 2006. *Chinese Islanders: Making a Home in the New World*. Charlottetown PE: Institute of Island Studies, University of Prince Edward Island.

Curry, Bill and Oliver Moore. 2011. PEI Rushed to Approve Thousands of Immigrants. Globe and Mail. September 16, 2011. http://www.theglobeandmail.com/news/politics/pei-rushed-to-approve-thousands-of-immigrants/article2169717/ (accessed February 20, 2014).

Duplain, Richard. 2008. No Recourse for Man Scammed by Foreign Workers. *Immigrant Watch Canada*, April 16. http://www.immigrationwatchcanada.org/2008/04/16/no-recourse-for-man-scammed-by-foreign-workers/ (accessed February 20, 2014).

Goss, Gilroy Inc. 2005. *Retention and Integration of Immigrants in Newfoundland and Labrador: Are We Ready? Final Report*. St John's, NL: For Atlantic Canada Opportunities Agency and Coordinating Committee on Newcomer Integration. http://www.nlimmigration.ca/media/12678/immigrationstudyfinal.pdf (accessed February 20).

Government of Prince Edward Island. 2008. *Opportunities PEI (formerly Population Secretariat)*. http://www.gov.pe.ca/popsec/ (accessed February 20, 2014).

Hirsch, Todd. 2011. How Alberta can "Retain" its Recent Arrivals. *The Globe and Mail*, November 7. http://www.theglobeandmail.com/news/opinions/opinion/how-alberta-can-retain-its-recent-arrivals/article2226316/ (accessed February 20, 2014).

Huffington Post. 2012. Cashing In: Inside PEI's Controversial Immigrant Partner Program, September 5. http://www.huffingtonpost.ca/2012/05/09/pei-immigrant-provincial-nominee-program_n_1499502.html (accessed February 20, 2014).

Ibbitson, John. 2005. *The Polite Revolution: Perfecting the Canadian Dream*. Toronto: McClelland and Stewart.

Islander by Choice Alliance. 2012. Our Mandate. http://peislanderbychoice.wordpress.com/author/peislanderbychoice/ (accessed February 20, 2014).

It's About Time. 2012. Promotional video for prospective immigrants to Prince Edward Island. http://www.youtube.com/watch?v=kotb1n4nTyA (accessed February 20, 2014).

Kim, Ann. H. 2008. Contemporary Issues in Korean Immigration: Advancing a Research Agenda. Power Point Presentation. Ottawa: Metropolis Brown Bag Series, Citizenship and Immigration Canada. December 16. http://canada.metropolis.net/mediacentre/ann_kim_dec16_08_e.ppt (accessed February 20, 2014).

Nanos, Nik. 2008. Nation Building Through Immigration: Workforce Skills Comes Out on Top. *Policy Options* June: 30-32. http://www.irpp.org/en/po/citizenship-and-immigration/nation-building-through-immigration-workforce-skills-comes-out-on-top/ (accessed February 20, 2014).

PEIANC. 2010. *Prince Edward Island Newcomers Guide.* Charlottetown, PE: PEI Association for Newcomers to Canada. http://www.peianc.com/content/page/guide_home (accessed February 20, 2014).

PEI Department of Finance and Municipal Affairs. 2011. *Prince Edward Island Population Report.* http://www.gov.pe.ca/photos/original/2011Census.pdf (accessed February 20, 2014). PEI-PNP. 2008. *Immigration Services: Prince Edward Island Provincial Nominee Program.* http://www.gov.pe.ca/immigration/index.php3?number=1014385 (accessed February 20, 2014).

PEI Population Panel. 1999. *A Place to Stay?* Charlottetown, PE: The Prince Edward Island Population Strategy.

PEI Provincial Government. 2010. *Prince Edward Island Settlement Strategy.* Charlottetown, PE: PEI Provincial Government. http://www.gov.pe.ca/photos/original/settlement_bro.pdf (accessed February 20, 2014).

Provincial Government of New Brunswick. 2008. *Be Our Future: New Brunswick Population Growth Strategy.* Fredericton, NB: Population Growth Secretariat. http://www.gnb.ca/3100/Promos/PS/Strategy-e.pdf (accessed February 20, 2014).

Provincial Government of Newfoundland and Labrador. 2007. *An Immigration Strategy for Newfoundland and Labrador: Opportunity for Growth.* St. John's, NL: Department of Human Resources, Labour and Employment. http://www.nlimmigration.ca/media/12684/strategydoc_mar07.pdf (accessed February 20, 2014).

Provincial Government of Nova Scotia. 2005. *Welcome Home to Nova Scotia: A Strategy for Immigration.* Halifax: Nova Scotia Office of Immigration. http://www.novascotia.ca/jobshere/docs/ImmigrationStrategy-WelcomeHomeToNS.pdf (accessed February 20, 2014).

Statistics Canada. 2006. Percentage of First Nations people in the Population: Canada, provinces and territories, 2006. http://www12.statcan.ca/census-recensement/2006/as-sa/97-558/figures/c6-eng.cfm (accessed February 20, 2014).

Tutton, Michael. 2008. Atlantic Canada Seeks Immigrants to Stem Out-Migration, but With Mixed Results. *The Guardian*. June 28, A11.

Wang, Shuguang and Lucia Lo. 2007. What Does it Take to Achieve Full Integration? Economic (under)performance of Chinese Immigrants to Canada. In *Interrogating Race and Racism*, ed. Vijay Agnew, 175-205. Toronto, ON: University of Toronto Press.

Weale, David. 1992. *Them Times*. Charlottetown, PE: Institute of Island Studies, University of Prince Edward Island.

———. 1981. *A Stream Out of Lebanon*. Charlottetown, PE: Institute of Island Studies, University of Prince Edward Island.

Woolcock, Michael and Deepa Narayan. 2008. Social Capital: Implications for Development Theory, Research, and Policy. *World Bank Observer* 15 (2): 225-49.

Wright, Teresa. 2009a. Are You an Islander? *The Guardian* (Charlottetown), August 22, A1-2. http://www.theguardian.pe.ca/Community/2009-08-22/article-1280545/Are-you-an-Islander/1 (accessed February 20, 2014).

Wright, Teresa. 2009b. Immigrant Retention Proving Difficult on PEI. *The Guardian* (Charlottetown), October 8, A5. http://www.theguardian.pe.ca/Faith/2009-10-08/article-1287314/Immigrant-retention-proving-difficult-on-PEI/1 (accessed February 20, 2014).

Yoon, In-Jin. 2006. Understanding the Korean Diaspora from Comparative Perspectives. *Asia Culture Forum*. http://www.cct.go.kr/data/acf2006/multi/multi_0201_In-Jin%20Yoon.pdf (accessed February 20, 2014).

Zachariah, Mathew. 1999. Things Fall Apart, the Centre Cannot Hold ... Break Down the Us and Them Attitude. *Revue Quebecoise de Droit International* 12 (1): 117-35.

Zhou, Min and Susan Kim. 2008. Community Forces, Social Capital and Educational Achievement: The Case of Supplementary Education in the Chinese and Korean Immigrant Communities. *Harvard Educational Review* 76 (1): 1-29.

# 10

# Is "Home" Where We Fill Our Stomachs? Turkish Professionals in Halifax and Toronto

*Serperi Sevgur*

## Introduction

B rah (1996) defines home as a place that encompasses our networks of family, kin, friends, colleagues and various "significant others," as well as the mundane and unexpected daily practices that can all contribute to a particular sense of rootedness. But what happens when one is born, raised and educated in a country for at least twenty-five years and then moves to another country? Can newcomers grow roots again? Once they are wrapped up in daily practices such as raising families, working in jobs, or once they exercise citizenship rights such as becoming engaged in the community and politics in this new country, what happens to their sense of belonging to their previous "home," (i.e., country of origin)? How does the longstanding, resident population view the impact of the new arrivals and how do these impressions, in turn, influence the immigrants' home-building practices? How do internationally inspired or home-grown[1] identity politics shape the immigrants' sense of belonging?

Although these may not be questions that immigrants consciously consider, the respondents of the study I conducted[2] were asked to address them systematically by reflecting on their personal experiences of immigration, their professional identities and ethnocultural attachments and, in turn, their perception of "home(s)." When probed further they were able to identify the foundational materials used to build their metaphorical "home(s)." While investigating the processes of building a home, the role of the respondents' networks and multiple identities were also explored.

This chapter provides an account of how the respondents of this study described their home(s) and how and why they cultivated their feelings of home(s). It begins with a theoretical overview and an introduction to the respondents, followed by a detailed examination of the factors and processes associated with the respondents' realization of where "home" is located. According to the Turkish immigrant professionals interviewed in this study, home, first and foremost, was where their loved ones were and where they were able to provide sustenance for themselves, especially the members of their nuclear family. All respondents had multi-local homes, one of which was Canada, and most did not feel a complete sense of belonging to either the country of origin or settlement. The length of time spent in Canada and timing in relation to one's life stages were identified as contributing factors to the feelings of home. How they built their sense of home was through acquisition, exercise and perception of citizenship rights in Canada. For the interviewees in this study, this was linked to positive feelings derived from being able to achieve a measure of economic and professional integration, as well as a sense of belonging that they traced to Canada's reputed multicultural commitments. In addition, a sense of home was achieved through participating in various networks on local, national, and international levels, which facilitated the expression of their compound identities.

**Theoretical Framework**

As a social construct, one's identity is shaped by one's various and multiple positions within the society. While cultural and gender politics play an important role, identity formations are also strongly mediated by class, age, generation, marital status and migrant status (Ehrkamp 2006). Furthermore, migrants are embedded in, identify with and hold multiple allegiances across national borders, to territories, ethnic and religious communities, and families. Migrants, as a result, are not just anchored in one national collectivity (Ehrkamp 2006) nor are they involved with any collectivity automatically, and they have a choice in the degree of importance they assign to different groups to which they belong (Phan and Breton 2009). Indeed, they use their agency and develop extended forms of identification and networking across multiple borders (Tastsoglou 2006). As migrants cross national borders, as well as "borders" of people, cultures, capital and commodities, they create a "diaspora space" where new forms of belonging and otherness are appropriated and contested with specific formations of power (Brah 1996). In the country of settlement, cultural categorization, state discourses, institutional settings and the politics of immigration and citizenship also shape migrant identities by contributing to the formation of the "other(s)," in relation to which identities are refined and sometimes contested and reconfigured (Yeoh and Willis 2005). With the ability of people to move between different frames of identity migrants use imaginative practices of reconceptualizing "home" in the process (Butcher 2009).

As evidenced in the literature, both transnational and local networks can be valuable resources for settlement (Conradson and Latham 2005; Collins 2008; Tastsoglou 2006). These networks are usually stratified along the lines of ethnicity, class and religious affiliation, reflecting the same social divisions that are present in the country of origin and in response to the conditions of the country of settlement (Gold 2001). While chain migration—the term coined by MacDonald and MacDonald (1964) for "that movement in which prospective migrants learn of opportunities, are provided with transportation, and have initial accommodation and employment arranged by means of primary social relationships with previous migrants" (82, qtd. in Johnston et al. 2006: 1228)—still continues to play a role in migration, it no longer plays the central role in migration of the highly skilled, relatively affluent migrants (Johnston et al. 2006). These migrants are found to rely more on their extensive and diversified networks consisting of, for example, professional colleagues and university alumni (Wong and Salaff 1998). Also, even though immigrants' lives are becoming more transnationally oriented, it is within local networks that they tend to ground their identities (Scott 2007). While the importance of ethno-cultural associations in the lives of immigrants (Ralston 2006) and robust involvement of the highly skilled in local professional networks have been commented on in the literature (Harvey 2008; Salaff and Greve 2004; Meyer et al. 2001) various types of local associations are also being formed to serve the specific needs of the diverse groups among highly skilled migrants (Scott 2007). As a result, there is more to be researched when it comes to highly skilled immigrants' networks, both at transnational and local levels, and in relation to their international and domestic moves, as well as their settlement and formation of belonging. This chapter offers a glimpse into the multiple and changing identities, as well as the complex networks at play, and their impact on the conceptualization and processes of building "home" on the part of Turkish immigrant professionals who live in two very different Canadian cities.

## Methodological Framework

This study is based on semi-structured interviews that were conducted with sixteen Turkish-origin professionals living in Canada, ten of whom were living in Toronto and six who were based in Halifax. The eight male and eight female participants were born in Turkey and earned their first university degrees in Turkey. Most spoke one of the two official languages (English or French) at the time of arrival in Canada, and a few spoke both. Nine had immigrated to Canada as skilled workers, while five came as graduate students. One respondent came after accepting a job offer, and one came as a Provincial Nominee. All were employed, except one who was between jobs, and another who had retired. The participants had lived in Canada for periods of time that ranged from four years to thirty-eight years. The majority had their Canadian citizenship, while others were permanent residents. Almost all respondents came from middle-class families, both in terms of their educational credentials and incomes in Turkey, and they maintained this economic level in Canada.

"Citizenship and Immigration Canada (CIC) statistics show that there has been a wave of Turkish immigrants to Canada after the financial crisis of 2001 and the rise of the social conservative party, Adalet ve Kalkinma Partisi (AKP) to political power in Turkey. This wave, which consists of more than 10,000 immigrants, seems to include mostly skilled workers and entrepreneurs (CIC 2008). The Federation of Canadian Turkish Associations (based on CIC statistics) reports that the number of Turkish Republic citizens living in Canada jumped from 24,910 in 2001 to 43,685 in 2006. More than half of the Turkish nationals (54 per cent) live in Ontario while the number of Turks in Nova Scotia more than doubled from 2001 to 2006. Although the number of Turkish immigrants is still very low in Nova Scotia, this wave of immigration, consisting mostly of skilled workers and entrepreneurs (CIC 2008), coincided with the regional immigrant inflows into Atlantic Canada, which rose about 60 percent from 2003 to 2009 (Akbari 2011).

Not surprisingly, the many differences between Toronto and Halifax caused some differentiation in the migration and settlement experiences of this study's participants. Toronto is a large urban centre, a prominent business and financial hub, and has been the major gateway for immigrant settlement in Canada since the 70s (Preston et al. 2011). By 2006, more than 45 per cent of Toronto's population was foreign-born and originated from many different countries and regions (Preston et al. 2011). Conversely, in Halifax, immigrants account for only 8 per cent of the population (Greater Halifax Partnership 2011), although this city attracts almost 78 per cent of all new immigrants to Nova Scotia. Demographic variables are found to have a stronger effect than economic variables on the location choice of Canadian immigrants, and immigrants from all classes are more likely to settle in areas with a larger foreign-born population share and a larger total population (Akbari and Harrington 2007). Not surprisingly, then, Toronto has historically drawn Turkish immigrants. The largest and oldest Turkish community of Canada lives there, whereas Turkish immigration to Halifax is very recent and occurs in very small numbers. Moreover, in this study, half of the Halifax respondents had lived in Toronto before moving to Halifax. With one exception (the interviewee who was a provincial nominee), all Halifax respondents had secured their jobs before moving to the city whereas only three out of ten Toronto respondents moved to Toronto with a secure job there. However, what is more surprising, and what this research contributes to studies of "home," is that these significant differences between Toronto and Halifax did not have a discernible impact on respondents' perceptions of home.

## What is Home?

In the words of this study's respondents, Canada was their home because: they had their nuclear family here (i.e., spouse and children) and friends; they had a house here (one that they either owned or rented); and because they were able to sustain themselves in Canada. This logic suggests that "home" is portable and is conceptually distinct not only from a "homeland" but also from affiliations with friends and the general community. In fact, for several participants "home" would be the next place that they would move to with their families to make a living. For example, this was how Gurbetci described "home":

> I inhabit here. There is a saying; you've probably heard this; "it is not where you were born but where your stomach is filled is your home." If you take this saying, my home is here. My wife and my children are here, they are going to school here. My life is going on in this neighbourhood. But, if, in

the future, I move to Turkey, or I don't know, to Germany, then my home will be there.[4]

Indeed, this echoes key aspects of home identified by other participants. Consider Matt's words, which also include emotions and values in this portable sense of home:

> We can say that wherever my spouse is, my family is, wherever we can find our food is our home. I mean, not only Turkey, not Turkish motherland.... If we go somewhere else, if we can continue there, if we can live there, there will be our home too. Home is not only a physical location, it is also formed with the construction of a set of feelings, values on it.

In other words, many of the respondents considered home to be where one was able to sustain family, not only in terms of economics, but also in terms of values and opportunities in society. Uncertainty aside, all of the participants were in the process of actively making a home in Canada, in their respective cities, even if there was the prospect of moving in the future.

For the respondents who were single, friends replaced family. Leibkorper, who was in his early thirties, lived in Toronto. He spoke about what happened after being in an accident:

> Twenty, twenty-five people were in the hospital from different nations, different religions.... They helped me a lot through those bad days. Because you are so vulnerable and weak. You need intimacy, care and warmth. And that's how I feel so connected to those people. So, it's like, your friends are your family basically.

Leibkorper highlighted his family-like feelings and solidarity while explaining the reasons for feeling at home in his city of residence. For those who did not have a nuclear family to sustain, family-like emotions and values mattered, in addition to the professional and lifestyle priorities which will be explored in the following sections. But first, a look at the characteristics and nature of multi-local homes, both geographically and biographically, is in order.

### Locating Home: Halifax versus Toronto, Canada and/or Turkey

Perhaps one of the most unexpected findings of this study is that, in terms of the identification of "home," there was no dramatic difference between Halifax and Toronto respondents. In fact, respondents in both Toronto and Halifax commented on the slow pace of their respective cities (compared to that of Turkish cities), the better conditions while raising children, people being friendly and respectful, the cultural and social activities of their respective cities, and the proximity to Europe as the initial factors in choosing and staying in the city of immigration. Alaturka, who visited Halifax before moving, explained how and why Halifax has become the choice of home for him and his family:

> We are coming from a very big city like Istanbul. We know the problems of a big city. The stress, the pollution, and the pressure that is present in a big city. When we came to Halifax we were suddenly taken by it. Because it has topographical, geographical characteristics that reminds us of Istanbul. Still people are respectful towards each other. We only left (Turkey) after deciding on Halifax. We did not see Toronto, Montreal.

Alaturka and his family had the good fortune of being able to choose, and having not seen Toronto and Montreal, first impressions of Halifax mattered immensely.

Canada itself also had much to offer in this respect. As much as the respondents felt at home in their respective cities, there was also an overarching feeling of being at home in Canada and being Canadian. All respondents thought of Canada as their home. While some saw Canada as the only "home" they had, others considered both Turkey and Canada to be home. Gunes was a thirty-year-old graduate student who considered moving within Canada upon graduation. He stated:

According to me, my home is both in Canada and in Turkey. I am used to both cultures. When I am in Turkey, sometimes, they make fun of me saying that "you have become a Canadian." Here too, sometimes they joke around with me, because of my use of English. Therefore, although it may not be possible to feel in harmony with both the homes a hundred percent I still see both of them as my home.

While some respondents found themselves in between—not feeling a full sense of belonging to either country—some came to terms with having two homes and accepted it as a fact of life. Seaport, an engineer in his early sixties, had been living in Halifax for more than thirty years. He stated that his home was Canada:

We have Canadian-style life here. We don't have a typical Turkish life, house and we are not connected to Turkish traditions here. Our children don't know Turkish. We were in a Turkish entourage very little here. And the years that we've spent here are more than those in Turkey. From these regards we are Canadian first, then we are Turks.

Seaport's statement captures two of the most important factors that helped many of the respondents feel at home: the degree of importance attached to ethno-cultural scripts and the number of years one spends in a place. The majority of the respondents ethno-culturally identified themselves as Turkish-Canadian or as Canadian with Turkish descent/heritage, suggesting that they, too, had developed attachments and had started to feel a part of Canadian society. Furthermore, many respondents mentioned that they had been in Canada for a long time, or that they were planning to be here for a long time. As they saw their future in Canada, they committed more to the formation and maintenance of an environment, society and country which they could call home.

## Locating Home: In Life

Many respondents mentioned going through a "trial period" whether they were in Toronto or Halifax. As they were evaluating their chances of staying, they were also going through milestones, such as transitioning from a student identity to acquiring or changing professional identities. For many respondents "home" was a reflection of their life stages, and its (re)establishment co-incided with events such as when they left their parents' home or started their married lives. For some respondents, formation of a Canadian identity coincided with these milestones and became part of their personal development. Lassie came to Halifax after having lived in Toronto. She explained why Toronto was her home:

> Istanbul is in a way past. And we did not stay there very long, only five years. T (home town), I am very much differ-ent than what (I was) there. I find that environment closed, like either the fundamentalists or nationalists or others etc. Here is new yet. For that reason I see Toronto as home at this moment (laughs).

As individuals go through various life stages they constantly question their personal development and identify with places that are more reflective of these developments. For some respondents, for example, the city they called home was tied to an understanding of "self" such as identifying with Toronto during a life stage that entailed becoming parents or grandparents, a career change or starting a relationship. For some, going through different life stages also meant changes in their philosophical outlook on life, such as changes in their worldview or political views. Moreover, both the Toronto and Halifax respondents had personal life stage changes (such as the graduation of children or themselves or retirement) where living arrangements could change accordingly (such as moving to another city in Canada or living part-time in Turkey and part-time in Canada) thus affecting the configuration of their future multi-local homes. I now turn to how the Turkish professionals in Canada construct their "home."

## Citizenship and Home

One of the processes by which the respondents constructed their sense of home was citizenship. It is reported in the literature that migrants perceive the acquisition of formal citizenship in their new state of residence as a prerequisite for achieving security (in both the place of settlement and abroad); allowing them to reunite with and extend this security to their loved ones; facilitating transnational practices such as visiting or returning to their home country; and as a prerequisite for equal access to social and political rights in the country of residence (Ehrkamp 2006). But citizenship entails more than possessing rights. It signifies membership in a community encompassing social, symbolic and even emotional/psychological dimensions (Dobrowolsky and Tastsoglou 2006) which includes feelings of belonging, values, principles, stories, myths, real and imagined communities, as well as personal and state-societal connections (Tastsoglou 2006). If citizenship is understood as a process with a psychological dimension, which includes the sense of belonging as well as other emotions intertwined with the acquisition of legal citizenship, then the firm belief in Canadian multiculturalism, along with the sense of satisfaction that comes with professional/economic integration, were sentiments expressed by the Turkish immigrant professionals to convey what Canadian citizenship meant to them. It was through these processes and sentiments around citizenship that their sense of belonging heightened and which, in turn, fostered these respondents' sense of feeling at "home." The three dimensions of citizenship will be examined in the following sections.

## From Paper to the Heart

Upon obtaining citizenship here, Turkish professionals in this study stated that they valued the possession of a Canadian passport (as a "western" passport to facilitate international travel) as much as they valued their right to participate in the civil and political life of Canada. On a symbolic level they thought that, as citizens, they officially qualified to be members of Canadian society and expressed feelings of being more accepted, included and comfortable in the country. In addition, they thought that Canada was a country where there was respect for people and ready access to justice. Trust in economic and political institutions (i.e., the perception that Canadian institutions are fair and just) is found to be an important factor in feeling included for Canadian immigrants (Reitz and Banerjee 2009).

Alaturka from Halifax talked about the emotional dimension of citizenship:

> The Canadian identity does not form easily. Because I am fifty years old. But, there are reasons for me to say I am a Canadian when asked. The first of these reasons is that I love Canada. Canada made me love itself (Canada). In fact, nobody could have made me take the Canadian passport, even by the force of a gun.

In fact, "love" was one dimension of citizenship that the Turkish professionals mentioned when they talked about their Canadian citizenship. The feelings of being included and comfortable in addition to contributing to a country that they loved and valued fostered the sense that Canada was now a home. Lassie explained how her Canadian identity has developed as a result of her feelings, and her knowledge of Canadian institutions and society:

> I worked in various schools, I am really aware of the Canadian reality. The problems in African Canadian population, the poverty, the hunger, the relationship problems... Whatever is happening in the hospitals. Because of this, when a Canadian comes, I know where s/he is coming from, when s/he talks about her/his problems, I can understand them. I see myself as a real Canadian in that sense.... I love it too.

To relate to fellow Canadians in order to understand each other, on various levels—at work or in the streets—translated into love and trust toward the society and country on the part of respondents as Canadian citizens.

## Multiculturalism

Canada's multicultural landscape, along with its official multicultural policy and practice, were identified as contributing factors in making the respondents feel more at home. Although multiculturalism has been criticized on both theoretical and practical grounds,[5] many respondents liked what Canadian multiculturalism offered: assurance of a secure cultural background and freedom and equality as preconditions for participating in public life (Faist 2000). Thus, they valued Canadian multicultural commitments and saw them working in tandem with political civic life. Insan Kaynaklari from Toronto explained why she felt more belonging to Canada and Canadian society:

> I live in Canada, at this moment as a Turk. But, as a Canadian citizen, I also integrated myself into the Canadian society. Because I work in Canada, I am with groups that are in Canada. This is an immigrant country. In this country you can see yourself comfortably as a Turkish Canadian. And I'd never want to lose my Turkish background. Because we belong to this society.

Feeling integrated but not assimilated helped this study group feel more at home. A few respondents mentioned the parallels between the tolerance that exists in the Turkish culture and Canadian multiculturalism. The context in which they, along with other immigrants, were able to keep their transnationally inspired belonging also strengthened the respondents' sense of Canada as home.

In addition, the respondents valued the opportunity to meet with people of different origins and be exposed to diverse cultures (e.g., through festivals, restaurants, etc.). They recognized that these encounters enriched their lives and contributed to their personal/professional development and identity. This was emphasized more by the Toronto respondents, especially when they were answering the questions regarding why they chose the city that they currently live in. Toronto respondents, while acknowledging the benefits of a (relatively, in their experience) "small" city, talked mostly about the ethnic diversity of other Torontonians and cultural activities. The respondents from Halifax not only extolled the benefits of living in a small city, but also underlined the physical beauty, as well as the friendly people. And, while Halifax has far fewer multicultural offerings than Toronto, respondents in Halifax did mention the former's diverse restaurants (Greek, Chinese, Turkish etc.). However, when noting multicultural landscapes and practices, Halifax respondents were more apt to refer to Canada in general, not Halifax specifically.

### Economic and Professional Integration

Bearing in mind that while economic integration does not guarantee social integration (Reitz and Banerjee 2009), this study concurs with others that have found that integration into the Canadian labour market or, at the very least, making a decent living financially in Canada, is still among the most important social processes by which immigrants make a "new home" for themselves (Tastsoglou 2006). The respondents employed in foundational institutions (such as education or health) felt that their jobs contributed to their sense of being part of a system that they valued. They not only benefited from these institutions but also contributed to the institutions' positive qualities which spoke to the trust that they felt towards these institutions (see above section: "From Paper to the Heart").

Siyah is a professor in her late thirties. She explained:

I am quite happy to be here and to be a part of this system. For example, lastly, in 2008, I was selected to the NSERC grant committee. It served to make me feel more as a Canadian. Yes, I am really a part of this society, if it was not so I would not be here, I would not be selected for this. It is not only an indicator of the point that I have reached in my career. At the same time, it is a proof that I have become a part of this society.

Many of the respondents, like Siyah, saw and valued this other measure of economic integration: not only being able to make enough to live comfortably but being able to feel part of the society through work. Positive contribution to Canadian society helped increase the sense of belonging that was felt toward this country of settlement.

Citizenship processes were not the only ways in which the respondents fostered their sense of "home." I will now turn to the discussion of networks, the other set of "home"-building processes as identified by the Turkish immigrant professionals.

## Networks and Home

Networks not only channel immigrants to new destinations and jobs, but they also facilitate settlement. In fact, by engaging in the construction and mobilization of networks, respondents were able to express their locally, nationally and transnationally-inspired identities, which, in turn, proved to be crucial in fostering their feelings of being at home. It was the presence of pre-migration transnational professional and social networks that was the most noticeable difference between the Toronto and Halifax respondents. Professional pre-migration connections—primarily ethnic, but in some cases also non-ethnic—and friends provided more help for those who landed in Toronto. The respondents who first arrived and lived in Toronto received the following forms of assistance: reception at the landing points (airport and train station); temporary accommodation; guidance about the general culture and daily living; guidance on the job market and job finding strategies/connections; and introduction to a circle of friends. Moral support was mentioned as the most important form of assistance. Halifax respondents received significantly less support. The help they did receive came via their places of employment (recall that all but one moved to Halifax after securing a job), and included assistance around handling visa issues, providing lists of rental properties and introduction to colleagues who offered their local knowledge around issues such as daycare locations; these colleagues often, in the long term, became friends. The initial difference between Toronto and Halifax residents, in terms of access to pre-existing transnational connections in the city, faded once the respondents started to participate in local networks and maintain their transnational networks.

Soon after their arrival, the respondents, like other immigrants (see Tastsoglou 2006), engaged in local and transnational networking practices which, in turn, were inspired and informed by transnational, national (Canadian) and local identifications. For example, professional identity was one of the paramount motives behind the migration of the respondents; thus all participants were part of local, national or transnational professional networks. By participating in these, they felt that they were fulfilling their duty to share their knowledge and expertise with other members of society. Thus, networks were not only to build connection, but also a means of exercising their sense of citizenship.

Seaport, from Halifax, who participated in several non-ethnic professional and volunteer organizations and believed he had benefited from them immensely, stated:

> I did this willingly even though it was difficult. I guessed that if I only went back and forth to work, without opening up (to outside) I would not be adapted any quickly. Or even if I did, maybe I would not be accepted by them. To know someone is the first key to open the door in Canada. It is more important for an immigrant. This, the issue of us, you, them is not there but if it happens this prevents it.

The professional networks, in fact, not only facilitated the respondents' professional development and improved their career opportunities, but also generated greater acceptance by the general community members, by contributing to community development, and fostering solidarity among members of specific professional groups. On many occasions, these professional connections also served ethno-cultural purposes through activities such as funding Turkish student-interns, participating in knowledge dissemination activities in Turkey, and providing a forum to represent Turkey. These networks became a medium through which transnationally-inspired identities were expressed. An observation was that there were more international professional associations which were locally active in Toronto as compared with Halifax. Torontonians mentioned high frequency and quite diverse professional activities, such as training opportunities, meetings, and seminars carried out by their subscribed associations, from which they could chose.

Ethno-cultural associations, in this case Turkish associations in Canada, were also of central importance to many respondents of this study. The Turkish associations with which most of the respondents were involved were mostly geared to cultural and artistic activities, as well as to contributing in general to community development and support in Canada. The respondents joined in order to enjoy themselves, commemorate national days, speak/hear the language, represent Turkey/Turkish culture within Canadian society, and to have their children and youth raised with familiarity of Turkish culture and art. Moreover, these networks also assisted the newcomers in settling, socializing, connecting and finding employment. Matt from Toronto gave an account of how transnationally inspired ethno-cultural associations further serve the cause of general community development:

It is an Association that is geared to facilitate civil community solidarity and communication. It is not like I only want to be with Turks. But, with respect to gather Turks together, to unify power I think that civil community activism is important. Turkish Society of Canada can produce services for a bigger mass.... I think that we can also be present in this society by emphasizing positive values in the Canadian society instead of making our presence dissociated.

While Halifax had only one Turkish Association, some participants in Toronto were able to choose between many. This was mostly due to the large number, diversity and longer presence of

Turkish migrants in Toronto. It is evident from the literature that more established migrant communities may fund a greater number of and more well-established organizations (Moya 2005) and that ethnically (Owusu 2000) and professionally, more diverse migrant populations establish more diverse organizations (Scott 2007). This was the case in Toronto. In addition, the presence of other ethnic groups in Toronto that could be considered in "competition with" or, arguably, detracting from, how the Turkish identity is being constructed and portrayed in Canada (e.g., the Greek, Armenian and Arab diasporas, to name a few) is another contributing factor to the burgeoning and strengthening of the various Turkish ethno-cultural associations, with or without the partisan political component. According to Moya (2005) this is a common occurrence because host societies rarely receive immigrants from only one source country, and the collective identities of arrivals become heightened not only by contrast to those of the native population but also by contrast to those of other newcomers.

As a final point, apart from networks which were used for multiple purposes, ranging from expressing identities to supporting local communities, all respondents had friends with varying degrees of closeness who supported them in various ways. Some respondents stated that they had tighter relationships with their Turkish friends, and therefore they mostly socialized with them. For others, the friend circles included other immigrants as well as native-born Canadians, whom they mostly met through work. Within these circles, respondents felt assured that they were not alone, that they could share their immigration experiences, have fun, get to know one another, and continue to be connected to their past and to their culture. The majority of respondents also kept in close touch with their overseas friends with whom they shared the highlights of their lives and exchanged information, help and support. Their local friends provided the respondents with a gateway (via accommodation, circle of friends and jobs) to the social processes with which the respondents quickly started to build their homes. But most important of all, friends provided moral support. With this note I conclude the discussion of processes which helped the Turkish professionals feel at home in their respective cities and focus on the other side of the coin: the factors that hinder the formation of home.

### Barriers to Feeling at Home

Economic and professional exclusion

This study's results also suggest that it is not the multiple attachments but the feelings of exclusion that hinder feelings of belonging. This finding is similar to that supported by Dion, Dion and Banerjee (2009), who found that the impact of unfair treatment and/or disrespectful behaviour from others based on group membership negatively contributes to a sense of being part of one's society and may be related to less confidence in others in the society.

The Turkish professionals interviewed for this study, by virtue of being a non-visible minority group, did not share some of the experiences of visible minorities, who are reported to have reduced attachments to Canada, show slower social integration into Canadian society, and attribute less importance to their Canadian identity than their white minority counterparts (Reitz and Banerjee 2009). Nevertheless, they still reported discrimination. The majority did not think they were well accepted in Canada. They concluded that Canadians do not trust them because they are immigrants. This they believe was reflected in their difficulty finding jobs in Canada, especially for the respondents from Toronto since, unlike the majority of respondents in Halifax, many had come to Toronto without having secured a job beforehand.

Bacus had been living in Canada for more than eight years. She had a Canadian degree. At the time of interview she was working in a job that was not related to her profession. She explained the reasons behind her not being able to find a job in her profession for almost a year:

I think one of the biggest factors is my name, my last name.

The fact that people cannot pronounce it, they don't know what it is. If I had a name like "Alice Smith," I would receive more phone calls (for interviews) in my job search process. Here they look at it two seconds, he's not going to push himself in order to pronounce it, or is that a girl or a boy, what, what kind of thing?

Once they obtained employment, although none of the participants had experienced blatant racism or discrimination, they worked extra hard to prove themselves at their work places and they had to keep more flexible working schedules and hours. They sensed that some individuals were not particularly comfortable with rising diversity and/or numbers of immigrants. Many Toronto respondents experienced a step backward in their careers—although not to the extent that they would lose their class status, and they thought that this was a loss not only for them but also for Canada. According to one respondent, there were many Turkish migrants who had left Canada because they could not find what they were looking for in terms of jobs/careers.

Ethnic exclusion

Even though the respondents of the study would not be considered as belonging to a visible minority group, many still did not feel like they looked "Caucasian" because they were not of European descent. They also remarked that they would always have an accent or that they would always feel different (in terms of schooling and in terms of culture/food preferences). A recurrent sentiment among the respondents was that they could not leave their Turkish identity behind even if they wanted to or even if they did not feel Turkish anymore, because others would see them as Turkish anyway. Siyah explained:

Sometimes there are difficulties of being Turkish Canadian. First, it is certain that you are a foreigner. Second, because you are Turkish, during the conversations people are more likely to bring up the subject of Armenian issue,[6] Kurdish issue,[7] the fall of Ottoman and what ever happened before and after that.... Even the Pope (laughs) (assassination attempt).[8] Sometimes people really ask in order to learn. But some others approach it with great prejudice. They already believe the other side.

The place of settlement plays a pivotal role when it comes to migrants' sense of transnational identity (Ghosh and Wong 2003). Indeed, the host society often thrusts upon individuals highly homogenized collective identities, particularly of "class" and "ethnicity," which may only remotely relate to their self-perceived (pre-migration) identities (Ghosh and Wong 2003). In the Canadian context, some respondents noted that they were attributed Turkishness by members of other ethnic communities even more often than by mainstream Canadians. This was particularly the case for the respondents living in Toronto where there are other ethnic communities of notable size. On a different level, the Canadian government's decision to recognize the Armenian genocide and its inclusion in the school curriculum created challenges for some respondents who had school-aged children.[9] These respondents felt that their children could be put on the spot by other children because of this information in the curriculum and that as parents they would have the burden of reconciling between the opposed positions of Turkey and Canada on this issue.

On the positive side, several participants found no discrimination in academia and/or technical places of work. In addition, there were instances where they were able to use their ethnic backgrounds to their advantage by building solidarity with people of similar ethnic backgrounds. They acknowledged the difference between being a Turk in Europe (in their words, particularly in Germany, where many Turks experience blatant racism and discrimination with little access to rights) and in Canada. They clearly appreciated Canada and called it home even though they experienced difficulties. In other words, transnational identity and references were both a source of discontent and strength, contributing to the development of sense of home in Canada on the part of Turkish professionals.

## Conclusion

> Life can change a lot of things but we are very content with Halifax, with our jobs, the environment that we live in. I can say that everything we dreamt of before coming here came true. In terms of living standard; in terms of work, it is extraordinarily satisfactory; grants, students.... It is a reality that we proved ourselves to Canada and worldwide as research faculty. (Siyah)

The presence of, and the ability to provide sustenance for, their nuclear family was a key defining feature of home, according to the respondents of this study. Notably, this was equally the case for participants from both Toronto and Halifax. More often than not, friends were considered very dear and their presence was incorporated into the definition of home as well. The extent to which home was multi-locational varied and was dependent on their individual ethno-cultural attachments, the time that they spent in Canada and their life stage. However, home was clearly portable and built through social processes of citizenship and networking. The former consisted of an emotional dimension, multiculturalism and professional/economic integration and was crucial in cultivating a feeling of "home" in Canada. In particular, respondents valued the Canadian political and civic life in which different ethnic groups live and work together—without the threat of assimilation—as well as their ability to participate in this system. Furthermore, professional fulfillment and acceptance constituted the cornerstones for feeling at home for this study group. The maintenance of local, national and transnational networking practices (family-friends, professional or ethno-cultural) by the respondents, who either saw Canada as their only home or as one of their two homes, was the other process which facilitated the building of a "new home." Turkish professional immigrants joined networks based on the identities that they cared for the most, and by the social processes of participating and being active in these networks, they felt more at home. Discrimination, on the other hand, both in public spaces and workplaces, based on the immigrant status and/or on being from Turkey specifically, constituted an obstacle to feeling at home in Canada.

Transnational ethnic and professional networks were more pivotal in directing the immigrants from Turkey to Toronto, and in providing more settlement help. Moreover, there were more international and local professional and ethno-cultural associations, which helped the respondents ground their identities in Toronto as compared to Halifax. Yet, paradoxically, while diversity in Toronto worked to facilitate belonging, Toronto was also where the Turkish identity had more negative connotations in the presence of other ethnic communities. These factors, both positive and negative, were not as apparent in Halifax.

Finally, the majority of the Halifax respondents especially made clear that professional pursuit and fulfilment were of utmost importance and constituted one of the main reasons to move to and stay in Halifax. The professional networks were instrumental in directing many respondents to their city of residence. Furthermore, it was via participating in these networks that the respondents were able to pursue and improve their careers and fulfil their professional and transnationally-inspired ethnic commitments, in addition to being accepted by the community. In this context, for the reasons reported above, increasing the presence, activities and visibility of transnational, national and local professional associations would help direct immigrant professionals to Halifax and provide them with more resources to feel at home.

## Notes

Acknowledgment: I am most in debt to Dr. Evangelia Tastsoglou for her help in crystallizing the concepts found in this chapter.

1. "Home" here is utilized in the sense of the "country of origin."

2. This study was conducted for my MA Thesis: Networking, Belonging and Identity: Highly Skilled Turkish Immigrants in Halifax and Toronto, submitted to Dalhousie University in April 2012.

3. (AKP) is the Justice and Development Party, a centre-right, Islamic-leaning conservative party under the leadership of charismatic Recep

Tayyip Erdogan. The party has stayed in power for three general elections, ever since first forming the government in 2002.

4. All quotations have been minimally edited to increase readability.

5. Anthias (2001), for example, reports that multiculturalism solidifies cultural differences by overemphasizing culture as a fixed and essential phenomenon, and it treats the dominant culture as the natural culture.

6. This refers to the forced deportation and consequent mass expiration of Armenian minority members on Turkish soil by the Ottoman forces during and shortly after the First World War. It is a highly politically-charged issue in Turkey's international relations, with some 20 countries recognizing this as "genocide" and pressuring Turkey to do so, which it rejects.

7. This is a reference to the Turkish government's refusal of Kurdish separatist groups' demands.

8. This alludes to the assassination attempt against Pope John Paul II on May 13, 1981, in Rome by a Turkish national.

9. A sour and tense period in the bilateral relations between Canada and Turkey started with the adoption of the "Armenian Genocide" Resolution (M-380) by the Canadian House of Commons on April 21, 2004, and the continuation of its full support since 2006 of the Resolution. This has been compounded by the memories of 1982 attacks on Turkish diplomatic missions in Canada by Armenian terrorists who are still at large. Since 2004, there have not been any "high level" visits between the two countries.

**References**

Akbari, Ather H. 2011. Labour Market Performance of Immigrants in Smaller Regions of Western Countries: Some Evidence From Atlantic Canada. *Journal of International Migration and Integration* 12 (2): 133-52.

Akbari, Ather H. and Jennifer S. Harrington. 2007. *Initial Location Choice of New Immigrants to Canada.* Atlantic Metropolis Centre, Working Paper Series No: 05-2007. Halifax: Atlantic Metropolis Centre.

Anthias, Floya. 2001. New Hybridities, Old Concepts: The Limits of "Culture." *Ethnic and Racial Studies* 24 (4): 619-41.

Boyd, Monica. 1989. Family and Personal Networks in International Migration: Recent Developments and New Agendas. *International Migration Review* 23 (3): 638-70.

Brah, Avtar. 1996. *Cartographies of Diaspora: Contesting Identities.* New York: Routledge.

Butcher, Melissa. 2009. Ties That Bind: The Strategic Use of Transnational Relationships in Demarcating Identity and Managing Difference. *Journal of Ethnic and Migration Studies* 35 (8): 1353-71.

CIC. 2008. Facts and Figures. http://www.cic.gc.ca/english/resources/statistics/facts2006/ (accessed August 25, 2012).

Collins, Francis Leo. 2008. Bridges to Learning: International Student Mobilities: Education Agencies and Inter-Personal Networks. *Global Networks* 8 (4): 398-417.

Conradson, David and Alan Latham. 2005. Friendship, Networks and Transnationality in a World City: Antipodean Transmigrants in London. *Journal of Ethnic and Migration Studies* 31 (2): 287-305.

Dion, Kenneth L., Karen Kisiel Dion and Rupa Banerjee. 2009. Discrimination, Ethnic Group Belonging, and Well Being. In *Multiculturalism and Social Cohesion: Potentials And Challenges of Diversity*, ed. Jeffrey G. Reitz, Raymond Breton, Karen K. Dion, Kenneth L. Dion, Mai B. Phan and Rupa Banerjee, 69-87. Dordrecht, London: Springer.

Dobrowolsky, Alexandra and Evangelia Tastsoglou. 2006. Crossing Boundaries and Making Connections. In *Women, Migration and Citizenship: Making Local, National and Transnational Connections*, ed. Evangelia Tastsoglou and Alexandra Dobrowolsky, 1-36. Hamphsire: Ashgate.

Ehrkamp, Patricia. 2005. Placing Identities: Transnational Practices and Local Attachments of Turkish Immigrants in Germany. *Journal of Ethnic and Migration Studies* 31 (2): 345-64.

———. 2006. Rethinking Immigration and Citizenship: New Spaces of Migrant Transnationalism and Belonging. *Environment and Planning* 38:1591-97.

Faist, Thomas. 2000. Transnationalization in International: Implications for the Study of Citizenship and Cultures. *Ethnic and Racial Studies* 23 (2): 189-222.

Ghosh, Sutama and Lu Wang. 2003. Transnationalism and Identity: A Tale of Two Faces and Multiple Lives. *Canadian Geographer* 47 (3): 269-82.

Gold, Steven J. 2001. Gender, Class, and Network: Social Structure and Migration Patterns Among Transnational Israelis. *Global Networks* 1 (1): 57-78.

Greater Halifax Partnership. 2011. http://www.greaterhalifax.com/en/home/economicdata/people/immigration.aspx (accessed December 7, 2012).

Harvey, William S. 2008. The Social Networks of British and Indian Expatriate Scientists in Boston. *Geoforum* 39 (5): 1756-65.

Johnston, Ron, Andrew Trlin, Anne Henderson and Nicola North. 2006. Sustaining and Creating Migration Chains Among Skilled Immigrant Groups: Chinese, Indians, and South Africans in New Zealand. *Journal of Ethnic and Migration Studies* 32 (7): 1127-50.

Kaya, Ilhan. 2003. *Shifting Turkish American Identity Formations in the United States.* Ph.D. Dissertation, Florida State University.

MacDonald, John, S. and Leatrice D. MacDonald. 1964. Chain Migration, Ethnic Neighbourhood Formation and Social Networks. *Milbank Memorial Fund Quarterly* 42: 82-97

Meyer, Jean-Baptiste, David Kaplan and Jorge Charum. 2001. Scientific Nomadism and the New Geopolitics of Knowledge. *International Social Science Journal* 53 (2): 309-21.

Moya, José C. 2005. Immigrants and Associations: A Global and Historical Perspective. *Journal of Ethnic and Migration Studies* 31 (5): 833-64.

Owusu, Thomas Y. 2000. The Role of Ghanaian Immigrant Associations in Toronto, Canada. *International Migration Review* 34 (4): 1155-81

Phan, Mai B. and Raymond Breton. 2009. Inequalities and Patterns of Social Attachments in Quebec and the Rest of Canada. In *Multiculturalism and Social Cohesion: Potentials And Challenges of Diversity*, ed. Jeffrey G. Reitz, Raymond Breton, Karen K. Dion, Kenneth L. Dion, Mai B. Phan and Rupa Banerjee, 89-121. Dordrecht, London: Springer.

Preston, Valerie, Rober Murdie, Silvia D'Addario, Prince Sibanda, Ann Marie Murnaghan, Jennifer Logan and Mi Hae Ahn. 2011. *Precarious Housing and Hidden Homelessness Among Refugees, Asylum Seekers and Immigrants in the Toronto Metropolitan Area.* CERIS Working Paper No. 87. Toronto: CERIS, the Ontario Metropolis Centre.

Ralston, Helen. 2006. Citizenship, Identity, Agency and Resistance Among Canadian and Australian Women of South Asian Origin. In *Women, Migration and Citizenship: Making Local, National and Transnational Connections*, ed. Evangelia Tastsoglou and Alexandra Dobrowolsky, 149-200. Hamphsire: Ashgate.

Reitz, Jeff G. and Rupa Banerjee. 2009. Racial Inequality and Social Integration. In *Multiculturalism and Social Cohesion: Potentials And Challenges of Diversity*, ed. Jeffrey G. Reitz, Raymond Breton, Karen K. Dion,
Kenneth L. Dion, Mai B. Phan and Rupa Banerjee, 123-55. Dordrecht,
London: Springer.

Salaff, Janet W. and Arent Greve. 2004. Can Women's Social Networks
Migrate? *Women's Studies International Forum* 27 (2): 149-62.

Scott, Sam. 2007. The Community Morphology of Skilled Migration:
The Changing Role of the Voluntary and Community Organizations
(VCOs) in the Grounding of British Migrant Identities in Paris (France).
*Geoforum* 38 (4): 655-76.

Tastsoglou, Evangelia. 2006. Gender, Migration and Citizenship: Immigrant Women and the Politics of Belonging in the Canadian Maritimes. In *Women, Migration and Citizenship: Making Local, National
and Transnational Connections*, ed. Evangelia Tastsoglou and Alexandra
Dobrowolsky, 201-30. Hamphsire: Ashgate.

Vertovec, Steven. 2004. Migrant Transnationalism and Modes of Transformation. *The International Migration Review* 38 (3): 970-1002.

Walters, David, Kelli Phythian and Paul Anisef. 2006. *The Ethnic Identity
of Immigrants in Canada*. CERIS Working Paper No 50. Toronto: CE-
RIS, the Ontario Metropolis Centre.

Wong, Siu-Lun and Janet W. Salaff. 1998. Network Capital: Emigrating
From Hong Kong. *British Journal of Sociology* 49 (3): 358-74.

Yeoh, Brenda S. A and Katie Willis. 2005. Singaporean and British
Transmigrants in China and the Cultural Politics of "Contact Zones."
*Journal of Ethnic and Migration Studies* 31 (2): 269-85.

## 11

## Why Here? Immigrants' Decisions to Stay or Leave Maritime Communities: Research from Miramichi, New Brunswick

*Natasha Hanson*

### The New Brunswick Context

Recognizing that it was facing a declining and aging population, the New Brunswick provincial government formed a Population Secretariat in 2007 to facilitate population and economic self-sufficiency (Premier/Business New Brunswick 2007; Province of New Brunswick 2007). The Population Secretariat, now known as the Population Growth Division, articulated a three-pronged approach to dealing with the ongoing population issues: retention, repatriation and immigration (Premier/Business New Brunswick 2007; Province of New Brunswick 2007).[1] While retention in Atlantic Canada commonly refers to attempting to keep immigrants from leaving the region, in New Brunswick, retention is primarily but not exclusively focused on people born in the province. This chapter, however, focuses on New Brunswick's broader immigration and immigrant retention challenges, and does so by way of a more specific study: the case of the Miramichi. Before turning to this case study, some additional background information on the province of New Brunswick is in order.

New Brunswick clearly has the attraction of immigrants as a goal but, as the subject of this book attests, the difficulty does not lie solely in getting newcomers to immigrate to the province; there is also the issue of retaining them, and ultimately making them feel at "home." In a June 2010 news article (Cormier 2010), a provincial official reiterated the goal set in the February 2008 government document entitled *Be Our Future: New Brunswick's Population Growth Strategy*: "[t]o increase the number of immigrants coming to the province with the goal of attracting at least 5,000 people per year by the year 2015" (Population Growth Secretariat 2008: 15). However, government officials, such as former Environment Minister Rick Miles speaking on behalf of former Post-Secondary Education and Training and Labour Minister Donald Arseneault (responsible for the Population Growth Secretariat), are well aware that "[b]eyond attracting immigrants, we need to ensure that they stay" (Cormier 2010). What is more, the current government continues to recognize the importance of retaining immigrants, as it included not only immigration and settlement, but also diversity and welcoming communities as "Areas for Consideration" in a recent discussion paper (Province of New Brunswick 2013: 6). To this end, since the establishment of the Population Growth Secretariat, and working in cooperation with the New Brunswick Multicultural Council, settlement services have received funding (Population Growth Secretariat 2007b).

This chapter focuses on a case study of the decision-making processes of immigrants to New Brunswick in terms of their reasons for coming, their experiences and their plans to stay. By probing immigrants' experiences and perceptions of immigration to the small city of Miramichi, located at a distance from larger, urban centres in New Brunswick, the aim is to provide further insight into government immigration programs and policies, as well as socio-cultural issues, related to retention and rural out-migration.

## Why Miramichi?

Miramichi, New Brunswick was chosen as the site for this case study because it is a small city of 17,811 whose population declined by 2 per cent between the 2001 and 2006 Censuses and further lost 1.8 per cent between 2006 and 2011 (Statistics Canada 2012, 2007). This loss reflects a common problem found outside of larger urban centres in Canada (Wulff et al. 2008; Flint 2007; Reimer 2007; Ouattara and Tranchant 2007). Immigration overall in New Brunswick almost doubled during the period from 2001 to 2006 and retention increased from 67 to 75 per cent (Akbari 2008), but the majority of immigrants to New Brunswick settled in the three cities of Fredericton, Saint John and Moncton; non-urban areas, such as Miramichi, did not see the benefits of this increased level of immigration. While the area of Miramichi attracted eighty new immigrants between 2001 and 2006, for a total of 645 immigrants, the area remained relatively homogeneous with only 340 people identifying as visible minorities and still consists of a predominantly English-speaking population (Statistics Canada 2007).[2]

The city of Miramichi is an example of a smaller centre, not near an urban area (or non-metro adjacent) within New Brunswick that is suffering from population loss and an aging population that could benefit from increased immigration. Yet, the community has several challenges in terms of attracting and retaining immigrants: the large forestry sector has suffered a major downturn in the past decade (Bruce 2010); the youth population is declining (Akbari 2014; Statistics Canada 2009) and people in the community believe this to be due to a lack of job prospects. Hence, the city of Miramichi finds itself in the contradictory position of needing an influx of population but not necessarily having the employment opportunities to support this influx.

However, the information collected in this study reveals that, contrary to popular assumptions, there are in fact job opportunities in Miramichi which are attracting immigrants. In addition, this research also suggests that the retention of newcomers who choose to move to the city or surrounding area does not solely depend on economic factors. This disconnect between non-immigrants' perception of a lack of local employment opportunities and the types of jobs that are in fact available in reality may relate to what kinds of employment are valued or available to non-immigrant community members. The employment drawing immigrants to the area is dichotomous: on one hand, there are very high-prestige health professional positions demanding high levels of qualifications; and on the other hand, there are service industry jobs that have few, if any, post-secondary education requirements. While there are also some mid-level positions, these are relatively limited in number. Therefore, the opinions held by non-immigrant community members regarding available job opportunities may reflect their dismissal of available low-paying service industry jobs, and their failure to factor in the existence of high-paying health professional positions for which they are likely not qualified. Non-immigrant community members' views that there are no jobs available is important as this, in turn, affects how they perceive immigrants to the community; for instance, as possibly "taking jobs away" from non-immigrant community members. This negative attitude of some non-immigrant community members also, at times, presented itself as a generalized pessimism toward the future of the community, as well as discouragement to those who immigrated to the area. However, there are those non-immigrant community members who recognize the potential benefits of immigration, particularly with regard to immigrant health professionals, as will be discussed further on in the chapter.

## Methodology and Data Collection

This chapter is based on qualitative data gathered in 2009 from immigrants living in Miramichi, New Brunswick and those providing them with settlement services.[3] The data collected serve as a case study of the complicated decision-making processes that occur in terms of where immigrants choose to live in Canada and their subsequent mobility decisions. It answers the call for further study of the motivating factors in rural retention (Depner and Teixeira 2012; Akbari et al. 2007; Reimer 2007). From a theoretical and methodological perspective, the data collected are framed by motivational analysis, described by Ouattara and Tranchant as investigating "the reasons and motivations that guide migrants in their choices" (2007: 98). This is in contrast to existing studies that compile demographic statistical data or take an economic approach using mathematical models to understand factors involved in migration decisions (Ouattara and Tranchant 2007). The benefit of a motivational analysis is that it emphasizes the personal and process-based nature of migration without the automatic assumption of economic or material motives (Ouattara and Tranchant 2007), allowing for a much more nuanced understanding of the decision-making process.

The concepts of social capital and social networks also informed the analysis of the data that were collected in order to investigate the decision-making process of immigrant interprovincial migrants (Granovetter 1983, 1973; Portes 1998; Bourdieu 2001; Putnam 2000; Smart 2008). Putnam defines social capital as the "connections among individuals—social networks and the norms of reciprocity and trustworthiness that arise from them" (2000: 19). The social networks themselves are social connections that involve mutual obligation (Putnam 2000). While social networks were not often found to influence, initially, the move to the community, as discussed later in the chapter, development of social networks is important in the retention of immigrants. Moreover, there is the possibility of encouraging further migration to the community through the social networks of those who have moved to the area. This concentration on the social aspects of the decision-making process for immigrant internal migration contributes to the literature on migration that is critical of emphasizing economic concerns over all else (Castles and Davidson 2000; also see Dobrowolsky, Bryan and Barber, this volume; Ramos and Yoshida, this volume) and presents new possibilities for informative, empirical investigation. The findings of the data collected indicate that non-economic factors often influence the decision of immigrants to stay in a community. This echoes the results of research on welcoming communities which note the importance of attitudes towards diversity and the quality and accessibility of local infrastructure and services, as well as the provision of effective settlement services (Bruce 2007; Lund and Hira-Friesen 2013; National Working Group on Small Centre Strategies 2007).

The qualitative data from this study consist of seventeen semi-structured interviews collected with people who immigrated to Miramichi and were living there during the fall of 2009. I also conducted two further interviews with people providing settlement services to the area, allowing further contextualization of comments by immigrants themselves. In addition, I engaged in participant observation at several community events and in the community at large.

It is important to note that I was not able to obtain interviews with immigrants who had moved out of the area. There were few reported incidents of immigrants moving away (from both immigrant and service provider respondents). Those instances of leaving discussed by interviewees living in the area cited employment opportunities elsewhere as the motivation for leaving in two cases, and missing urban living in the other. In most cases those immigrants who had left the community had not maintained any social ties. This could indicate that they had not formed social networks in Miramichi with other immigrants or through the local multicultural association (see Ramos and Yoshida, this volume for further discussion on the significance of social networks).

The interviews for this study were conducted with immigrants, the majority of whom (thirteen out of seventeen) had moved to the area in the past five years, and were guided by the broad themes of immigration decision-making, as well as community reception and resettlement decision processes. These themes relate to the concept of welcoming communities, as mentioned above, and the information gathered shows that the factors associated with this concept were considered during the ongoing decision-making processes by interviewees about staying and leaving Miramichi.

## Miramichi Immigrant Interviewees

The immigrants interviewed had varied backgrounds, and in order to contextualize the demographic profile of the interviewees, some general information about them as a group is provided below. For the majority of those interviewed, Miramichi was the initial area of residence in Canada (twelve out of seventeen). The participants ranged in age from twenty-five to seventy-eight years old, with the majority (thirteen out of seventeen) between the ages of thirty-one and fifty. Eleven of the interviewees were men and six were women. Of these six women, five were not employed outside of the home. Four of these five women were stay-at-home mothers. Overall, in terms of paid employment, only two interviewees were unemployed at the time of the interview and were actively job hunting.

The interviewees were at various stages of immigration and two (out of seventeen) had obtained their Canadian citizenship. Those who were not Canadian citizens stated that they wished to be and were actively pursuing this goal. In terms of where interviewees were in the immigration process, nine currently had work permits, six had permanent residency and two were Canadian citizens. This is not surprising, as the majority had moved to the area only within the past four years. The majority of interviewees (eleven out of seventeen) had moved to Miramichi with their nuclear families and all but one were part of a nuclear family unit. Two people were separated from their families at the time of the interview, with their partners living in their country of origin waiting to come to Canada. The countries of origin were diverse, reflecting the general statistical patterns of immigrants to New Brunswick (Akbari et al. 2007), and there was no discernible pattern to where people had moved from. The occupations of interviewees were also diverse but could be divided into three categories: of the nine employed outside of the home, one third were medical professionals, one third were in the food service industry, and the others worked in a range of industries. Given this occupational information and the above breakdown of citizenship status, it becomes clear that the majority of interviewees were economic immigrants.

## Decisions: Reflections on the Good, Bad and Surprising Elements of Living in Miramichi

General immigration decision processes

Immigration to Miramichi is typically explained by one of three situations: employment offers; moving there with a partner who has a job offer; or marrying someone from the area. Only in three cases did people move without employment offers; this indicates that there are job opportunities available in Miramichi despite the common community perception to the contrary. Interviewees cited better job prospects, finding a good place to raise their children, and seeing a different part of the world as the motivations behind moving to Canada.

The occupation of the interviewees or their spouse, in many cases, informed the immigration experiences of these people. For example, and most notably, medical professionals described overall easier transitions into the community in terms of initial work permit immigration processes and community reception. They mentioned that the community was very supportive of them and appreciated their willingness to practice in the area. This speaks to the general knowledge and concern within the community about medical professional labour shortages. These professional interviewees and their spouses are indicative of overall trends in highly skilled immigrants making up increasingly large numbers of overall immigrants to New Brunswick (Akbari 2014; Akbari et al. 2007).

Those people hired by companies, agencies or the local health authority clearly had an advantage, as the employer helped (to varying degrees) with the initial immigration paperwork. Also, medical professionals had the advantage of being offered a site visit to the local hospital which was responsible for their hiring, and there was mention of a monetary signing bonus. However, aside from site visits for medical professionals, employers seldom provided newcomers with substantial information about the community. Information that workers received about the community was limited to the low cost of living in the area, and the fact that the winters were long.

The interviewees reported that they typically found information about the Canadian immigration process and the community by searching the Internet, contacting the Canadian embassy, and asking friends living in Canada. Yet, some of the interviewees stated that the information found on government websites was lacking and even conflicting, as there were inconsistencies between web pages, making the process of finding accurate information difficult. This could be indicative of what one interviewee saw as a lack of cooperation between the provincial and federal levels of government with regards to immigration programs. However, the New Brunswick government has recognized that its website information requires work, and beginning in 2007, it signed an agreement with the federal government that over the next four fiscal years there would be the "implementation of the New Brunswick immigration portal designed to make current online information for prospective immigrants and newcomers to New Brunswick more user-friendly" (Population Secretariat 2007: 1).

Many of the interviewees also noted that there was little information about Miramichi online, and as such many lacked information about the city before arriving. In fact there was no mention of immigration at all on the municipal website of the City of Miramichi, or indication of what services may be available, at the time of this research (City of Miramichi 2010). However, the city website now mentions moving to the city from another country and has a link to the Miramichi Regional Multicultural Association (MRMA) website and its *Newcomer Guide* (City of Miramichi 2011). This indicates that there have been some steps taken to address the previous disconnect, between the provincial mandate for increased immigration and the municipal govern-ment. The initial lack of promotion of the city as a destination for immigrants, along with little community information through the municipal website for those moving to the city, was not helpful in the attraction or retention of newcomers.

In terms of using social networks to gather information/ support on immigration to Canada in general, and Miramichi in particular, eleven out of the seventeen interviewed knew people living in Canada before moving; however, of those, only two knew people living in Miramichi. Hence, most interviewees did not move to the area in order to join family or friends. This is not surprising considering the small population of immigrants in the area. Thus, social networks do not appear to have played a major role in the choice of destination for those newcomers interviewed. However, one of the interviewees told me that she had encour-aged friends from her country of origin to move to the city, and that one nuclear family had indeed moved to Miramichi at their encouragement. This positive story indicates that building up the community through immigration could become a self-fulfilling process due to the positive experiences of those living in the area.

Community reception and resettlement decision processes

Despite not knowing much about the community prior to arrival, interviewees generally found themselves welcomed, specifically in terms of how friendly people were on an individual basis. In fact, fifteen out of the seventeen immigrants interviewed stated that they found the community welcoming. In their answers respondents generally mentioned how well individuals treated them. One interviewee explained how people in the community were immediately welcoming:

> Really the people were amazing ... we bought this house and even before we moved in the people on the street gave us a house warming. I mean that is just so, so strange, something I'm not used to at all. And it was the same everywhere we went, we really were welcomed. Which is great, you never

had to fight for a place, you were part of the community, that's it.

In contrast to this, one interviewee stated that he found the community insular rather than welcoming:

> I don't think it is welcoming. We have two families whom we consider as extremely good friends, I mean like maybe even part of our family now, that close but they're just two and one of them is obviously, obviously one of them is a foreigner herself so, and I have to say that the other couple is not from New Brunswick. They're from some other province.

This interviewee pointed out that while people in Miramichi were pleasant, they were seemingly unwilling to create friendships with newcomers; hence his closest friends were also "from away."

When asked about the positive qualities of the community, interviewees frequently mentioned that the area was "nice" in terms of both the people and the physical space, which they described as quiet, with a simple way of life, safe with low crime rates and low cost of living. As one interviewee explained:

> It's nice and quiet; I think it's a great place for small children. To commute to almost anything is like five minutes or three minutes. I mean my daughter's school is two minutes. I think that it's relatively safe, compared to other bigger cities. The people are very, very friendly and hospitable. They don't make you feel like you are not from here or anything. You're not a stranger; they make you feel very welcome.

There was also mention that the various levels of government provided good social services, including healthcare and education. Furthermore, most interviewees positively commented on the services of the Miramichi Regional Multicultural Association (MRMA). In 2008, the MRMA began to provide settlement services and many of the interviewees were involved in some way with the Association. As a result, several noted that the Association was important to them in the provision of English language classes, information and who to contact about immigration generally, as well as being a space to form friendships with other immigrants (which was emphasized). This is an important point: not only did the organization help to provide information and services, but it also provided a social space for immigrants to find others with common experiences and build social networks. The providers of settlement services interviewed recognized that the most sought-after services were English language instruction and socialization. As one worker noted, socialization was an important part of their mandate because "social isolation is a problem among newcomers." Due to the relative newness of the provision of settlement services in the area, workers acknowledged that they were working to respond to needs and improve services.

In addition to providing services to new immigrants, an important part of the MRMA mandate is to provide education to the community about the benefits of immigration. As one Association employee stated, community education is imperative because it helps to facilitate a welcoming community, which is essential to successful immigration and retention. There seems to be a common misunderstanding generally that immigrants take jobs away from Canadians (Vukets 2010). This is despite the fact that there are measures in place to ensure that Canadian citizens are given preference in hiring, with employers first having to prove they are unable to find suitable Canadian citizens for the job (Vukets 2010). The provincial government also realizes the importance of educating the public about the benefits of diversity; for example, funding was announced for multicultural resources in public libraries (Cormier 2010). In fact, promotion of diversity and multiculturalism is officially part of the provincial population growth strategy (Population Growth Secretariat 2008).

While interviewees experienced the above positive aspects of their new community, they also found that there were negative aspects to the community as a whole. When it came to describing the difficulties that they had experienced in the immigration processes or within the community, several commonalities became evident. In terms of socially-based problems, a few interviewees cited instances of racism in local social institutions that they, their family members, or other immigrants had experienced. Interviewees felt that these issues were not being dealt with within those institutions, which was disappointing to those involved. This is reflective of a study on racism experienced by visible minority adolescents in New Brunswick that found authority figures dismissed racist incidents such as name-calling as harmless (Baker et al. 2009). Despite these instances of reported discrimination, the vast majority of the respondents still felt welcomed in the community, including one whose family had been subjected to discrimination; she considered the instances not representative of the community as a whole. Clearly, authority figures within the community need to address racism, and as Baker et al. (2009) suggest, there needs to be an acknowledgement of the racism inherent in such actions as name-calling, and development of policies in order to formally deal with such behaviour within social institutions such as schools. The remainder of difficulties cited by respondents dealt more with the practicalities of living in this particular municipality, as discussed below.

Interestingly, an important issue for the respondents was the defeatist attitude displayed by the municipal government, where it seemed that local government representatives did not think the city could grow and prosper. While one interviewee enjoyed living in Miramichi, she noted that the

> downside for me is I just sometimes I just feel like, ah like I don't know, like the council whoever, has just given up, like what's the point of fixing the roads. This is just a little town with nothing going, you know.

Some interviewees recalled their disbelief in being asked by provincial officials and local community members why they would actually move to Miramichi. One interviewee mentioned that, via email with provincial government immigration representatives, he was "asked for a reason why [he'd] come here rather than going anywhere else." This negative or defeatist attitude shocked the interviewees, as their impression was that the community needed more people and should be trying to attract them, not being negative about people moving to the area. Some interviewees linked this negative/defeatist attitude to the aging population of the city and what they saw to be a lack of young people staying in the area. This attitude is also likely linked to perceptions in the community of scarce employment opportunities and fears around immigrants "taking" away employment from non-immigrants. However, as noted previously, this employment perception does not reflect the labour market realities which lead to immigrants being employed in the area.

Due to the small size of the city, participants often mentioned the fact that cultural and social events, shopping venues and rental housing were relatively limited. Also likely linked to the small size of the community were comments by interviewees that the lack of personal or social connections made finding employment difficult, even if they were highly qualified for the position in question (for a discussion of the Prince Edward Island context see Baldacchino, this volume). As one frustrated interviewee noted, "It's not what you know in Miramichi, it's whom you know basically and I've had that experience, I have friends who are immigrants here who had the same experience." Those providing settlement services also noted this as problematic. Related to this were issues surrounding credential recognition, which one immigrant interviewee mentioned as a problem. Other immigrant interviewees did not mention this issue but this is not surprising given that the majority of those interviewed were employed within their chosen fields. However, settlement service providers said the issue of credential recognition was difficult to deal with because there were no clear guidelines (government or otherwise) as to how immigrants should proceed if their professional or educational credentials are not recognized.

A couple of interviewees thought it was problematic that the city does not have a university because a university would encourage educational aspirations of young people and retain some high school graduates. It was also suggested that establishment of a post-secondary institution could act as a possible means to revitalize the area. Some interviewees cited poor municipal infrastructure, particularly roads, as a problem. Additionally, the location of the community was said to make air travel inconvenient, given that it is a two-hour drive to one of the airports in the province. The geographic area is also prone to quite a long and snowy winter, and some interviewees considered this a negative factor. One noted that the winter weather made it very difficult to get around the city.

While there has been implementation of a municipal bus system recently, its coverage and frequency are still inadequate resulting in poor accessibility to public transport. Many interviewees therefore mentioned that having a car and driving was almost a necessity to live in the city. Yet, access to vehicles was problematic given that many interviewees expressed the requirement of building an entirely new credit history upon moving to Canada, an issue written about in the literature on Canadian immigration (Atallah and Rebelo 2006). Given this situation, obtaining a lease on credit for a vehicle was impossible for some. An interviewee who moved to the area before the implementation of the municipal bus system noted the difficulties this created:

> The other side of it is that the first thing that I noticed is that basically there was no public transport. Which means that I have to go and buy a car, I mean how do you go and buy a car just like that? You move from a country, the bank wouldn't give you anything, you can't just pay cash and buy a [car] and it was, winter was coming so you need [it] and we're a big family so we need a fairly decent car. The insurance was extremely high because they wouldn't accept the insurance from [name of country] ... and I had letters and everything from big companies, reputable worldwide companies and they wouldn't accept that. The ... some of the banks wouldn't let you open an account.

Compounding the matter, there was mention that getting a driver's licence itself required a wait time that was very inconvenient, and the people who did buy vehicles ended up paying for very expensive car insurance because of the discounting of their previous experiences, as noted in the above quotation. Furthermore, some banks made it difficult to open accounts for the interviewees, also noted above.

In terms of issues with government immigration procedures almost all interviewees mentioned that a more streamlined approach was needed. Some interviewees stated specifically that immigration documents and websites at both levels of government were difficult to understand in that the language used was obtuse, and that examples given did not reflect the intended culturally diverse audience. Also, some interviewees had problems getting responses from both levels of government to immigration questions either by telephone or email.

When asked if they were going to stay in Miramichi, seven said they were definitely staying for the foreseeable future, and seven said that they may stay but it depended on several factors, the most cited of which was employment. Two of the interviewees said that they were definitely going to move at some point in the future, so their children could go to university.

### But Will Newcomers Stay?

In conclusion, this research provides case study evidence that even if newcomers have secure employment, there are socio-cultural factors that will influence the retention of immigrants in smaller communities. The lure of good employment was clearly an important factor in influencing many respondents to initially move to Miramichi; however, in speaking to them about living and possibly staying in the community, interviewees emphasized the welcoming nature of Miramichi's communities, as well as the sense that it provided a safe and secure setting to raise a family. Interviewees also mentioned that they enjoyed living in the quiet, small community. Hence, while employment is important in trying to attract and retain immigrants in non-urban areas, there are clearly socio-cultural elements, as listed above, which are of importance, specifically to the issue of retention.

This case study also points to elements that could be improved to advance the attraction and retention of immigrants to Miramichi and the province generally. There needs to be a change in negative and defeatist attitudes by provincial officials and local community members, acknowledging the potential damage these attitudes have in discouraging immigration. This also could be addressed through further education about the positive impact immigration has in communities, that immigrants are not "taking" employment from the local community but instead filling vacant positions. Further promotion of Miramichi as an immigration destination could be implemented, emphasizing the positive qualities mentioned by interviewees: the area is "nice" in terms of both people and physical space; quiet, with a simple way of life; safe with low crime rates; and has a low cost of living. Government websites, at the federal and provincial levels, need to ensure that they contain detailed and accurate information and that they do not contradict one another. Also, the language used in websites and documents needs to be simplified and the examples used should reflect the culturally diverse audience at which they are aimed. When people need further assistance with immigration processes, this should be accessible and if communications occur via email, there should be a system in place to acknowledge receipt and give a timeline of response to the email.

Regionalization policies should also take into account that targeting families for settlement in lower populated areas may be a good strategy, as the lifestyle of smaller communities appears to coincide with the needs and desires of this group (see also Ramos and Yoshida, this volume). Also of key importance are settlement services both in terms of provision of services and as a source of social networking. Immigration has the potential to effect positive change in non-urban communities such as Miramichi; there just needs to be further recognition of this at the municipal level, and the above suggestions would go a long way toward making this city more welcoming and able to retain those moving to the area.

## Notes

1. The Province of New Brunswick established a consultation process on a new population growth strategic plan in 2013, which included soliciting responses to the *New Brunswick Population Growth Strategy 2013-2018: Discussion Paper* (2013). A formalized strategic plan document has not yet been produced from this process.

2. The 2011 Census did not collect any information regarding the number of immigrants who moved to the city and as such cannot be used in comparison to the 2006 Census results.

3. This research was made possible through the provision of a pilot project grant from the Atlantic Metropolis Centre with Dr. Pauline Gardiner Barber of Dalhousie University as principal researcher. Earlier, truncated versions of this data were presented at the National Metropolis Conference in Montreal, Quebec, March 2010 in a presentation entitled "Why Immigrants Stay or Leave Maritime Communities: Research from Miramichi, New Brunswick" and at the Atlantic Metropolis Symposium in May, 2010 in a presentation entitled "Immigrants' Decisions to Stay or Leave: Research from Miramichi, New Brunswick." An earlier version of this chapter is available through the Atlantic Metropolis Centre as a working paper entitled *Why Stay? An Ethnographic Analysis of the Settlement Decision-Making Process.*

## References

Akbari, Ather H., Scott Lynch, James McDonald and Wimal Rankaduwa. 2007. *Socioeconomic and Demographic Profiles of Immigrants in New Brunswick.* Atlantic Metropolis Centre Working Paper. http://community.smu.ca/atlantic/documents/NB_Report_Final_Dec.pdf (accessed November 12, 2012).

Akbari, Ather H. 2008. *Immigrant Inflows and Their Retention Rise in Atlantic Canada.* Atlantic Metropolis Centre, Working Paper. http://atlantic.metropolis.net/ResearchPolicy/Akbari__Immigration_Trends_(2001-2006).doc (accessed July 8, 2010).

———. 2014. Human Resource Deficit in Atlantic Canada: A Challenge for Regional Economic Development. *Journal of International Migration and Integration* 1:1-12.

Atallah, Nabiha and Sarita Rebelo. 2006. Recognition of Credit History for New Immigrants. *Metropolitan Immigrant Settlement Association, Atlantic Metropolis Centre.* isisns.ca/documents/RecognitionofCredit HistoryforNewImmigrants.pdf (accessed July 8, 2010).

Baker, Cynthis, Manju Varma-Joshi and Connie Tanaka. 2009. Sticks and Stones: Racism as Experienced by Adolescents in New Brunswick. *Canadian Journal of Nursing Research* 41:1.

Bourdieu, Pierre. 2001. The forms of capital. In *The Sociology of Economic Life,* 2nd ed., ed. Mark S. Granovetter and Richard Swedberg, 96-111. Boulder, CO: Westview Press.

Bruce, David. 2007. The Challenges of Immigration as a Rural Repopulation Strategy in Maritime Canada. *Our Diverse Cities* 3:90-96.

———. 2010. Nurturing the Animation Sector in a Peripheral Economic Region: The Case of Miramichi, New Brunswick. In *The Next Rural Economies: Constructing Rural Place in Global Economies,* ed. Greg Halseth, Sean Markey and David Bruce, 128-41. Oxfordshire, U.K.: CABI International.

Campbell, David. 2010. Population is Starting to Rebound, So Are We Turning a Corner? *Telegraph-Journal* (June 30).

Castles, Stephen and Alastair Davidson. 2000. *Citizenship and Migration: Globalization and the Politics of Belonging.* New York: Routledge.

City of Miramichi. 2010. City of Miramichi, New Brunswick, Canada: A Great Place to Live, Work and Play! http://miramichi.org/en/ (accessed July 8, 2010).

———. 2011. Moving to Miramichi. miramichi.org/en/living/moving-tomiramichi.asp (accessed February 27, 2014).

Cormier, Molly. 2010. Libraries Receive Funding for Initiatives. *The Daily Gleaner* (June 21).

Depner, Wolfgang and Carlos Teixeira. 2012. Welcoming Communities? An Assessment of Community Services in Attracting and Retaining Immigrants in the South Okanagan Valley (British Columbia, Canada), with Policy Recommendations. *The Journal of Rural and Community Development* 7 (2): 72-97.

Flint, David. 2007. *Rural Immigrants Who Come to Stay: A case study of recent immigrant to Colchester County, Nova Scotia.* Atlantic Metropolis Centre, Working Paper. atlantic.metropolis.net/WorkingPapers/Flint_AMC_WP7.pdf (accessed July 8, 2010).

Granovetter, Mark. 1973. The strength of weak ties. *The American Journal of Sociology* 78 (6): 1360-80.

———. 1983. The strength of weak ties: A network theory revisited. *Sociological Theory* 1:201-33.

Lund, Darren E. and Parvinder Hira-Friesen. 2013. Measuring the Welcoming Capacities of Host Urban and Rural Communities. *Canadian Ethnic Studies* 45 (3): 65-80.

National Working Group on Small Centre Strategies. 2007. *Attracting and Retaining Immigrants: A Tool Box of Ideas for Smaller Centres*, 2nd ed. Victoria: Inter-Cultural Association of Greater Victoria. http://icavictoria.org/sites/icavictoria.org/files/documents/toolbox/en-toolbox.pdf (accessed July 8, 2010).

Ouattara, Ibrahim and Carol Tranchant. 2007. Immigration to Rural Communities: A Distinctive and Distinctly Promising Phenomenon. *Our Diverse Cities* 3:97-103.

Population Growth Secretariat. 2007. Agreement to Enhance Online Tools for Newcomers to Province (07/05/28). http://gnb.ca/cnb/news/pg/2007e0664pg.htm (accessed June 26, 2010).

———. 2007b. Main Estimates 2007-2008 / Population Growth Secretariat (07/05/10). http://gnb.ca/cnb/news/pg/2007e0587pg.htm (accessed June 26, 2010).

———. 2008. Be Our Future: New Brunswick's Population Growth Strategy. http://gnb.ca/3100/Promos/PS/Strategy-e.pdf (accessed June 26, 2010).

Portes, Alejandro. 1998. Social Capital: Its Origins and Applications in Modern Sociology. *Annual Review of Sociology* 24:1-24.

Premier/Business New Brunswick. 2007. New Brunswick to establish Population Growth Secretariat (07/02/16)." http://gnb.ca/cnb/news/pg/2007e0193pg.htm (aAccessed June 26, 2010).

Province of New Brunswick. 2007. *Our Action Plan to be Self-Sufficient in New Brunswick*. http://nb.ca/2026/OSSPDF/report-E.pdf (accessed June 26, 2010).

———. 2013. *New Brunswick Population Growth Strategy 2013-2018: Discussion Paper*, 2. http://gnb.ca/content/dam/gnb/Departments/petlpft/PDF/PopGrowth/NBPG_Strategy_2013-18.pdf (accessed February 27, 2014).

Putnam, Robert. 2000. *Bowling Alone: The Collapse and Revival of American Community*. New York: Simon and Schuster.

Reimer, Bill. 2007. Immigration in the new rural economy. *Our Diverse Cities* 3:3-8.

Smart, Alan. 2008. Social capital. *Anthropologica* 50 (2): 409-16.

Statistics Canada. 2007. Miramichi, New Brunswick (table). 2006 Community Profiles. 2006 Census. Statistics Canada Catalogue no. 92-591-XWE. Ottawa, 12. http://statcan.ca/english/census06/data/profiles/community/Index.cfm?Lang=E (accessed August 15, 2009).

———. 2009. Miramichi, 2006 Census. Presentation given in Miramichi, NB, October 21, 2009.

———. 2012. Focus on Geography Series, 2011 Census. Statistics Canada Catalogue no. 98-310-XWE2011004. Ottawa, Ontario, 12. http://statcan.gc.ca/census-recensement/2011/as-sa/fogs-spg/Facts-csd-eng.cfm?LANG=Eng&GK=CSD&GC=1309050 (accessed February 27, 2014).

Vukets, Cynthia. 2010. Newcomers Don't Take Jobs Away: Employers. *Times and Transcript* (July 3).

Wulff, Maryann, Tom Carter, Rob Vineberg and Stephen Ward. 2008. Special Issue: Attracting New Arrivals to Smaller Cities and Rural Communities: Findings from Australia, Canada and New Zealand. *International Migration and Integration* 9:119-24.

# ACKNOWLEDGMENTS

Our sincere thanks to our core contributors, as well to a wide array of supporters, who saw the need for work of this kind- critical, analytical and yet accessible- on immigration in Atlantic Canada, and without whom this book idea would never have become a reality. We are very grateful for the revealing research and analyses, as well as the persistence and patience, of all of the chapter authors. And, of course, we are extremely thankful for the insights of the hundreds of interviewees who agreed to participate in the range of research projects showcased in this volume.

We are also indebted to the (former) Atlantic Metropolis Centre (AMC) and the Social Sciences and Humanities Research Council (SSHRC) for the research funding that, directly and indirectly, provided invaluable support to all the researchers and research assistants who contributed to this collection. We would also like to acknowledge the generous AMC/SSHRC subvention given to Cape Breton University (CBU) Press which served to defray key, publication-related expenses, and to thank the Press for all its efforts.

Many thanks to the students, too numerous to mention by name, who worked on this volume in various capacities, from researching and writing, to completing book production related undertakings. However, in relation to the latter, we would like to express our ex- plicit appreciation of the onerous tasks completed by Serperi Sevgur. Alexandra would also like to make specific mention of Catherine Bryan to acknowledge her impeccable work in multiple regards.

Finally, as the three of us are not only immigrants to Atlantic Canada (and indeed, with two of us first generation immigrants to Canada, and one the daughter of immigrants), but we are also all long-standing residents of this region, we would like to thank our families, friends, and communities for the strength, support and sustenance they have provided, which have generated, in turn, the profound warmth, meaning and substance to our respective homes.

Evangelia, Alexandra and Barbara

# Contributors

GODFREY BALDACCHINO is an Island Studies Teaching Fellow at the University of Prince Edward Island where he served as Canada Research Chair (Island Studies) (2003-2013). His research focus includes the experiences of recent newcomers to Prince Edward Island, as well as the challenges faced by internationally educated health professionals. He also served as Vice-President of the PEI Association for Newcomers to Canada (PEIANC).

PAULINE GARDINER BARBER is a Social Anthropologist and Professor at Dalhousie University. For several decades she has studied the transnational implications of Philippine migration to Canada and globally, with a focus upon how migration shapes local lives and livelihoods in migrant-sending communities.

CATHERINE BRYAN is a PhD candidate in Social Anthropology at Dalhousie University in Halifax, Canada. She has a BA Honours in Women's Studies from the University of Winnipeg, and a Bachelor and Masters of Social Work from McGill University. Her research interests include migration, transnationality, feminist political economy, social reproduction and changes to the Canadian rural economy. Her dissertation is a multi-sited ethnography exploring the origins of a Filipino community in a small town in Manitoba.

BARBARA COTTRELL has conducted numerous projects including *Violence in Immigrant Families* and is the author of *When Teens Abuse Their Parents* (2004). Barbara is Past President of the NS Chapter of the Canadian Evaluation Society and a member of the Research Advisory Committee of the Canadian Centre for Policy Alternatives – NS.

ALEXANDRA DOBROWOLSKY is a Professor of Political Science at Saint Mary's University, and an Adjunct Professor in the Schulich School of Law, Dalhousie University. She teaches in the areas of Canadian, Comparative and Women, Gender and Politics and has published on themes of representation and citizenship, and in policy areas that range from constitutional and social policy to security and immigration policy.

J. DAVID FLINT is an adjunct professor of sociology at Saint Mary's University. He has been studying the socioeconomic conditions in rural and coastal communities in the Atlantic Provinces for the past twenty years. He lives in Tatamagouche, NS, where he is active in the Transition Town movement.

KAREN GALLANT is a specialist in Recreation and Leisure Studies and an Assistant Professor in the School of Health and Human Performance, Dalhousie University. Her research is primarily focused on civic engagement and community health, particularly the role of volunteers in community building, and community inclusion of marginalized populations.

NATASHA HANSON is currently an adjunct faculty member of the Department of Sociology and Anthropology at the University of Prince Edward Island. She completed a Postdoctoral Fellowship studying the impacts of employment-related geographic mobility within the Prince Edward Island trucking industry, as part of the national "On the Move Partnership." Her research interests include migration, livelihood, identity and political economy.

PERUVEMBA S. JAYA is an Associate Professor in the Department of Communication, Faculty of Arts, at the University of Ottawa. Among the projects she is working on is a Social Sciences and Humanities Research Council of Canada funded project on multicultural media in Ottawa.

HOWARD RAMOS is an Associate Professor in the Department of Sociology and Social Anthropology at Dalhousie University. He has published on, and researches, issues of social justice, including immigration, indigenous and environmental protest, transnational human rights, equity, and race and ethnicity.

BRENDA ROBERTSON served as a leisure studies professor at Acadia University in Nova Scotia for thirty years prior to retiring in July 2012. As a scholar her work reflects a social psychological analysis of leisure functioning of disenfranchised groups. As a practitioner, her work reflects a social psychological analysis of leisure functioning of disenfranchized groups, in an effort to improve professional practice by eliminating factors that serve to marginalize certain populations.

SERPERI SEVGUR holds an MA in International Development Studies, and is currently a PhD candidate in Sociology at Dalhousie University. Her research interests include international migration of the highly skilled and their networks, and the intersectional analysis of migration and settlement experiences.

CHARLENE SHANNON is an Associate Professor in the Faculty of Kinesiology at the University of New Brunswick. Her research has focused in the areas of youth development, family leisure, the links between leisure and health and well-being (e.g., illness, childhood obesity), and most recently, bullying in recreation and sport settings.

ANNE-MARIE SULLIVAN is an Associate Professor and teaches leisure theory, leadership, research methods, and therapeutic recreation at Memorial University of Newfoundland. Her current research interests include therapeutic recreation practice issues, problem gambling, deviant leisure and women's lived experiences of motherhood.

EVANGELIA TASTSOGLOU is a Professor in the Department of Sociology and Criminology at Saint Mary's University. She has published widely in the areas of gender and international migration, immigrant and minority women and citizenship, Canadian immigration, settlement and integration with a feminist and intersectional perspective, and on diasporas and diasporic identities.

SUSAN TIRONE is a Professor and Associate Director of the College of Sustainability at Dalhousie University. She has taught courses in Community Development and Leisure Studies for more than fifteen years. Her research and scholarship focus on race, ethnicity, disability and immigration status and how these affect well-being.

STACEY WILSON-FORSBERG is an Assistant Professor of Human Rights and Human Diversity at Wilfrid Laurier University Brantford campus. Her research focuses on multiculturalism in Canada, specifically the role of citizen engagement and social capital in the integration experiences of immigrants, the acculturation experiences of Latin American immigrants, and more recently, the school to work transitions of African immigrant youth.

MARIA JOSEFA YAX-FRASER is a PhD student in the Department of Social Anthropology at York University and part-time professor at Saint Mary's University. She is the chair of the Halifax Immigrant Women's Organization and a member of the Maritime-Guatemala Breaking the Silence Network. Her interests includes migration and integration, gender and development, mothering, human rights and peace, homelessness and Latin American history.

YOKO YOSHIDA is an Assistant Professor in the Department of Sociology and Social Anthropology at Dalhousie University. She also serves as the Academic Director of the Atlantic Research Data Centre in Halifax. Her research interests include social statistics applied in the areas of socio-economic inequality, inequality in health and integration processes of immigrants.

# Index

www.ingramcontent.com/pod-product-compliance
Lightning Source LLC
Chambersburg PA
CBHW020657270326
41928CB00005B/164